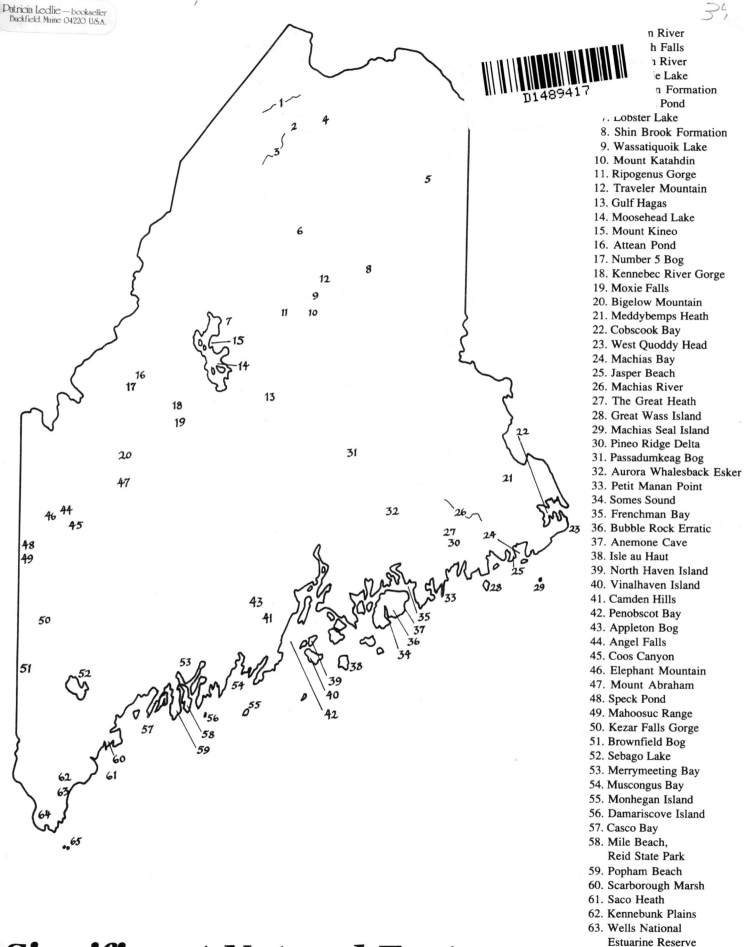

n River
h Falls
n River
e Lake
n Formation
Pond
7. Lobster Lake
8. Shin Brook Formation
9. Wassatiquoik Lake
10. Mount Katahdin
11. Ripogenus Gorge
12. Traveler Mountain
13. Gulf Hagas
14. Moosehead Lake
15. Mount Kineo
16. Attean Pond
17. Number 5 Bog
18. Kennebec River Gorge
19. Moxie Falls
20. Bigelow Mountain
21. Meddybemps Heath
22. Cobscook Bay
23. West Quoddy Head
24. Machias Bay
25. Jasper Beach
26. Machias River
27. The Great Heath
28. Great Wass Island
29. Machias Seal Island
30. Pineo Ridge Delta
31. Passadumkeag Bog
32. Aurora Whalesback Esker
33. Petit Manan Point
34. Somes Sound
35. Frenchman Bay
36. Bubble Rock Erratic
37. Anemone Cave
38. Isle au Haut
39. North Haven Island
40. Vinalhaven Island
41. Camden Hills
42. Penobscot Bay
43. Appleton Bog
44. Angel Falls
45. Coos Canyon
46. Elephant Mountain
47. Mount Abraham
48. Speck Pond
49. Mahoosuc Range
50. Kezar Falls Gorge
51. Brownfield Bog
52. Sebago Lake
53. Merrymeeting Bay
54. Muscongus Bay
55. Monhegan Island
56. Damariscove Island
57. Casco Bay
58. Mile Beach,
    Reid State Park
59. Popham Beach
60. Scarborough Marsh
61. Saco Heath
62. Kennebunk Plains
63. Wells National
    Estuarine Reserve
64. Mount Agamenticus
65. Isles of Shoals

Significant Natural Features

Maine's Natural Heritage

Maine's Natural Heritage

Rare Species and Unique Natural Features

By Dean B. Bennett

For the Maine Critical Areas Program
State Planning Office

ILLUSTRATIONS BY LUCIA DELEIRIS

*Inventories, photography, and preparation of the
manuscript were paid for, in part, by funds appropriated
by the Maine State Legislature for the Maine State
Planning Office and funds provided to the Maine Coastal
Program by the U.S. Department of Commerce,
Office of Ocean and Coastal Resource Management.*

DOWN EAST BOOKS
CAMDEN, MAINE

Copyright © 1988 by the State of Maine
ISBN 0-89272-228-2
Library of Congress Catalog Card Number 86-50855

Design by Lurelle Cheverie

Printed in Singapore by
Singapore National Printers Ltd
through Four Colour Imports Ltd., Louisville, Ky.

5 4 3 2 1

Inquires about reprinting any portion of
the text or illustrations from this book
should be addressed to: Maine Critical
Areas Program, c/o Down East Books,
P.O. Box 679, Camden, ME 04843.

To all those, past and present,
who have endeavored to preserve
Maine's natural heritage.

Contents

Foreword

In the morning, after a storm had savaged the Maine coast, the fog settled in again unexpectedly. A couple of clamdiggers appeared in our dooryard, one of them carrying an open cardboard box. Inside the box crouched a small, dark bird.

I recognized the bird faster than I did its custodian, although it was the first close view I had ever had of that tiny subarctic seabird called a dovekie. These birds, near relatives of puffins, are sometimes blown inland by storms and stranded there, unable to get airborne again among the trees.

"It reminded me of a baby puffin," said the young clammer after I had identified the bird for him. "I found it sitting in the middle of the road and I figured you would know what it was."

Then I recognized him. Years before, Wilbur Hutchins had taken part in a local children's nature program my wife, Ada, and I had organized in the coastal town of Milbridge. He and his twin brother, Roy, had spent a memorable week with us on Machias Seal Island, watching puffins and the other seabirds about which we were writing. Wilbur had left town for a while, and I had lost track of him. Now, we took the dovekie to the shore, put it in the water, and watched it swim back into the fog, where we knew it was at home.

The dovekie's unexpected appearance that day was one of the many dividends Ada and I have received over the years since that first plunge into environmental education. The magical aspect of the experience was its reverberation—the way that one strand of a web woven years ago is touched and sends along signals to all the other parts.

The simple act of beginning such a nature program alerted the town's citizens to many of the natural wonders—tide pools and bogs teeming with life, for instance—lying almost at their doorsteps. A move to sell the town park on the shore (because it was "worthless") was turned back when newspaper stories about kids exploring the tide pool convinced parents of its value. Children who had never put their feet in salt water, even though their fathers were commercial fishermen, learned something about the ecology of the coast.

One girl in the program went on to major in Wildlife Management at the University of Maine at Orono. Others who took part in the program have had children of their own, and they tell them something about the natural treasures that make their state something special.

Imagine, then, the impact that Dean Bennett has had on Maine. The children and adults he has taught about the way nature works have spread the message on to others, and now they, too, are passing it on. Reverberations again.

Whenever Maine's citizens get behind an important piece of environmental legislation, I have to wonder whether it would have drawn any notice at all a quarter of a century ago. Today, because of environmental education, men and women receive a respectful hearing on their concerns about environmental degradation, whereas a decade ago they would have been laughed at (as we were). Now, referenda proposing funds for pollution control are passed routinely and critical areas are set aside.

And now we have this book, *Maine's Natural Heritage*. I wish that Ada and I had had it two decades and more ago when we were trying to open the eyes of kids (and their parents) in Milbridge. Dean Bennett's book will pull all the strands together for many people who hunger for ecological wisdom. Most of us know that Maine's supposedly thin soils produce a large variety of plants—but why? The sportsman may curse the black fly, and yet he wouldn't want it totally eradicated in certain places. But why? Dean Bennett answers these and thousands of other questions that are of concern to all of us who value our experiences in the out-of-doors.

So read, enjoy, and spread the word. The results are sure to be rewarding, like the sight of a young man coming out of the fog, carrying a dovekie in a cardboard box.

Preface

I don't pretend to know much about the State of Maine . . . a territory almost
the size of England. . . . What little I do know about Maine, however, I like—
like so well that I have never found any section of the world in which I could
live as happily, or seen any part of one other country, no matter how beautiful,
in which I felt the same contentment.[1]

—Kenneth Roberts

Human history contains a long and detailed record of our ties to the natural
world, not only our physical connections but our emotional ones as well. We
look to nature to be stable, supportive, self-renewing, and enjoyable, seeking
to find contentment as did Kenneth Roberts. Our experiences with nature help
us to discover ourselves. Our perceptions, our emotions, our capacities to
understand are challenged and revealed when we encounter new and varied
environments.

Ecologically, Maine contains a natural diversity we have long appreciated
but are only beginning to understand. We do know, however, that the
interrelationships of diverse organisms are important phenomena of ecological systems, including those in which humans participate. And only in recent
years have we begun to discover the full extent of Maine's unique and rare
natural qualities.

It is to this end that this book was written—to increase awareness and
capture interest, to inform and to instill appreciation and respect, and to
develop a sense of responsibility for the future of our precious natural heritage.
It is designed to help the reader identify critical natural features in Maine and
to know where and how to see and experience some of them. Perhaps its most
important aim is to develop public motivation to participate actively in
discovering and conserving the diversity of Maine's natural history.

Safeguarding our natural inheritance is a privilege we have by virtue of our
unique position in the ecosystem. It requires awareness, understanding, and

vigilance on the part of all people. Every citizen shares a caretaking role in the management of a growing number of lands held in the public trust. Furthermore, private landholders may also find themselves directly entrusted with the care of one or more of nature's heirlooms.

As we work to protect those qualities we value in nature, our route is often long with many twists and turns and unmarked pathways, but the basic steps are relatively easy to discern. First, we must identify the elements in our environment that are rare, unusual, and significant. Second, we must recognize and understand the problems threatening their existence. Third, we must exercise stewardship and take effective conservation action. All of these steps depend upon educating the public.

Most people know of Mt. Katahdin, which, in the words of former Governor Percival Baxter, "stands above the plain unique in grandeur and glory." Fewer people, however, are aware that on its slopes and spectacular tableland live uncommon species of animal life—the northern bog lemming, the secretive yellow-nosed vole, the Katahdin arctic butterfly—and some of the rarest arctic alpine tundra communities in eastern North America. This region is but one of hundreds of areas now officially recognized as harboring especially significant elements of Maine's natural environment.

Selection of these sites is the work of Maine's Critical Areas Program, managed by Hank Tyler—who goes by Harry R. Tyler, Jr., on his official correspondence. This book is Hank's dream, for behind his quiet manner lies a fervent dedication to the state's priceless natural heritage, as well as a wealth of experience and background that makes him superbly qualified for his position.

Hank Tyler's job starts in the field, and it is obvious to those who know him that he is more comfortable slogging in a bog with his camera and worn sack of paraphenalia than sitting behind a desk. Only after he or one of the program's planning consultants has investigated firsthand a waterfall, old-growth forest, nesting area, or other feature can a detailed planning report be prepared and the importance of an area be established.

After tracking down the landowner or landowners and discussing the issues involved in protecting a significant area, the Critical Areas Advisory Board decides whether or not to include that area on the Critical Areas Register. Once designated, these lands are monitored by the Critical Areas Program. Since most critical areas are on private land, the program is particularly sensitive to respecting the rights and privacy of property owners. Also, the balance in some particularly fragile areas can be disturbed by any visitors, no matter how well-meaning their intentions.

The Critical Areas Program is not the only organization engaged in identifying and protecting Maine's special natural features. Hank Tyler works closely with a number of other equally knowledgeable and dedicated individuals. They represent public organizations, including state and federal resource agencies and institutions of higher education, as well as those from the private sector, such as the Maine Chapter of The Nature Conservancy, Maine Audubon Society, the Natural Resources Council of Maine, and the Maine Coast Heritage Trust.

The purpose of the Critical Areas Program and similar efforts is, in some respects, to place a magnifying glass on environmental change. Looking at natural features and species of plants and animals that are rare, unusual, or threatened sharpens our focus on the effects of human activities as well as those of other natural events occurring in the world around us; we become more aware of the value of natural things and the consequences of their loss.

How many have been captivated by the changing panorama of a flight over a checkerboard landscape, tilled fields and farmsteads alternating with untamed forest? Or marveled at the peaceful coexistence of nature and human life in the nooks and crannies of the state's wrinkled coastline? Who has not experienced the excitement of wondering what lies just around the next bend of a river or turn in a trail? Maine has a long history of providing such pleasures, as seen in James Rosier's account of Captain George Waymouth's discovery of the St. George River in 1605: "Our Captaine discovered up a great river trending alongst into Maine about forty miles, . . . the beauty and goodness whereof I cannot by relation sufficiently demonstrate. . . . The farther we went, the more pleasing it was to every man, alluring us still with expectation of better."[2]

It is to that spirit, of fortuitous discoveries already made and expectation of better still to come for ourselves and our children, that this book is dedicated. I hope it will be a starting point for those just becoming interested in the world of nature, and enlarge the perspectives of others already familiar with the beauty and mystery of Maine's natural environment. Above all, I hope that through the images presented here the less-known and more intricate details of the delicate film of life on this earth will be seen more clearly.

A book of this scope obviously depends on far more than the expertise of any one individual. The task of sifting through and evaluating the enormous amount of available scientific information was compounded by the rapid rate at which new data are being generated. During the seven years of planning and writing, I called on the assistance and advice of many professionals in a variety of fields, not only to acquire and assess information but to seek their advice on the selection of the natural features and species to include. On several occasions I visited the natural areas being discussed to gain a firsthand impression. Inevitably, in spite of my most careful attempts at collecting and objectively dealing with information, there will be mistakes and matters of judgement for which I, as author, must assume responsibility.

I am indebted to many people. First and foremost, I thank Hank Tyler for his patience, valuable advice, gentle criticism, and constant encouragement. Also I express my thanks to staff at the State Planning Office for their active interest, support, and encouragement: Richard E. Barringer, Holly Dominie, Naomi A. Edelson, R. Alec Giffen, and Carolyn Woodwell. To the following, who also interrupted their busy lives to give their time, expertise, and advice on all or portions of various drafts of the manuscript, I owe a special thanks: John J. Albright, Jane Arbuckle, Archie W. Berry, Jr., Harold W. Borns, Jr., Betty J. Brown, Christopher S. Campbell, L. M. Eastman, Thomas E. Eastler, Susan C. Gawler, Susan Hayward, Malcolm L. Hunter, Arthur M. Hussey II, Marc Loiselle, Thomas McAndrews, Peter G. McConnell, John R. Moring, John Mudge, Carroll J. Schell, Douglass Stafford, Woodrow B. Thompson, and Barbara St. John Vickery. Others who assisted with my research, readily answering my questions and providing information, were Robert W. Boettger, William P. Hancock, John H. Hunt, Al Hutchinson, Frederick W. Kircheis, Carolyn LePage, Janet S. McMahon, W. Thomas Shoener, Thomas S. Squiers, Charles Todd, and Marshall Wiebe.

I must also thank Pat Morgan and Karin Womer of Down East Books for their careful attention to content, organization, and style, and from whom I learned much about writing as they patiently guided me through the work. I am indebted to Sylvia Hodgkins who, in her pleasant and efficient manner, made illegible pages of handwritten manuscript readable. Finally, my wife, Sheila, was a patient and constant companion during the process, and with perceptive advice and encouragement she helped me through my difficulties; to her I owe a special thank-you and debt of gratitude.

—Dean Bennett, Mt. Vernon, Maine

Unusual Features of Land and Water

Perspective

One doesn't expect to find a gold mine in western Maine, yet according to an 1876 county atlas there is one, in a remote, mountainous region. Could it still be found, after a century of inactivity? My companion and I thought so. On a hot summer day we started out, following a mere trickle of a stream—a stream that on a later trip would yield a fleck of gold. Through the cool, thick forest canopy we caught glimpses of our landmark—a sharp, hilly peak off to the right; the mine was supposed to be opposite it.

We tramped on for several hours, searching, but it looked hopeless. The woods seemed endless, an unlikely place for a mine. Suddenly, in a wet, dark, mossy sag on the top of a ridge, the ground took on a peculiar lumpy shape. We rolled back the two-inch-thick carpet of moss and duff between the trees and exposed aged and iron-stained chunks of feldspar, encrusted with thousands of needle-like crystals of druse quartz. Glints of gold flashed as we pawed over them. Then reality caught up with us: they were only pyrite crystals—fool's gold. Still, we sensed we were on the right track. On closer inspection, the irregular surface revealed the configuration of an old sluiceway. We followed its outline to a dark, wooded pool surrounded by aging timbers. And there it was: the mine shaft, all but submerged, disappearing into a moss-covered ledge. We probed with a stick, but couldn't reach the end of the tunnel. What treasures had been removed from inside? What might still remain?

— D.B.

Although gold is rare in Maine, the state's land and waters contain other treasures equally stimulating to the senses and emotions. Stand on the peak of one of Maine's four-thousand-foot mountains on a clear day, for example, and soak up the exhilarating beauty of the lakes and forests spread out as far as the eye can see. Or, creep to the rim of any one of Maine's twenty or so outstanding gorges and acknowledge the power of water working the land. Such experiences strengthen our awareness of the truly remarkable diversity of Maine's natural landscape.

Great Sand Beach, Roque Island, Washington County. A classic example of fringing pocket beach. L. Kenneth Fink, Jr., photo.

Graptolite fossil, Westmanland, Aroostook County. Graptolites were planktonic animals with primitive nervous systems and backbones. The fossils at Westmanland are from the Silurian Age and are over 400 million years old. Hank Tyler photo.

Screw Auger Falls Gorge in Grafton Notch State Park, Oxford County, is a registered Critical Area because of its scenic and scientific attributes. Thomas Brewer photo.

An eagle's view of the state's topography shows clearly that sometime in the distant past powerful forces of upheaval and fracturing produced a prominent, mountainous backbone. But one must look with an even more careful eye at the subtle orientations, shapes, and patterns of lakes and hills to connect them with the slow-moving, grinding sheet of ice that covered the area twenty thousand years ago and formed the basic contours and perimeters of the land as we know it today.

Maine's southeastern boundary, the only one bared vulnerably to the sea, is a rough-hewn coastline of spectacular beauty. Here the ancient crustal folding that formed the mountain chain is evident also in the placement of peninsulas and coastal islands. Between these two great powers, the mountains and the ocean, lies a mediating plain, cushioned by a thick mat of forest and stitched with winding streams, quiet lakes, ponds, and wetlands.

Seen closer up, the terrain is equally impressive. Geologists, foresters, and others who explore the land have created for us an amazingly detailed record of the state's complexity, but one doesn't have to be an expert to strip the coverlet of soil and vegetation from the surface and view firsthand fascinating specimens of sedimentary, igneous, and metamorphic rocks, magnificent gemstones, and dramatic evidence of ancient life preserved in the rocks. Other features, no less dramatic, were formed by the movement and melting of ice and the effects of wind and water. These include glacial cirques, eskers, deltas, beaches, rapids, waterfalls, and gorges.

Even amidst this natural wealth of geologic formations, certain exceptional features stand out. Their significance lies in their beauty, their rarity, and above all in the history they record. To the practiced eyes of geologists and

paleontologists they are benchmarks in time—events frozen in rock. Long-extinct volcanoes, mountains, coastal plains, continental shelves—the list grows longer as our eye for reading the landscape becomes more experienced. We see climates of long ago, oceans that opened and closed, shallow seas that once covered the land, different environments, and early life forms.

The importance of preserving these features cannot be overemphasized. They are all authentic remnants of the past; only through careful and repeated study can we expect to fully understand and appreciate their meaning. Upon this natural legacy is based our knowledge of Maine's geologic history.

Little Bigelow Mountain, Franklin County, part of Maine's mountainous backbone. L.M. Eastman photo.

Raven's Nest, Schoodic Point, Acadia National Park. Courtesy of National Park Service.

1

Patterns in the Rock

Portion of the world during the middle Cambrian period (around 550 million years ago). Redrawn from A.M. Hussey II, The Geology of the Two Lights and Crescent Beach State Parks Area, Cape Elizabeth, Maine, *Bulletin 26 (Augusta: Maine Geological Survey, Dept. of Conservation, 1982).*

Wherever they occur, exposed rocks of cliffs, roadside ledges, gorges, and water-worn tidal areas of the coast provide bits of information about the past. From these widely scattered pieces, geologists, paleontologists, and other scientists are patiently assembling a remarkable story of Maine's geologic history.[1] It's a formidable task but one filled with stimulating discoveries, ideas, and questions. Imagine the excitement when formations of rocks in the greater Casco Bay area proved to be essentially identical to counterparts in southern Ireland and England. Finds of this nature generate all kinds of interesting theories about how and why ancient happenings affected the state's bedrock. Scientists still do not have all the details, but the evidence does suggest a fascinating sequence of events.

About 700 million years ago and for a few hundreds of millions of years later, an ocean which geologists have named Iapetos (in Greek mythology, the father of Atlantis) existed off the eastern edge of the ancient continent of North

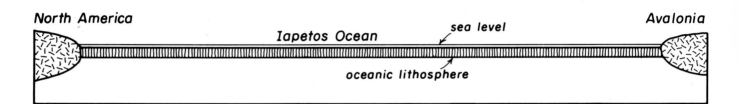

America. Far to the east lay a land mass called Avalonia, which included parts of present day Newfoundland, Britain, New Brunswick, Nova Scotia, Maine, and Massachusetts. From late Precambrian time through the Cambrian period,

Bedrock Geology of Maine. Generalized from P.H. Osberg, A.M. Hussey II, and G.M. Boone, 1985, Maine Geological Survey, Augusta. Redrawn, by permission, from a map published by Hearne Brothers, Warren Mich.

Igneous Rocks

Mesozoic plutonic-volcanic rocks.

Late Silurian to Carboniferous intrusive rocks, chiefly consisting of the mineral feldspar.

Late Silurian to Devonian intrusive rocks consisting of minerals with magnesium and iron.

Ordovician intrusive rocks.

Sedimentary/Metamorphic Rocks

Middle Devonian to Carboniferous (?) sedimentary rocks.

Early Devonian sedimentary rocks of central and northern Maine

Silurian and early Devonian rocks of the coastal volcanic belt.

Silurian-Devonian sedimentary rocks of central and northern Maine.

Middle Ordovician to upper Silurian sedimentary rocks of Aroostook County

Ordovician and Silurian limestones and sedimentary rocks of Aroostook County.

Late Precambrian, Cambrian, and Ordovician sedimentary rocks.

Precambrian rocks of the Chain Lakes massif.

Fault

GEOLOGIC TIME SCALE

ERA	PERIOD		EPOCH	YEARS B.P. (in millions)		GEOLOGIC EVENTS SHAPING MAINE
CENOZOIC	QUATERNARY		HOLOCENE	0.01	.011	— Glacial ice melts in Maine.
			PLEISTOCENE		.025	— Late Wisconsin-age glacier enters Maine. — Glaciers form over colder regions of northern continents. — Global cooling.
				1.6		
	TERTIARY					
				66.4		
MESOZOIC	CRETACEOUS				120	— Final volcanic activity in Maine.
				144	150	— Continents split again; Atlantic Ocean forms.
	JURASSIC					
				208		— Continental crust cracks: rift basins, Bay of Fundy.
	TRIASSIC					— Basaltic magma intrusions — dikes (Schoodic Point). — Intrusions of igneous rocks — Mt. Agamenticus.
				245		
PALEOZOIC	PERMIAN					— Erosion continues.
				286		
	CARBON-IFEROUS	PENNSYLVANIAN				— Plants abundant.
				320		
		MISSISSIPPIAN				
				360		
	LATE DEVONIAN					— Erosion; faulting; sediments of Mapleton Formation in Presque Isle area.
				374		
	EARLY DEVONIAN				390	— Acadian Orogeny: continents collide, Merrimack Sea closes; Appalachian Mts. built; granite and pegmatite intrusions; metamorphism; volcanic activity in Katahdin area.
				408		
	SILURIAN					— Continued closing of Iapetos Ocean creates Merrimack Sea over what is now Maine; sedimentary rock corridor formed — Waterville to Aroostook; fossil deposits, Rangeley deposition.
				438		
	LATE ORDOVICIAN					— Taconic Orogeny; collision of island arc of western New Hampshire with old North America.
				458		
	EARLY ORDOVICIAN					— Deformation of Casco Bay Group and Shin Pond formation by collision of Avalonia with Casco Bay Island arc. — Deposition of Casco Bay Group sediments. — Rocks with serpentine formed in central western Maine. — Volcanism builds island arcs along what is now coastal Maine and western New Hampshire. — Continents begin migrating toward each other, narrowing the Iapetos Ocean.
				505		
	CAMBRIAN					— Late Precambrian through Cambrian, ancient land masses moving away from each other, Iapetos Ocean expanding.
				570		
PRE-CAMBRIAN	PROTEROZOIC					— Iapetos Ocean existed off ancient continent of North America, Avalonia lies far to the east.
				2500		
	ARCHEAN					Dean B. Bennett Copyright 1986

these land masses were moving away from each other as the Iapetos Ocean expanded.

The mechanism for this continental movement is called sea-floor spread-

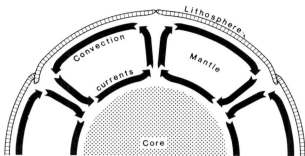

Convection currents in the earth's mantle. From A.M. Hussey II, The Geology of the Two Lights and Crescent Beach State Parks Area, Cape Elizabeth, Maine, Bulletin 26 *(Augusta: Maine Geological Survey, Dept. of Conservation, 1982).*

ing, caused by convection currents in the earth's mantle that result in upwelling of molten rock at mid-ocean ridges. As new ocean crust forms, it spreads to either side of the ridges, powerfully enough to force movement of continental plates. Completing the convection cycle, these same rocks that once rose to form the oceanic crust eventually slide down again (a process called subduction) into the mantle to depths where they melt. Deep ocean trenches are

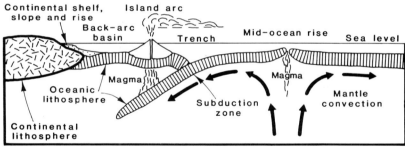

Generalized diagram of events forming large structural features of the earth. From A.M. Hussey II, The Geology of the Two Lights and Crescent Beach State Parks Area, Cape Elizabeth, Maine, Bulletin 26 *(Augusta: Maine Geological Survey, Dept. of Conservation, 1982).*

formed and earthquakes and volcanic eruptions occur as the edge of one crustal plate is pushed underneath an abutting plate. These forces, along with erosion, played a powerful role in the development of the bedrock of these ancient continents, just as they continue to do today.

Along the margins of ancient North America and Avalonia, sediments from the eroding land masses were deposited in the ocean, creating ideal habitat conditions for numerous marine organisms. The now extinct trilobites, relatives of lobsters and crayfish, were among the more common and distinctive animals that crawled and swam around the muddy bottom of this Cambrian sea. The shells of these and other bottom dwellers were buried by accumulating sediments, and today the fossil remains of some of these ancient marine organisms have assumed importance as indices of geologic time. The trilobites, for example, were abundant and widely distributed during a period lasting over 300 million years, before they became extinct at the end of the Paleozoic era. The occurrence of appreciable numbers of their fossils (several locations of trilobite fossils have been found in Maine) is especially helpful in dating geologic events.

By early Ordovician time, the continents—Avalonia and the ancestral

Silurian trilobite species (actual length 4.5 inches). Several locations of trilobite fossils have been discovered in Maine.

North America—had begun migrating toward each other. With this reversal of continental movement, the Iapetos Ocean began to close. At this time, most of the land that would become Maine lay beneath this ocean.

Although geologists are not yet able to give precise details of the geologic setting and events, they hypothesize that as the continents moved closer the huge slabs of oceanic plate floating on the mantle broke and were subducted into the mantle. The crust and sediments of the ocean floor were carried to depths where intense heat and pressure were sufficient to melt them. The resultant magma worked its way to the surface, causing volcanic eruptions and creating island arcs. One long, narrow belt of active volcanoes, closer to the Avalonian continent, extended from present-day Newfoundland to Alabama and included parts of coastal Maine. As the volcanic mountains eroded, an apron of sediments was deposited around the edge of the arc. Today, these sediments make up a thick belt of metamorphic rock formations, known as the

The Casco Bay Group of rock formations extends from Saco to the vicinity of Belfast. Hank Tyler photo.

Portion of the world from the late Cambrian period to the early Ordovician period (around 500 million years ago). A long, narrow belt of active volcanoes, closer to the Avalonian continent, included parts of coastal Maine. Eventually sediments eroded from the volcanic mountains formed a thick belt of metamorphic rock formations, known as the Casco Bay Group. Redrawn from A.M. Hussey II, The Geology of the Two Lights and Crescent Beach State Parks Area, Cape Elizabeth, Maine, Bulletin 26 *(Augusta: Maine Geological Survey, Dept. of Conservation, 1982).*

Casco Bay Group, that extends from Saco northeastward to the vicinity of Belfast.[2]

During this early Paleozoic time, in what is now the Chain of Lakes region in central western Maine near the Canadian border, rocks containing the mineral serpentine were formed by processes resulting from movement of the oceanic plate.[3] Serpentine, derived from the hot-water alteration of magnesium silicates, has a silky, waxy to greasy luster and feel and varies in color from cream white through all shades of green to black. Since the 1940s, fibrous forms of the mineral located in the region have received attention as a source of asbestos. Geologists conjecture that the presence of this deposit of serpentine marks an important tectonic line extending northeast and southwest throughout much of the northern Appalachians.

Probably during early Ordovician time, between 500 and 480 million

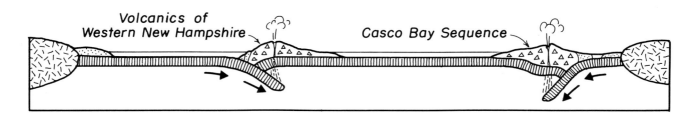

Volcanics of Western New Hampshire   Casco Bay Sequence

years ago, the Avalonian landmass collided with the island arc located off its coastline. As the land buckled and folded, underlying rocks were depressed to deep levels where intense heat and pressure metamorphosed them. Geologists call such an event an orogeny, meaning the birth of a mountain.

The impact of the collision had a profound effect on the geology of Maine. For example, the rocks of the Casco Bay Group underwent their first deforma-

Metamorphic rock of the Casco Bay Group that has been deformed three times. The rock was deposited originally at the end of the Cambrian or early Ordovician, about 500 million years ago. Hank Tyler photo.

tion at this time. And in northern Penobscot County, evidence of an early Ordovician disturbance can be seen in exposures of rocks known as the Shin Brook Formation.[4] Here, layers of rock formed of volcanic ash were deformed and strongly metamorphosed. The formation is also significant because of its

The Casco Bay Deformation during the early Ordovician period (500 to 480 million years ago) had a profound impact on the geology of Maine. Redrawn from A.M. Hussey II, The Geology of the Two Lights and Crescent Beach State Parks Area, Cape Elizabeth, Maine, Bulletin 26 (Augusta: Maine Geological Survey, Dept. of Conservation, 1982).

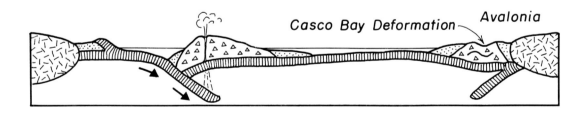

unique assemblage of fossils of marine invertebrates, a grouping unusual in North America. Identification of the imperfectly preserved fossils in the rock sequences shows large numbers of brachiopods, with trilobites, gastropods, sponges, corals, and other species in lesser abundance.

Fossil of the bachiopod Platystrophia *from the Shin Brook Formation. The Paleozoic seas of Maine abounded with brachiopods, also known as "lampshells." The Shin Brook Formation has yielded several poorly preserved specimens of this small marine invertebrate of Ordovician times. Platystrophia is characterized by a thick, strongly ribbed shell up to 1.7 inches long. Rocks of the Shin Brook Formation also show evidence of an early Ordovician disturbance.*

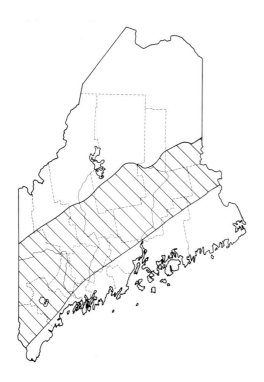

Belt of fossils. Today a corridor of weakly
metamorphosed sedimentary rocks,
containing fossils of marine animals
buried in thousands of feet of sediments
beneath the Merrimack Sea some 400
million years ago, cuts across the state.

In late Ordovician time, as the distance between the two continents continued to close, another island arc, closer to ancient North America in what is now western New Hampshire, collided with that continent. This deformation and mountain-building event is referred to as the Taconic Orogeny.

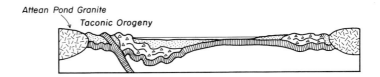

Attean Pond Granite
Taconic Orogeny

For some 40 million years, extending from the Ordovician through the Silurian and into the early Devonian periods, the continents continued their lateral migration. The Iapetos Ocean became a long, narrowing body of water with a new name: the Merrimack Sea. It is thought that much of Maine, as we know it today, lay beneath this sea. Slowly the processes of erosion wore down

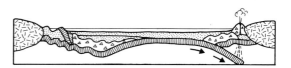

the mountains and carried their materials into the sea, where the sediments formed continental shelves. Underwater mudslides occurred along the unstable edges of these shelves, as they still do today. Often marine animals were buried in the thousands of feet of accumulating sediments, eventually to be unearthed as fossils. High temperature and pressure formed the deeply buried sediments into sandstones, shales, and other sedimentary rocks. Later events caused some metamorphism of the rocks in this area, and the result is a 160-mile-wide corridor of weakly metamorphosed sedimentary rocks extending from Waterville to Aroostook County, in which are found the majority of the state's fossil localities.[5]

Studies of exposures of this thick sequence of rocks in the Kingsbury, Skowhegan, and Waterville areas have contributed to an understanding of the geology of New England.[6] Fossils in the complex strata are now used to date rocks as far south as Connecticut, and the character of the rock materials and their styles of folding provide evidence of assistance to scientists unraveling the sequence and timing of deformations.

To the west, in the Rangeley area, several extensive formations of sedimentary rocks in this same lower to middle Paleozoic age range are also found.[7] Studies of the strata show that a deep basin in the area received deposits of sediment washed off an ancient mountain range to the northwest. Rocks from these sediments are generally well preserved despite complex deformation and metamophism and are among the best exposed and most easily seen sequences of rocks of this age in the northern Appalachians.

Around 390 million years ago, in the early Devonian period, the Merrimack Sea was squeezed into extinction as Avalonia collided with ancient North America. This event occurred during the formation of a supercontinent called Pangaea. The event is known as the Acadian Orogeny, another major period of upheaval and volcanic activity that deformed most of Maine. Beneath

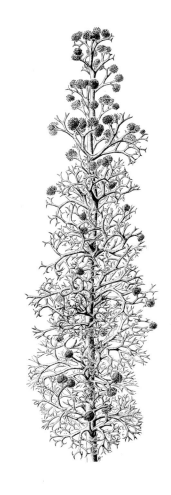

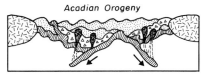

Acadian Orogeny

Maine's state fossil, Pertica quadrifaria, *is a primitive plant that lived about 390 million years ago. It probably grew to a height of about six feet, making it the largest land plant at that time. The fossilized remains of* Pertica *were first discovered in Maine in 1968. Reprinted, by permission, from A. E. Kasper, Jr., and H.N. Andrews, Jr., "Pertica, a New Genus of Devonian Plants in Northern Maine,"* American Journal of Botany, 59. *Mary Hubbard artist.*

The Acadian Orogeny during the early Devonian period (around 390 million years ago) deformed most of Maine. Redrawn from A.M. Hussey II, The Geology of the Two Lights and Crescent Beach State Parks Area, Cape Elizabeth, Maine, Bulletin 26 *(Augusta: Maine Geological Survey, Dept. of Conservation, 1982).*

the surface, the old sedimentary rock metamorphosed as it was cooked, folded, and altered under great heat and pressure. The sedimentary rocks of the Casco Bay Group were recrystallized into a host of new and very different appearing rocks.

Deeply depressed sediments began to melt, forming large quantities of magma that intruded under great pressure into the metamorphic rocks, penetrating joints, cracks, and crevices. As the magma gradually cooled and crystallized, huge masses of granite were formed, along with relatively small amounts of pegmatite rock, with its larger crystals of quartz, feldspar, and gem minerals. Rarer still were rocks containing metal ores—gold, silver, copper, lead, and zinc—seldom found in large quantities in Maine.

At the conclusion of all this activity, prominently in view, was the Appalachian Mountain Range, of which the Longfellow Mountains are a part. These mountains were then considerably higher than today; in fact, amazing as it may seem, the mountains of southwestern Maine at that time probably rivaled the heights of the present Rocky Mountains and Sierra Nevadas. Perhaps even more unbelievable, evidence suggests that the huge plutonic masses of granite rock that make up many of our mountains today were then

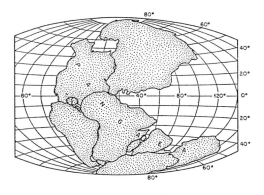

The supercontinent Pangaea as it may have looked sometime after the Acadian Orogeny. After an illustration in R.C. Dietz and J.C. Holden, "The Breakup of Pangaea," © Scientific American, Inc. *(October 1970). Tom Prentiss, artist.*

A recumbent fold of metamorphic bedrock along the York County coastline. Note the narrow white bands of quartz that were later intruded into cracks in the bedrock layers. Hank Tyler photo.

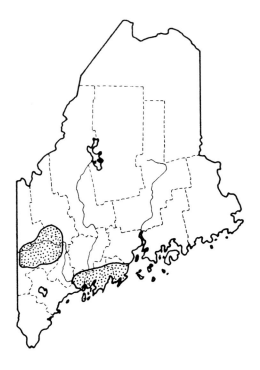

Major pegmatite districts in Maine. Such areas of coarse-grained granitic bodies are among the best sources of gem minerals in the East. From W.B. Thompson, Maine Critical Areas Program, (1977). Redrawn from E.N. Cameron et al., Pegmatite Investigations, 1942-45, New England. *U.S. Geological Survey Professional Paper 255 (1954).*

located several miles beneath the surface—now revealed by millions of years of erosion.

Today, in the region of Baxter State Park, a "lucky" combination of the "right" depth of erosion and a fortuitous effect of the Acadian Orogeny affords a unique view into a dissected and nearly complete volcanic system—one of the largest known volcanic centers on the earth.[8] The volcanic activity began in the region about 405 million years ago and lasted 30 to 40 million years. Scientists theorize that magma originating in the mantle raised the temperature near the base of the earth's crust, causing its partial melting, eventual intrusion to shallow levels, and subsequent volcanic eruption at the surface. In time, the melt beneath the volcano cooled and solidified, forming the Katahdin granite of the area. Forces associated with the Acadian Orogeny tilted the entire volcanic system by three to eight degrees toward the northeast. The influence of this tilt and ensuing erosion removed most of the volcanic rock pile, with the exception of a small block in the Traveler Mountain area. Erosion also revealed the magma chamber, once underneath the volcano, that now forms the Katahdin Mountain area. Today, we have access to essentially the entire cross-section of this fossil volcanic cone and its internal features. There are only a

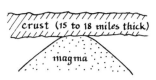

1. *Magma (molten rock), perhaps basalt, originates beneath the earth's crust.*

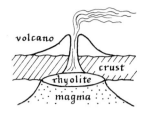

2. *The magma melts some of the crust, forming the volcanic rock, rhyolite, which is forced upward to erupt at the surface.*

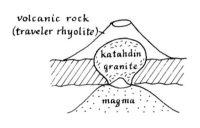

3. *The igneous rock deep within the volcano cools and crystallizes, forming Katahdin granite.*

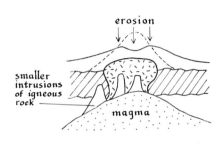

4. *Erosion begins. (Eventually most of the volcanic rock pile was removed.)*

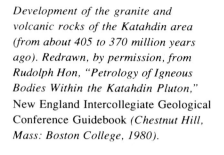

Development of the granite and volcanic rocks of the Katahdin area (from about 405 to 370 million years ago). Redrawn, by permission, from Rudolph Hon, "Petrology of Igneous Bodies Within the Katahdin Pluton," New England Intercollegiate Geological Conference Guidebook (Chestnut Hill, Mass: Boston College, 1980).

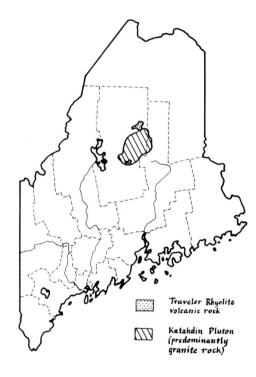

Granite and volcanic rocks of the Katahdin area. Redrawn, by permission, from Rudolph Hon, "Petrology of Igneous Bodies Within the Katahdin Pluton," New England Intercollegiate Geological Conference Guidebook (Chestnut Hill, Mass: Boston College, 1980).

handful of similarly documented cases anywhere around the world where both a volcano and its subvolcanic regions beneath may be observed.

Following the Acadian Orogeny came a somewhat quieter interlude, although some breakage and slippage (faulting) of the bedrock occurred until possibly the Permian period. The erosive actions of wind and water continued their inescapable leveling processes. Of special interest is the deposition of an alluvial fan complex by rivers and streams in a mountain valley in the vicinity of Presque Isle. Today, the rocks formed from this deposition are known as the Mapleton Formation and are the oldest known sedimentary rocks in the northern Appalachians that were clearly deposited on the older Acadian-deformed bedrock.[9]

Gradually, as millions of years passed, rock and overburden were removed, revealing the granitic mountains and roots of volcanoes we see today. The evolution and extinction of life forms continued, especially during the Carboniferous period when land plants were abundant. However, the continental land masses were still unsettled, and in Triassic time, for example, magma was forced into the metamorphic rocks and older granites in the Mt. Agamenticus area of York County.

Something over 200 million years ago, at the end of the Triassic period, hot material in the mantle once again began to rise on convection currents and

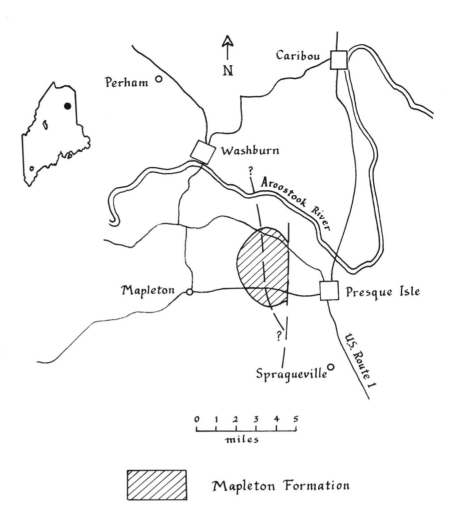

N

Perham ○

Caribou

Washburn

Aroostook River

Mapleton ○

Presque Isle

U.S. Route 1

Spragueville ○

0 1 2 3 4 5
miles

Mapleton Formation

The Mapleton Formation (about 380 million years old), the oldest sedimentary rocks found anywhere in the northern Appalachians that were deposited on bedrock deformed during the Acadian Orogeny. Redrawn, by permission, from K.J. White, "The Mapleton Formation: An Immediately Post-Acadian Basin Fill." Unpublished master's thesis, Boston College, 1975.

spread out beneath the joined continents. Basaltic magma was injected into numerous fractures in older metamorphic and igneous rocks. These intrusions, or dikes, can be seen in a number of places along the coast of Maine. The continental crust cracked and rift basins formed, including the Connecticut

Right: Basalt dikes in granitic bedrock, Saco River watershed. Janet McMahon photo.

Far Right: Cleft in granite created by the erosion of a basalt dike on Little Moose Island, Acadia National Park. Hank Tyler photo.

River Valley and Fundy Basin. As the rift basins filled with sediments, they probably became shallow marshes and mudflats—ideal habitat for dinosaurs, which first appeared during this period.

At the end of the Jurassic period, 150 million years ago, the rift basins spread open and the large continent began splitting apart again. This time the halves divided along new lines, leaving identical specimens of rocks and fossils on both sides of the newly formed Atlantic Ocean: in the Americas and in Europe and Africa.

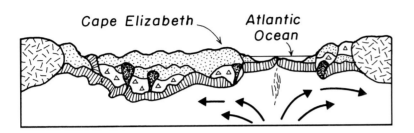

Continental split during the late Jurassic period (about 150 million years ago). During this time the continent separated, splitting along new lines and leaving the same rocks and fossils in Maine and on the continental edges of Europe and Africa. Redrawn from A.M. Hussey II, The Geology of the Two Lights and Crescent Beach State Parks Area, Cape Elizabeth, Maine, Bulletin 26 (Augusta: Maine Geological Survey, Dept. of Conservation, 1982).

From late Triassic through the Jurassic and Cretaceous periods, ocean spreading continued and the present-day Atlantic Ocean formed. Dinosaurs still roamed through shallow marshes on the continents, though by the end of the Cretaceous period, some 70 million years ago, they were gone. During this same period, about 120 million years ago, volcanic activity occurred in southern sections of Maine—the final eruptions in the state. From that time to the present, through the Cenozoic era, ("time of recent life"), the continents have continued to shift.

It is possible that the complex sequence of continent building and erosion, cooling and remelting of rock has happened many times, for the rock cycle, as it is called, continues today. We hear and feel the rumblings inside the earth. We know that new rock is being made and the character of the old is being changed. We witness the slow and often subtle processes of erosion, which provide the raw materials for new sedimentary rock, and—as we shall see in the next chapter—create features of remarkable beauty and geologic interest.

2

The Works of Glaciers

In comparison to mountain building, the subtle erosive activities of wind and water do little to capture our attention, much less our imagination; yet they continue to refine the details of the earth's surface—slowly disassembling the creations of more spectacular geologic events. However, there were times in the earth's history when an unusual combination of climatic conditions on a massive continental scale punctuated the relatively undramatic work of weather. This powerful phenomenon, known as glaciation, was responsible for some of Maine's most fascinating geologic features.

For reasons still being researched, sometime around 2.5 million years ago—toward the end of the Tertiary period—global temperatures began to

Somes Sound, on Mount Desert Island, is Maine's only fjord. Now flooded with seawater, it is a glacially carved valley formed during the last period of glaciation. Hank Tyler photo.

cool. Over Greenland, Antarctica, and northern regions of Europe and North America, annual snowfall exceeded the yearly rate of melting and evaporation. Here, covering enormous areas, the snow accumulated to a depth where compaction produced glacial ice. Fed continually by more and more snow, huge continental glaciers thousands of feet thick formed. Under the pressure of its own tremendous weight, glacial ice can actually become "plastic" and flow, like a river of ice. Spreading across northern areas of North America and Eurasia, the glaciers ground their way over the land. Rock fragments wedged into the base of the ice, turning it into an enormous abrading tool.

Each successive glacier added its softening touch to the contours of the earth's surface—polishing the ancient bedrock, eroding the tops and faces of hills to produce streamlined, asymmetrical profiles, and recarving the valleys into a U-shape in cross-section. Several times the continental glaciers made their powerful assaults on the landscape, retreating and melting as they encountered warmer climates to the south. So much of the earth's water was tied up in ice during periods of glaciation that global ocean levels fell as much as 300 feet.

The late Wisconsin-age glacier, which advanced southeastward across the St. Lawrence lowland about twenty-five thousand years ago, was the last ice

The U-shaped valley and cirque of the North Basin on the Mt. Katahdin massif. The valley was carved by alpine glacial ice. Hank Tyler photo.

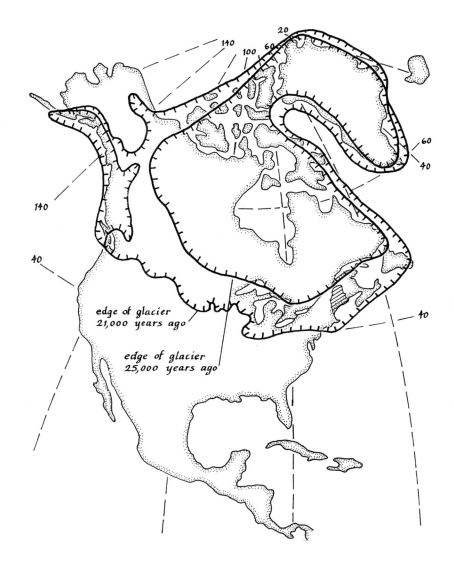

edge of glacier 21,000 years ago

edge of glacier 25,000 years ago

Glaciation in North America.

sheet to affect Maine. As it grew, thick white lobes of ice flowed radially outward from its center. Advancing slowly across the landscape, the glacier eventually engulfed the highest mountains, blanketing a major portion of the North American continent with a sheet of snow and ice as much as three miles thick. Evidence that the glacier overtopped Mt. Katahdin was gathered by the geologist Ralph S. Tarr, who found foreign rock fragments at the mountain's summit in 1897 and 1899.

The glacier is believed to have first entered Maine about twenty-five thousand years ago. By twenty-one thousand years ago, it had ground its way across the state and terminated well out on the continental shelf, covering most of what is now the Gulf of Maine. (Much of the gulf was dry land at that time because such vast quantities of the earth's water were tied up in ice.) The tremendous weight of the ice mass depressed Maine's bedrock by as much as two thousand feet, forcing it into the somewhat plastic mantle beneath. On the surface, the advancing ice sheet scraped the bedrock clean of weathered material. Grooves and small scratches, called glacial striations, were gouged out by the

Glacial scratches in bedrock, House Island, Casco Bay. Tammis Coffin photo.

rocky material held in the ice beneath the glacier. During this process, the glacier picked up more material in some places than it could transport and dropped the excess—forming a veneer of random, unsorted, but compact deposits of clay, sand, and rocks.

Mountains were shaped into dull saw-toothed profiles as the glacier rode up their north-facing slopes and plucked off their tops, leaving south-facing cliffs. Valleys were widened and deepened by fingers of glacial ice moving through them. The freezing and thawing of these valley glaciers chipped away at the mountains, forming open bowl-shaped features called cirques, which were occupied by small mountain glaciers. Where the highlands above the cirques were narrow, thin ridges, called aretes, were produced. This is the case with the Knife Edge, probably Baxter State Park's most spectacular feature.[1]

About eighteen thousand years ago, in response to a warming climate, the Wisconsin glacier began to melt. The glacier's effects as it receded were no less pronounced than when it had bulldozed its way across the state earlier. And as the glacier slowly left the still-depressed land, the ocean, now rising with the

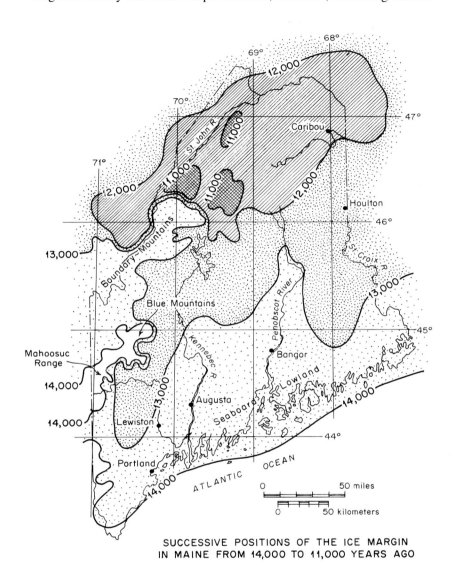

SUCCESSIVE POSITIONS OF THE ICE MARGIN
IN MAINE FROM 14,000 TO 11,000 YEARS AGO

Inferred extent of ice cover during deglaciation. The map shows successive positions of the late Wisconsin ice margin in Maine from 14,000 to 11,000 years ago (adapted from Davis and Jacobson and from Denton and Hughes). Extent of ice cover is based on limiting radiocarbon dates, inferred ice-surface gradients, and topography. Number and configuration of ice remnants at 11,000 years ago are conjectural. Generalized from W.B. Thompson and H.W. Borns, Jr., 1985, Maine Geological Survey, Augusta.

addition of water from melting glaciers, continued to lap at its edges, drowning lowland areas of southern Maine and following the retreating ice sheet as far inland as Grindstone in the Penobscot basin and Bingham in the Kennebec.

Soils and rocks of all sizes, previously picked up and transported by the glacier, were released from the melting ice and deposited in other locations by streams. Interestingly, many glacial deposits are stratified; that is, they consist of layers of materials sorted by size. The reason for this is quite simple: during warmer months, the glacier melts more rapidly, and because the resulting meltwater flows faster and stronger, it can move the larger rocks and coarser gravels further distances. As cooler seasonal climate slows the icemelt, the rate and force of meltwater flow decreases and the streams gradually drop their sediment loads—the larger, heavier materials settle out first, followed by the finer, lighter sands and silts.

Rivers of meltwater carried some of the debris to the sea, where it was

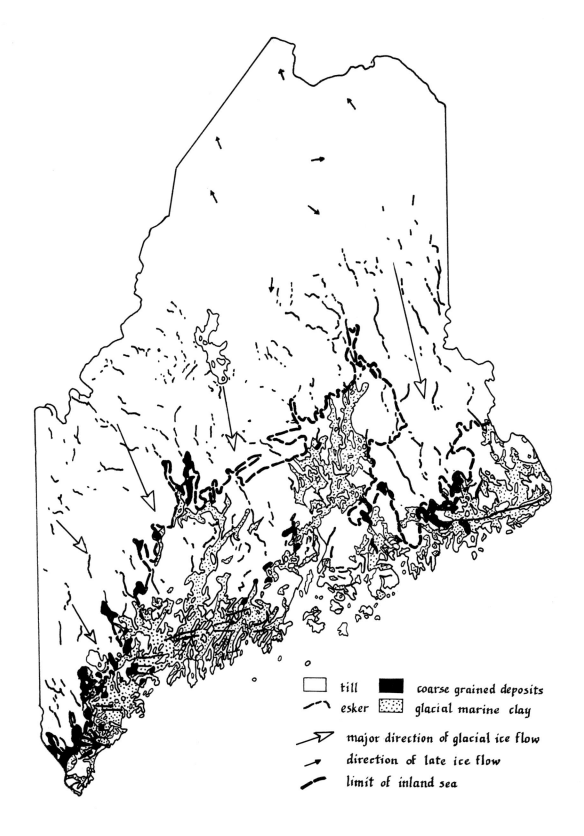

	till		coarse grained deposits
⌇	esker	⣿	glacial marine clay

⇨ major direction of glacial ice flow

→ direction of late ice flow

⌇ limit of inland sea

Maine Surficial Geology. Generalized
from W.B. Thompson and H.W. Borns, Jr.,
1985, Maine Geological Survey, Augusta.
Redrawn, by permission, from map published
by Hearne Brothers, Warren, Mich.

Columbia Falls Delta, Washington County, one of Maine's three outstanding glaciomarine deltas, was formed by glacial meltwater twelve thousand years ago. Note the delta's flat top and the sloping face on the left. Hank Tyler photo.

deposited as deltas composed of gravel, sand, and finer materials. Three of the many glaciomarine deltas thus formed in Maine are now considered to be unique in the United States: Pineo Ridge Delta, Columbia Falls Delta, and Gray Delta.[2]

Pineo Ridge, near Cherryfield, is an outstanding example of a glaciomarine delta. At about sixteen thousand acres, it is also Maine's largest. The

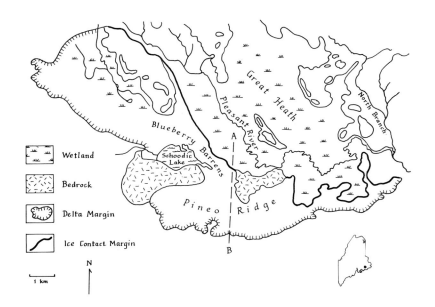

Pineo Ridge Delta, an outstanding example of a glaciomarine delta. Redrawn from H. W. Borns, Jr., Maine Critical Areas Program (1977).

topography of its northern edge is chaotic, composed of mounds and pits formed as sediments were deposited in direct contact with the melting edge of the glacier. Special features of this delta include remnants of old wave-cut cliffs and beaches, iceberg depressions, springs, and preserved braided-stream channels, showing the spreading of a stream as it became choked with sediment.

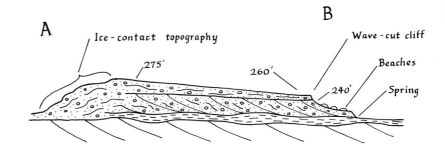

A
Ice-contact topography
275'
260'
240'

B
Wave-cut cliff
Beaches
Spring

Geological cross-section of Pineo Ridge Delta. Redrawn from H. W. Borns, Jr., Maine Critical Areas Program (1977).

In other situations, close to the retreating ice front but in quiet waters away from the mouths of streams, layers of very fine glacial sediment slowly settled on the sea floor. Clams, mussels, and other marine mollusks, whose modern forms live in the subarctic, were often buried by these accumulating sediments. Today this marine clay and silt, containing abundant remains of shells, is named the Presumpscot Formation and can be found throughout coastal Maine as well as at some inland locations. In addition to marine clay, large amounts of stratified sand and fine gravel, called outwash, were deposited in front of the melting ice sheet.

Beneath the melting glacier, many streams flowed over the ground surface in tunnels of ice, the walls of the ice acting to contain the deposits of sediment, which accumulated in layers on the streambeds. The courses of many of these ancient glacial streams can still be traced across the landscape, where long ridges of sand and gravel, called eskers, were left behind.[3] Maine has two dozen or so examplary eskers, which are outstanding in part because of their unaltered condition.

An esker, a serpentlike glacial deposit of sand and gravel, on Meddybemps Heath. This area has been designated a National Natural Landmark by the National Park Service. Elizabeth Thompson photo, courtesy of Maine Fish and Wildlife *Magazine.*

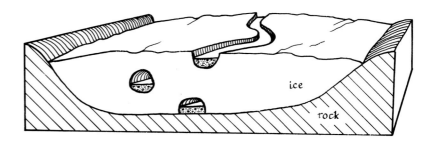

ice

rock

Possible location of esker channels in a glacier

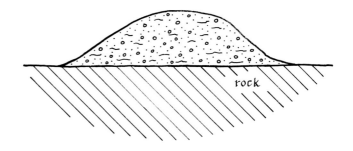

rock

Formation of eskers. Redrawn from H. W. Borns, Jr., Maine Critical Areas Program (1979).

Esker after deposition (cross section)

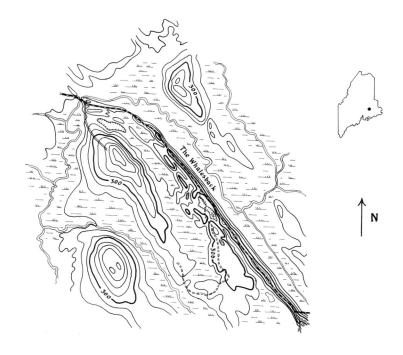

Dissipation of the glacier was not steady. It would sometimes pause, reform, perhaps even advance a little, then retreat again. Evidence of this behavior can be seen today in the form of moraines—ridges of rock debris carried forward by the ice flow and dropped along its melting edge.

In other cases, great chunks of ice broke off and were buried beneath layers of glacial sediment. Thus insulated, they sometimes lingered for years. When they finally melted, depressions in the landscape were left; some of these kettleholes are now ponds, and others bogs.[4] Kettleholes are abundant in Maine. Aside from their geological significance, kettles provide ideal conditions for the formation of bogs, which support highly specialized plant and animal life.

Most kettleholes are associated with kame topography, another glacial feature. As the melting glacier diminished, the meltwater flowing off its surface carried sediments to streams and ponds at its edges. Along the sides of valleys, steplike deposits of sands and gravels, called kame terraces, were left when the glacier finally melted away. In other cases, debris washed into depressions and openings in the ice. After the ice melted, these were left as

A complex of kettlehole ponds and an esker in central Kennebec County. This area has been designated a National Natural Landmark by the National Park Service. Hank Tyler photo.

A kettlehole bog in Somerset County. Hank Tyler photo, courtesy of Maine Fish and Wildlife *Magazine.*

mounds, called kames. Although these deposits were originally stratified, parts that were once in contact with glacial ice collapsed into a hodgepodge of unsorted sands and gravels when the ice melted.

As the glacier retreated from Maine, the land began to rebound, lifting slowly out of the sea as it was relieved of its enormous ice burden. As a result, the coastline was moved seaward. Today, much of southern Maine is composed of this uplifted and exposed ocean floor. Marine clay of the Presumpscot

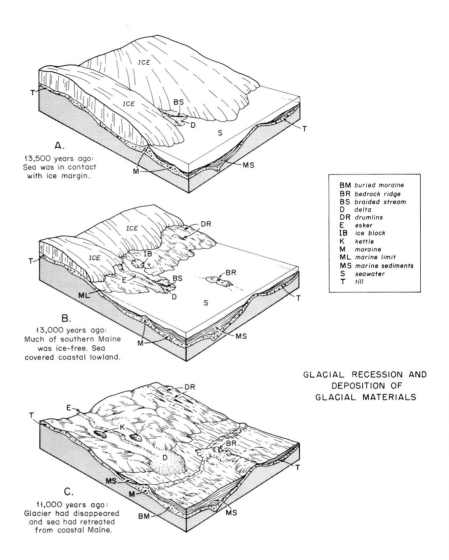

A.
13,500 years ago:
Sea was in contact
with ice margin.

B.
13,000 years ago:
Much of southern Maine
was ice-free. Sea
covered coastal lowland.

C.
11,000 years ago:
Glacier had disappeared
and sea had retreated
from coastal Maine.

BM	*buried moraine*
BR	*bedrock ridge*
BS	*braided stream*
D	*delta*
DR	*drumlins*
E	*esker*
IB	*ice block*
K	*kettle*
M	*moraine*
ML	*marine limit*
MS	*marine sediments*
S	*seawater*
T	*till*

GLACIAL RECESSION AND
DEPOSITION OF
GLACIAL MATERIALS

Sequence of glacial recession and deposition of surficial materials in southern Maine. Redrawn from R.D. Tucker, Surficial Geologic Map of Maine *(Augusta: Maine Geological Survey, Dept. of Conservation, 1985).*

Formation can now be found at elevations as high as three hundred feet above sea level along the coast. Further inland, rebound tilted up the clay deposits as much as five hundred feet. In recent times, this land has been the dumping ground of lazy, meandering streams no longer able to carry their loads of silts, sands, and gravels.

By ten to eleven thousand years ago, the glacier had melted completely in Maine. As the ice disappeared to the north beyond the Appalachian Chain, the deglaciated landscape probably was revegetated by tundra species. There were expanses of layered sand and gravel, as well as silt and clay. Other areas were strewn with rocks and boulders, called glacial till; centuries later these were arranged into the neat stone walls typical of early New England. Still larger

Bubble Rock, Acadia National Park, is a prominent example of an erratic. Dean Bennett photo.

boulders, appropriately named erratics, were distributed haphazardly across the land.

Eight thousand years ago, after the earth's crust had completed its rebound, the sea lay approximately three hundred feet below its present level. Five thousand years ago, glacial meltwater had brought it to within eight to twelve feet of what it is today. Since that time the sea has risen more slowly, permitting the formation of beaches—a fascinating process described in detail in Chapter 4. Due to the previously lower sea level, these began to develop several hundred feet offshore from their modern positions. Starting as barrier islands, or spits formed off rocky points, the beaches gradually moved landward as the sea level rose, covering the marshes that had formed in the shallow lagoons behind them.

Today the fine shaping of the intricate details of the surface goes on. Weather continues to do its part, cycling water and other matter, spurred on by the sun and the uneven solar heating of the earth's surface. The sea is still rising from the ongoing melting of glaciers and thermal expansion of the oceans. Tides continue their erosive action on the coast, drawing energy from the gravitational forces exerted by the sun, moon, and earth.

As an added factor, there is some evidence that parts of the coast are sinking. From Casco Bay southward, it appears to be sinking at the rate of about eight inches per century. However, surveys indicate that east of Machias the land is sinking at a much more rapid rate—possibly as much as three feet per century in the Passamaquoddy Bay area. These processes are known as coastal warping, and they, along with the waves, the winds and storms, the currents, and the freezes and thaws, contribute to the design of Maine—and to the formation of the special features that make the state unique.

3

Inland Waters

Clouds dump more than 200 trillion pounds of water over Maine each year—
enough to cover the state's thirty-three thousand square miles to a level waist
deep. Fortunately, nearly 60 percent of it either returns to the atmosphere as
water vapor or sinks into the ground, while the remainder runs off the land back
to the oceans whence it came.

Water in any one place, whether in the ground or on the surface, is
influenced by geologic events of the distant past. The mountain building
periods of several hundred million years ago established the fundamental
orientation of Maine's largest watersheds. (A watershed is a land area that
drains to a given point, such as the mouth of a river.) The direction of flow of
these river-basin waters is profoundly affected by the northern mountains of
the Appalachian Chain, cutting diagonally across the state in a northeast
direction and terminating in north-central Maine. The headwaters of the St.
John River drain off the northwestern flank of these mountains into a vast
watershed incorporating the north-flowing waters of several well-known tributaries—the Allagash, Fish, and Aroostook rivers. To the south, the mountain
slopes give rise to the south-flowing Androscoggin, Kennebec, and Penobscot
rivers, their expansive basins covering much of the remainder of the state.

In more recent times, glaciers reshaped the river basins and altered the
courses of their rivers and streams. The last glacier, entering Maine about
twenty-five thousand years ago, followed the ancient contours of the mountain
valleys, scouring and channelizing the bedrock. And when it melted, between
ten and fifteen thousand years ago, powerful rivers of glacial meltwater
dumped their loads of abrasive materials. The deposits often dammed valleys
and redirected the courses of streams. Deltas formed where the rivers met the
sea as it followed the retreating glacier inland over the present-day coastal
region. Wave action further worked the sediments. Where the deposits of
permeable sand and gravel were sufficient to conduct significant quantities of
ground water, aquifers were formed, their flows generally following the slope
of the land within the watersheds, though considerably slower than waters on
the surface.

Today the powerful hydrologic cycle, once responsible for sustaining the glaciers, replenishes the rivers and streams that continue to carve the land; it fills the lakes and ponds and nourishes the plants that turn them into wetlands. The results of all this activity include some of the most unusual examples of water-related features in the country.

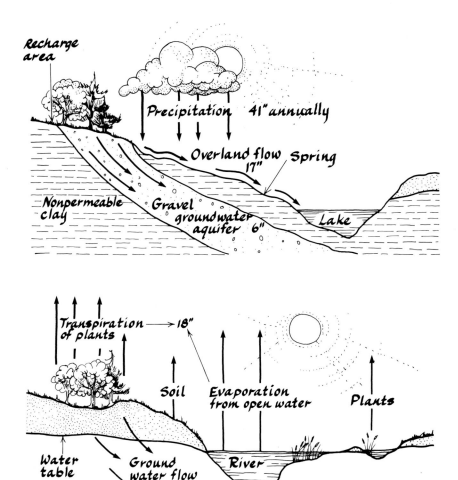

The hydrologic cycle is the source of Maine's abundant water supply.

Rivers and Streams

Ripogenus Gorge, located near the southwestern tip of Baxter State Park, is one of Maine's most spectacular gorges. Between nearly vertical rock walls, up to 280 feet high, it controls the wildly tumbling West Branch of the Penobscot for well over a mile. The exposed rocks, ranging in age from 500 to 350 million years, provide valuable clues to understanding the geology of central Maine. In addition to its scenic beauty and geologic significance, the gorge is legendary in the log driving history of the state. Ripogenus Dam, constructed above the gorge in 1917 to provide sluicing water for logs, was at that time a major engineering feat for such a remote wilderness area.

The lower segment of the West Branch includes one of the least developed river corridors in the state and contains a variety of geologic and hydrologic features. In addition to Ripogenus gorge, a number of significant waterfalls are located on the river and its tributary streams. These include

Katahdin Falls on Katahdin Stream and Nesowadnehunk Falls on the West Branch.

Grand Falls on the Dead River in Somerset County. This classic horseshoe falls is one of Maine's widest waterfalls. Thomas Brewer photo.

Maine has an estimated thirty-two thousand miles of flowing waters, and more of these rivers and streams are undeveloped and free-flowing than in any other state in the northeastern United States. A joint study by the Maine Department of Conservation and the National Park Service identifies more than four thousand miles that possess significant natural values.[1] In addition to geologic features—bedrock formations, fossils, waterfalls, gorges, and rapids—these values include important habitats for rare and unusual plants and animals, scenic and recreational attractions, and historic sites. The lower West Branch is but one of thirty-eight rivers or segments of rivers displaying characteristics unique not only within the state but also beyond its boundaries. The majority of these rivers, highly rated for their distinctive features, are concentrated in the four largest and least developed drainage basins: the Eastern Coastal River Basin, the Kennebec River Basin, the St. John River Basin, and the Penobscot River Basin.

1. Allagash
2. Aroostook
3. Dead
4. Dennys
5. East Machias
6. Lower Kennebec
7. Upper Kennebec
8. Machias (Washington County)
9. Moose
10. Narraguagus
11. East Branch, Penobscot
12. West Branch, Penobscot
13. Upper West Branch, Penobscot

14. Main stem, Penobscot
15. Pleasant (Washington County)
16. West Branch, Pleasant
17. Saco
18. St. Croix
19. St. John
20. Sheepscot
21. Aroostook
22. Carrabassett
23. Crooked
24. Damariscotta
25. Fish
26. Grand Lake Stream

27. Kennebago
28. Kennebec
29. Mattawamkeag
30. North Branch, Penobscot
31. South Branch, Penobscot
32. Piscataquis
33. Rapid
34. St. Francis
35. St. George
36. St. John
37. Sandy
38. West Branch, Union

Maine's outstanding waterfalls, gorges, rapids, and other important river-related features, such as fossils and scenic views, are spectacular evidence of the state's geologic history. During the mountain-building periods 300 to 500 million years ago, the durable metamorphic and igneous rocks over which our rivers flow were formed, but it was glaciation, a relatively recent geologic event, that profoundly influenced the shape of the formations we see today.

In the case of waterfalls, their existence is based on one of two conditions:

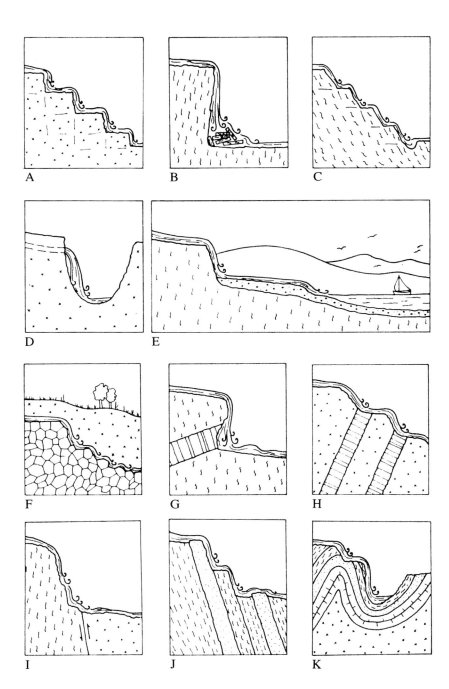

Development of waterfalls.
Redrawn from Thomas Brewer,
Maine Critical Areas Program (1978).

A. Falls developed on jointed crystalline bedrock. (Examples: Nesowadnehunk Falls, Step Falls, Damariscotta Falls.)

B. Falls developed on foliated bedrock with cleavage dipping upstream. (Examples: Angel Falls, Big Wilson Falls.)

C. Falls developed on foliated bedrock with cleavage dipping downstream. (Examples: Cold Stream Falls, Grand Pitch on the East Branch of the Penobscot, Screw Auger Falls in Gulf Hagas, Smalls Falls.)

D. Falls developed from a hanging valley where a stream enters a deep glaciated valley. (Example: Cascade Brook Falls in Grafton Notch.)

E. Falls developed on an old sea cliff originally cut by waves along the shoreline as it followed the retreating glacier inland. When the land rebounded after being relieved of the glacier's weight, the sea cliffs emerged. (Example: Cascade Stream Falls.)

F. Falls developed along the strike of a columnar jointed dike. (Example: Big Falls.)

G. Falls developed due to undercutting of a jointed dike. (Example: Cobb Brook Falls.)

H. Falls developed across the strike of dikes due to erosion of the dikes. (Examples: Hiram Falls, Union Falls, Old Falls Pond Dam.)

I. Falls due to the excavation of a fault zone. (Example: Little Wilson Falls.)

J. Falls developed across contacts. (Example: Old Roll Dam on the West Branch of the Penobscot.)

K. Falls developed across folds. (Examples: Sawtelle Falls, Moxie Falls, Houston Brook Falls.)

either the flow of water and sediment load have not yet proved powerful enough to erode the underlying shelf of bedrock over which the water tumbles; or the position and nature of the bedrock is such that the falls maintains itself even as erosion proceeds.[2] Throughout geologic time, the land has been

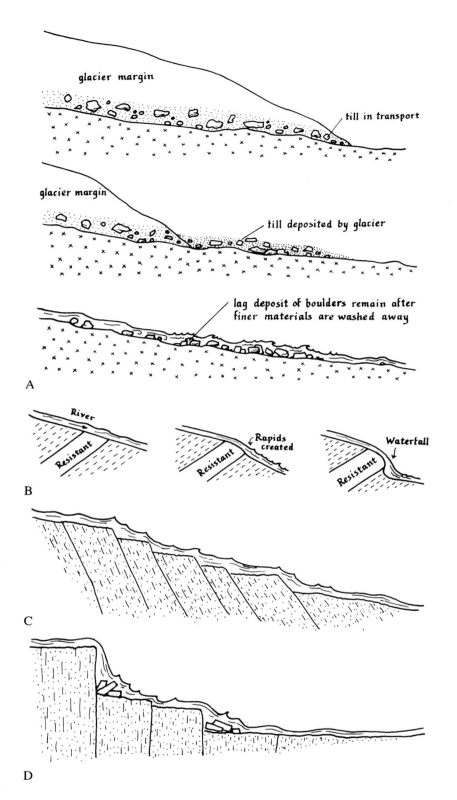

A

B

C

D

Development of whitewater rapids.
Redrawn from Janet McMahon, Maine
Critical Areas Program (1978).

A. Rapids developed over glacial
deposits. Pockwockamus Falls, on
the West Branch of the Penobscot,
is a good example, as are Wigwam
Rapids (Machias River), Limington
Rips (Saco River), and Aziscohos
Falls (Megalloway River).

B. Development of rapids due to differential
erosion. Wassataquoik Stream and the
Cribwork, on the West Branch of the Penobscot
River, show this type of rapids.

C. Rapids developed on foliated bedrock
with cleavage dipping upstream. Portions
of the Heater, on the Mattawamkeag
River, were formed in this manner.

D. Rapids developed on foliated
bedrock with cleavage dipping downstream.
Stair Falls, on the East Branch of the
Penobscot River, is a good example.

subjected to a continuous leveling process. Erosion of glacial deposits and
bedrock causes the landscape to become flatter, and so, too, waterfalls
degenerate into rapids, eventually becoming meandering streams. (In some
situations rapids develop first, followed by the formation of a falls as the
weaker zones of rock in the riverbed begin to wear.) Many rapids were formed
over glacially deposited boulders that were too large and heavy to wash away

with other glacial debris.[3] Because these lagged behind, in a sense, they are called lag deposits. Generally, it is difficult to determine the exact set of factors governing the formation of falls and rapids because of the complex and erratic action of rivers over long periods. Both falls and rapids, however, are only temporary features on the ever-changing landscape.

Gorges, like rapids and falls, result from the erosion of glacial debris and bedrock.[4] But unlike falls, which are primarily cut *back* by erosion, gorges are cut *down* into the bedrock, often appearing as deep, narrow passages with steep, rocky sides. Some gorges were created as a direct result of glaciation, either by the movement of a valley glacier or by large volumes of abrasive glacial meltwater. These tend to exist on steep south-facing slopes of hilly or

Large potholes like this one are evidence of the powerful erosion caused by torrents of glacial meltwater. Courtesy of Maine Bureau of Parks and Recreation

At Moxie Falls, in Somerset County, Moxie Stream plunges fifty feet. Thomas Brewer photo.

mountainous areas. Others formed during the normal wearing away of waterfalls, fault zones, or igneous dikes, which often are weaker than the rocks that surround them.

Studies by the Maine Critical Areas Program show that within Maine's boundaries are about forty whitewater rapids, more than sixty waterfalls, and perhaps as many as twenty gorges—all singled out for their exceptional qualities. Many are important for their scientific significance as well. Gorges and waterfalls, in particular, contain large areas of exposed bedrock, which is usually difficult to study because it is normally covered by glacial deposits and developed soils. The location and characteristics of gorges provide important clues to the geologic history of an area.

Moxie Falls, in the upper Kennebec River Basin, is probably one of the best structural-geology teaching sites in the state, revealing information about two large-scale folded rock structures in the area. One is an upwardly convex fold of layered rocks (an anticline), and the other is a syncline, an upwardly concave fold. The falls is also one of Maine's highest and most scenic.

The upper Kennebec River Basin is part of the third largest watershed in New England and contains the unique Kennebec River Gorge, a prime geologic locality and one of the finest rafting areas in the eastern United States. Cold Stream Falls, also in the basin, is small but exceptionally scenic.

Pockwockamus Falls Whitewater Rapids, on the lower West Branch of the Penobscot River, is also of scientific interest; it is one of the state's best examples of rapids formed over a lag deposit. The half-mile stretch consists of two distinct drops, both surging over boulder-strewn riverbeds.

Upper Pockwockamus Falls Whitewater Rapids, along the West Branch of the Penobscot River, has an exceptionally steep pitch of fast-moving water. Janet McMahon photo.

Kezar Falls Gorge, on the Kezar River in the Saco River Basin, is another feature of scientific and scenic interest. A deep, sinuous gorge over thirty feet deep and six feet wide, it was ground out of bedrock by a debris-loaded stream during the last phases of the glacier's recession. Evidence of this action remains, in the form of an esker pointing directly into the mouth of the gorge. This gorge demonstrates the origin of several similar gorges in the state, including Screw Auger Falls in Grafton (shown in Section I Perspective) and Snows Falls in Paris.

The seventy-five-mile-long Saco River Basin also contains Hiram Falls, an excellent locality for studying the origin of granite. In addition, the Saco River offers some of the most outstanding examples of meandering river channels in the Northeast. Though close to Maine's most densely populated region, the stretch of river from Hiram to Fryeburg is, surprisingly, one of the least developed in the state. Its stretches of natural shoreline, clean and easily navigated waters, and accessible location all contribute to the Saco's status as Maine's most heavily used canoe-touring river.

Another geologic asset found along Maine's rivers and streams is fossil-bearing bedrock. Several areas along the East Branch of the Penobscot have yielded fossils: brachiopods, trilobites, and coral found in exposed bedrock of limy shale, sandstone, and conglomerate.

The East Branch system has one of greatest concentrations of geologic and hydrologic features in the state. It is located in the Penobscot River Basin, Maine's largest watershed and the second largest in New England (only the Connecticut is larger). The headwaters of the East Branch include Allagash Stream and Allagash, Chamberlain, and Telos lakes, which were part of the St. John River watershed until 1841.[5] At that time, the business climate in northern Maine was one of intense competition among powerful lumbering interests

Located in Grafton Notch State Park, scenic Screw Auger Falls Gorge was ground out of granite and pegmatite bedrock by a glacial stream carrying large sediment loads. Courtesy of Maine Bureau of Parks and Recreation.

vying for control of the waterways and access to virgin timber. Dams were built at chamberlain and Telos lakes, cutting them off from the Allagash and St. John rivers. The lakes were thus raised to a level where the water could be dumped into an old glacially incised gorge between Telos Lake and Webster Lake on the East Branch. Two hundred and seventy square miles of Allagash River drainage were added to the Penobscot watershed by this engineering maneuver, enabling loggers to drive the timber to mills and ports in Maine instead of Canada, where profits were lower.

Haskell Rock Pitch is a whitewater rapid located in an exceptionally scenic area along the East Branch. Haskell Rock itself (reportedly named after a logger who was stranded there during high water and drowned) is a distinct mass of heavily eroded conglomerate.

Upstream from Haskell Rock Pitch is Stair Falls Whitewater Rapids, a striking example of how rapids develop over resistant rock layers that dip

Left: Stair Falls Rapids, East Branch of the Penobscot River, is a good example of how rapids are formed over resistant rock layers. Janet McMahon photo. Courtesy of Down East *Magazine.*

Haskell Rock, at Haskell Rock Pitch on the East Branch of the Penobscot River, illustrates the sculpturing effect of the river on sedimentary rock. Janet McMahon photo.

downstream. The most unusual characteristic of this set of rapids is the regularity of its series of drops, giving the falls the appearance of stairs.

Many of Maine's rivers and their special features have played distinctive roles in the state's history. Human activity has long been associated with waterways. Early peoples were well aware of the waterfalls, gorges, and whitewater rapids along their canoe routes; for centuries the Wabanakis judged distances by them, established campsites near portage trails, and took fish from the rapids and pools. They called whitewater rapids Abol ("where the water laughs in coming down"), Debsconeag ("carrying place"), and Passamagamet ("at the place of many fish").

European explorers, penetrating the wilderness, viewed falls and rapids as obstacles to their inland excursions, but the early entrepreneurs who followed recognized them as sources of power to move logs and turn the wheels of machines. Today, many of Maine's waterfalls have been inundated by dams, and they and numerous other geologic features now lie drowned beneath engineered lakes. The waters behind Ripogenous Dam, for example, now cover Pine Stream Falls and Chesuncook Falls in the West Branch region. But a great many remain, reminding us of a past rich in legend and history: log running, political intrigue, and fortunes made and lost.

Debsconeag Falls Whitewater Rapids, along the West Branch of the Penobscot. The name comes from a Wabanaki word meaning "carrying place." This section of rapids is approximately two hundred feet wide and thirteen hundred feet long and is a good example of how rapids develop over resistant rock layers and eroded debris. Janet McMahon photo.

Gulf Hagas, Piscataquis County. One of Maine's most spectacular gorges, Gulf Hagas contains a series of waterfalls and small rapids. Thomas Brewer photo.

The Maine Tourmaline Necklace is crafted from gold panned in the Swift River and twenty-four tourmaline gemstones from the famous Plumbago Mine in Newry. Photo by G.M. Hart, Maine State Museum.

Debsconeag Falls Whitewater Rapids is one such formation with historic significance. Its name is derived from the Indians, who portaged around this carrying place because of its steep pitch and turbulent, high-standing waves. Debsconeag, on the lower West Branch of the Penobscot, also has the dubious distinction of being the site of many log jams. To avoid the jams, massive log booms were used to hold back the logs until the water level was high enough to carry them over the rapids. Today, remnants of the huge boom logs and the chains that held them together can still be seen on the eastern bank of the river.

Another historic logging site is Old Roll Dam, located on the upper West Branch of the Penobscot. This falls, a series of nine six-foot drops over bedrock with cleavage dipping upstream, is the former location of an old log-driving dam—one of many constructed with simple tools and great effort thoughout the state.

The upper West Branch flows into Chesuncook Lake. Chesuncook Village, located on the northwest shore of this lake, thrived during times of heavy logging in the 1800s and is now on the National Register of Historic Places.

The Pleasant River, also in the Penobscot River Basin, flows through one of the state's more remote areas. Like the Penobscot River, the Pleasant played an important part in Maine's logging industry. Its West Branch and tributaries offer a number of significant natural features, including Screw Auger Falls, on Gulf Hagas Stream, and Hay Brook Falls. Gulf Hagas Gorge, on the West Branch, is spectacular: a canyon eight miles long and up to 130 feet deep, probably formed during a late- or post-glacial period by the release of a huge volume of water from an ice-dammed lake to the north. The river flows over five major falls as it makes its way through the nearly vertical walls of the gorge. In addition, this region contains a state-maintained historic site, the Katahdin Iron Works, and the Hermitage, location of an old-growth stand of white pine and site of an old hunting camp.

Some areas along Maine's rivers are noted for their superb aesthetic qualities. Coos Canyon, on the Swift River in Byron, is one. This gorge is about fifteen hundred feet long and over twenty feet deep, with many excellent examples of erosional features, such as potholes—smooth-sided hollows in the bedrock formed by abrasion from pebbles and other rocks caught in the swirl of eddies. The Maine Department of Transportation maintains a roadside rest area by the gorge.

The Swift River is also famous for its gold-panning history; in fact, it supplied the gold in the Maine Tourmaline Necklace.[6] This beautiful piece of jewelry, a gift to the state in 1977 by the Maine Retail Jewelers Association,

is crafted from twenty-four pink, red, green, and blue tourmaline gemstones from the famous Plumbago Mine in Newry. The stones are set in a chain of pure gold, panned in the Swift River over a period of twenty-seven years. Forty-three unaltered nuggets were incorporated into the design while others were refined and smelted to make the settings.

The Swift River is a tributary of the Androscoggin, one of Maine's largest rivers. The Androscoggin flows 164 miles from Umbagog Lake to its outlet near Brunswick. Its headwaters include the beautiful Rangeley Lakes region. A number of outstanding features associated with the Androscoggin and its tributaries include Aziscohos Falls Whitewater Rapids on the Magalloway River and Big Falls on the Cupsuptic River.

One falls of exceptional beauty in the Androscoggin River watershed is Angel Falls on Mountain Brook in Franklin County. With two large drops, one almost forty feet and the other nearly a hundred feet, Angel Falls is the state's highest. It also appears to be a hanging falls, unusual in Maine. These occur where a river valley is deepened by glaciation at a rate faster than the channel

Angel Falls, Oxford County, is one of Maine's highest waterfalls. E.T. Richardson, Jr., photo.

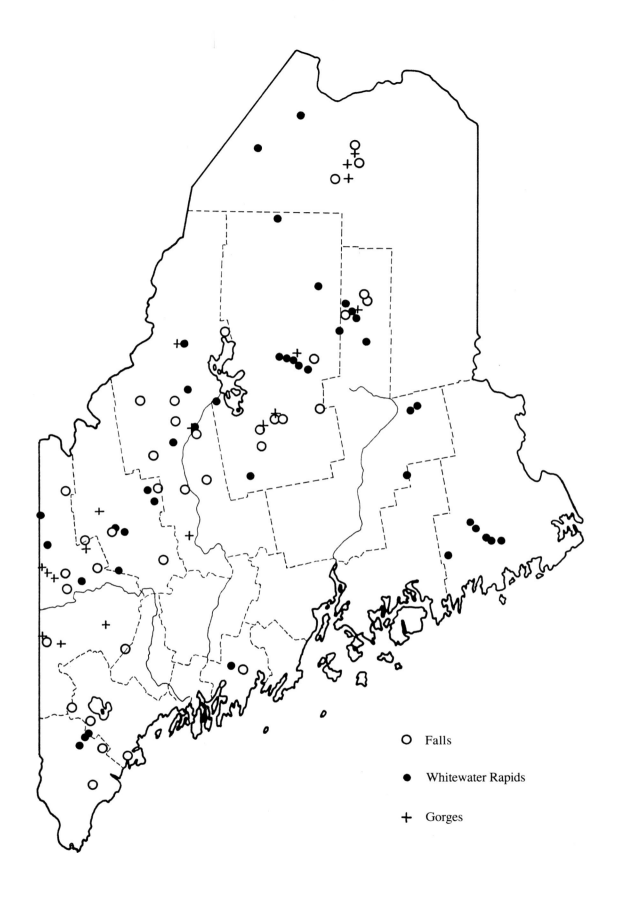

Significant falls, whitewater rapids, and gorges in Maine. From Maine Critical Areas Program.

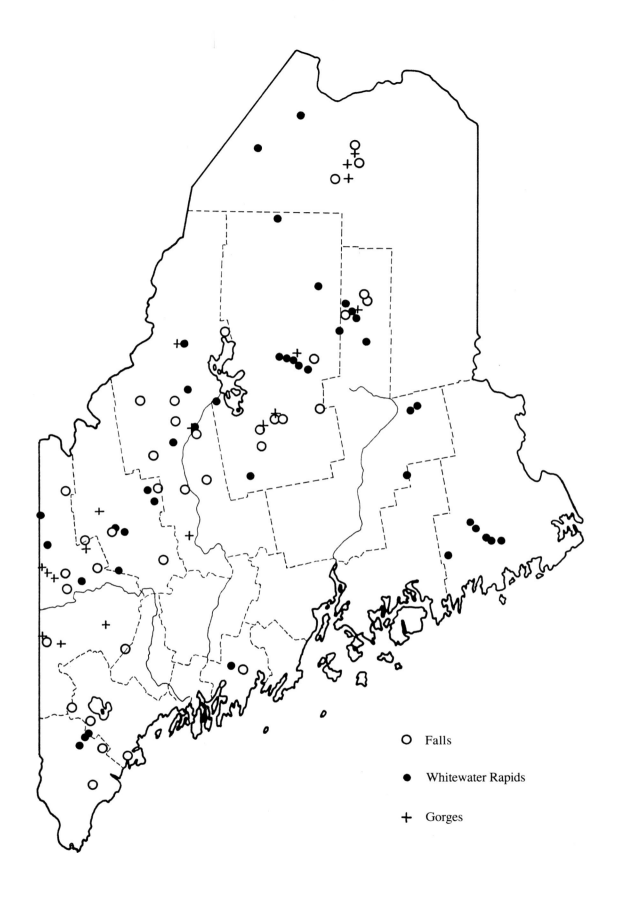

Falls

Whitewater Rapids

Gorges

U N U S U A L   F E A T U R E S   O F   L A N D   A N D   W A T E R

of an entering tributary stream, thus creating a drop where the stream joins the main valley.

Many of Maine's scenic features are seldom seen because of their remoteness. Dunn Falls is one of these, a spectacular series of waterfalls and cascades on a mountain stream in Andover North Surplus. The falls consists of two large vertical drops of approximately fifty-five feet and seventy-five feet. In certain sections the bedrock walls are nearly three hundred feet high.

The St. John River Basin contains many such remote and beautiful scenic features. It is an impressive watershed, draining over twenty-one thousand square miles in Maine and the Canadian provinces of Quebec and New Brunswick. The river itself is approximately 450 miles long. The Aroostook, Allagash, and Fish rivers are the upper St. John's major tributaries in Maine.

The Machias is another of the state's longest free-flowing wild rivers. One thirty-mile-long segment, from Whitneyville Dam to Tug Mountain in Washington County, is not crossed by even a single bridge. The river lies in the Eastern Coastal Watershed, which encompasses the basins of all the rivers east of the Penobscot that empty into the Atlantic Ocean. The St. Croix River is the largest in the basin and is recognized as an outstanding river for backcountry excursions (others include the Allagash, the East and upper West branches of the Penobscot, and the St. John).

Maine's whitewater rapids are also popular among those who enjoy canoeing, kayaking, rafting, and fishing. Improved access to once-remote locations has resulted in statewide (and, in some cases, nationwide) reputations. Rivers identified as outstanding for whitewater canoeing include the Carrabassett, Dead, East and West branches of the Penobscot, upper Kennebec, Machias, Rapid, Sebois, and Wassataquoik.

The St. John River is the largest, least developed, and longest free-flowing river system east of the Mississippi. The natural, unregulated water flow accounts for low water conditions in the summer. Hank Tyler photo.

Rapid River, Oxford County, is one of Maine's spectacular whitewater-rapids rivers. Hank Tyler photo.

Despite their diverse and unique features, Maine's rivers and streams are not the only waters to capture our interest and attention; the state's lakes and ponds, numbering in the thousands, also display many inviting and useful qualities.

Lakes and Ponds

Maine is covered with lakes and ponds, many of which have figured strongly in the state's history. Those who have seen Maine's forest wealth laid out before their eyes in the form of acres and acres of logs —rafted up, boomed, and being towed across Chesuncook, Moosehead, and any number of other lakes and ponds—will never forget this once common sight from the log-driving past.

The formation of most of Maine's lakes and ponds (terms that in this state generally mean the same) can be linked to a single cause: glaciation. In fact, Maine has the second largest number of natural glaciated lakes of any state east of the Mississippi River: about three thousand lakes and ponds over ten acres in size and another two thousand between one and ten acres. The last glacier scraped out the basins of many of these when it moved across the region; others were widened and deepened by the ice sheet. Some basins were created when glacial deposits blocked off river valleys, and many, called kettles, were formed when huge, isolated blocks of melting ice were buried in glacial outwash.

Northwestern Maine's Moosehead Lake, covering about 117 square miles (76,295 acres), is the state's largest—in fact, the largest lake in New England to lie wholly within the boundaries of a single state. Of Moosehead Lake, Thoreau wrote in 1853: "a suitably wild-looking sheet of water, sprinkled with small, low islands, which were covered with shaggy spruce and other wild wood,—seen over the infant port of Greenville with mountains on each side and far in the north, and a steamer's smokepipe rising above a roof."[7]

Sebago Lake, in southern Maine, is second to Moosehead in size, with a surface area of over forty-four square miles (29,526 acres). However, it holds the distinction of being the deepest, at 316 feet, and its deepest point is forty feet below sea level. Geologists believe that Sebago was created in part by a dam of glacial drift filling an old preglacial outlet at the south end of its Lower Bay.

Speck Pond, near Grafton Notch State Park in the Mahoosuc Mountains, at 3670 feet, is Maine's most elevated body of water. It lies in a cirque—a steep-walled, half-bowl-shaped depression formed by the erosive action of a mountain glacier. Speck Pond is one of less than a dozen cirque lakes (tarns) in Maine.

Speck Pond, Maine's highest (3670 feet), is in the Mahoosuc Mountains, Oxford County. Fred Bavendam photo.

UNUSUAL FEATURES OF LAND AND WATER

Some of Maine's lowest lakes (those near sea level) are called bar-dammed lakes. Sediments deposited by ocean waves become bars, which dam coastal rivers to form lakes. Two examples occur on Mount Desert Island: Hunters Beach Cove and Sandy Beach at Newport Cove.

Maine is famous for its remote, pristine lakes and ponds, where the silence of many a summer's night is broken only by the echoing tremolo of the loon. In northwestern and northern Maine, due to the character of the bedrock and peculiarities of glaciation, small ponds, rather than large lakes, dot the landscape. A good example of this can be found in the isolated, 22,000-acre Deboullie Township in northern Maine.[8] Twenty-one ponds are located in this publicly owned territory, several characterized by steep, cliffy shorelines and surrounding forest containing stands of old-growth trees, sharp ridges, and rare plants. The deep waters of some are inhabited by the rare blueback charr.

Deboullie Pond, in Aroostook County, is especially deep. It is one of ten lakes in Maine supporting a population of landlocked arctic charr. Deboullie Pond is surrounded by state land managed by the Bureau of Public Lands. Hank Tyler photo.

A talus slope of broken rock at Deboullie Pond. This slope, like others in the area, supports numerous lichens and bog-type plants. Deboullie Pond is highly scenic because of the surrounding mountains. Hank Tyler photo.

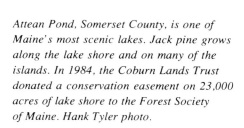

Attean Pond, Somerset County, is one of Maine's most scenic lakes. Jack pine grows along the lake shore and on many of the islands. In 1984, the Coburn Lands Trust donated a conservation easement on 23,000 acres of lake shore to the Forest Society of Maine. Hank Tyler photo.

Other examples of remote, picturesque bodies of water are Attean Pond, near Jackman; Lobster Lake, just east of the northern tip of Moosehead Lake; and First Debsconeag Lake, near the lower West Branch of the Penobscot south of Mt. Katahdin. All three have large undeveloped sections of shoreline, scattered sand beaches, dispersed stands of jack pine, and nearby scenic mountains.

Lobster Lake, Piscataquis County, with Big Spencer Mountain in the background. Noteworthy beaches and unusual jack pine forests are found along its shores. In 1981, Great Northern Paper Company granted a conservation easement on the lake's shores to the State of Maine, and in 1984 the state purchased more shoreland to complete protection of the lake. Hank Tyler photo.

All lakes and ponds go through a natural aging pattern, producing a condition called eutrophication—a situation in which a large population of aquatic plant life, fed by an excess of nutrients from natural erosion and runoff, depletes the dissolved oxygen supply in the water. This normally slow process

UNUSUAL FEATURES OF LAND AND WATER

A sand beach at Lobster Lake.
Hank Tyler photo.

can be hastened by pollution and other human activities that increase deposits of sediments and inflow of nutrients such as phosphates. At some point most ponds will succumb, becoming wetlands and (in many cases) eventually dry land. The record of this metamorphosis is easily read on the landscape. In fact, because so many wetlands exist today, it is speculated that Maine once had thousands more lakes and ponds. Later sections of this book will identify and describe the uncommon plants and animals these wetlands harbor.

The diversity and character of Maine's inland waters and their unique geologic and hydrologic features are truly valuable assets in terms of the state's natural wealth. But it doesn't stop there; Maine is also fortunate that it has a coastal shoreland with hundreds of other remarkable features carved by the never-ceasing work of ice and water.

4

The Coast

Petit Manan Point, a Washington County National Wildlife Refuge. Spectacular granitic cobble and boulder beaches fringe the shoreline of this wild and exposed peninsula. Jack pine, coastal plateau peatlands, and subarctic maritime plants can be found here. L. Kenneth Fink, Jr. photo, courtesy of Maine Critical Areas Program.

In the natural world, areas of transition between ecosystems—where grassland meets forest or forest meets wetland—provide a rich diversity of habitat for an increased variety of species. These belts at the boundaries of distinct natural systems are always rewarding to study and explore, but none is more fascinating than the region where land encounters the sea.

"It's like geography. . . . The interesting parts are the edges," muses carpenter Jim Locke in Tracy Kidder's book, *House.* The parallel drawn between a craftsman adding the finishing touches to a building and the refinements produced by the natural forces that shape the rim of a continent is apt. The basic processes that form a coastline—actions of wind and wave, erosion and fabrication—occur throughout the world, but in Maine, special grace notes appear. These include unusual sea caves, spouting holes, thunderholes, and marine arches. Combined with other coastal features, such as beaches, headlands, and islands, they create an "edge" that is interesting indeed.

Maine's "rockbound coast" is legendary, a setting of restless and raw beauty. Here the surf drums the shore in slow time; here the winds and breezes shift continuously between land and sea at the slightest cooling or warming, and mists materialize and fade with the currents of air and water. This coast is a place for the senses and emotions to be turned both inward and outward.

Much of the shoreline is broken, scarred, and strewn with rocky debris, the result of glacial erosion, wave action, and weathering. Deeply notched bays and narrow toothlike reaches alternate with elongated necks and jagged headlands, multiplying by a least a factor of fifteen the 230-mile coastline. Offshore, the tops of drowned ridges, hills, and mountains break the surface of the sea as islands.

Most of the coastal rock is metamorphic, as at Pemaquid Point, or igneous, like the fine-grained granite and outstanding basaltic dikes that characterize Schoodic Point. High wave-cut cliffs are not as common here as in California, for this shoreline rebounded only comparatively recently from glacial pressure. Instead, along much of its length the land slopes gradually to meet the sea.

SOME SIGNIFICANT GEOLOGIC FEATURES OF THE COAST OF MAINE

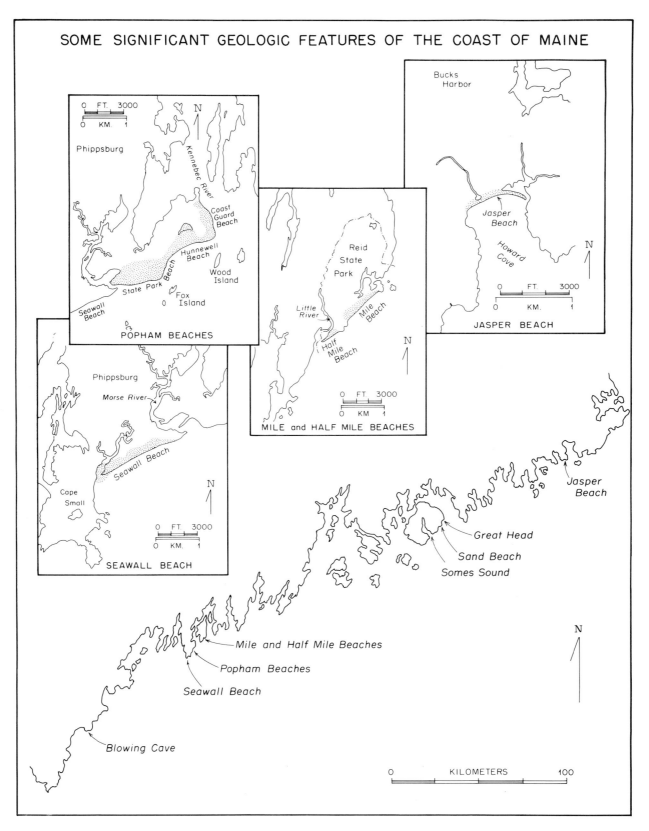

Some significant geologic features
of the coast of Maine. Based on
information from the Maine Critical
Areas Program. Marie E. Litterer, artist.

Great Head Cliff on Mt. Desert Island, one of the highest headlands on the eastern seaboard, rises 145 feet above the ocean. Courtesy of National Park Service.

Seawall Beach and Popham Beach, near the mouth of the Kennebec River, are two of Maine's best preserved beach systems. Seawall Beach is protected by a conservation easement to The Nature Conservancy and managed as an educational and research area by Bates College. L. Kenneth Fink, Jr., photo.

Exceptions do occur east from Machias Bay, where cliffs characterize the shoreland, and at Great Head on Mt. Desert Island. One of the highest headlands on the eastern seaboard, Great Head rises 145 feet above the ocean.

Sand Beaches

Despite this abundance of rock, sand beaches are found nestled among the numerous bays and inlets—their smooth, curving profiles adding scenic relief to the juts and jags that characterize much of Maine's coastline.[1] Sand beaches are most prevalent on the southern coast from the New Hampshire border to Portland. Here the early post-glacial Androscoggin River, which probably at that time drained south through Sebago Lake, deposited abundant quantities of sand along the present coastline. The southern beaches are also generally longer, due in part to a relatively straight coastline produced by bedrock folds paralleling the sea's edge. While most of the glacially derived sand for these beaches comes from nearby sources, two of the largest beach systems in the vicinity of Casco Bay are formed of sand carried from upland deposits. These are the Popham Beach system, near the mouth of the Kennebec, and the Old Orchard Beach system, supplied by the Saco.

North of Casco Bay, where sand is limited, beaches are fewer. The highly irregular coast has deep embayments, and the beaches are primarily formed by wave action at the heads of bays. This activity, in conjunction with the erosion of rocky headlands, tends to straighten the coastline. Erosion of bedrock usually provides only minor amounts of sediment to Maine's beaches, but Sand Beach on Mt. Desert Island is an exception; its sand contains 60 to 70 percent (by weight) from nearby bedrock.

Sand Beach also illustrates another derivation of beach sediment: mollusk shells. It is one of few Maine beaches composed of a high percentage (by volume) of carbonate shell fragments from marine organisms—a composition unusual along the northeast coast but typical of tropical regions. Several other carbonate beaches are found on islands in Penobscot Bay.

Other, smaller sand beaches are scattered along the coast. In all, over two dozen sand beaches remain in an undeveloped state; these are of special importance because of identified geological, botanical, and zoological values. Some, for example, provide habitat for the least tern and the piping plover, both on the Federal Endangered Species list. Because sand beaches are among Maine's most valuable recreational, as well as environmental, resources, many have been damaged by careless or improper use. Compared with more southerly states, Maine has relatively few of these fragile ecosystems, yet the varied shape and geological character of the state's coastline, coupled with the influence of wind, waves, and currents, have produced unusual beach forms and features of both scenic and scientific interest. For many, sand beaches are one of Maine's indispensable attributes; as such, they require sound management and development policies to preserve their special qualities.

In order to fully appreciate sand beaches, it is helpful to become acquainted with the materials that create, the forces that shape, and the features that identify them.

A beach results from a precise correlation between the size of particles of glacial sediment—sands, silts, and clays—and the speed of moving water. The finer silts and clays are carried away, while the coarser grains of sand are left behind to form the beach. Waves are the most important agent in the process of building beaches as well as eroding them. Steep, high-energy waves, such

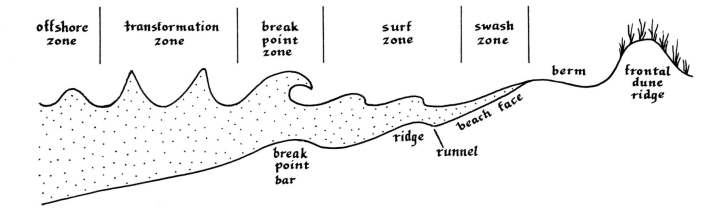

offshore zone | transformation zone | break point zone | surf zone | swash zone

berm
frontal dune ridge
beach face
ridge
runnel
break point bar

as those produced by storms, can remove large amounts of sand from beaches very quickly. In general, beaches are eroded in winter and built up during the summer months. Winds are of secondary importance; however, they do influence the shape and movement of dunes as well as the height of waves striking the beach.

Beaches are classified into several types according to their appearance when viewed from above. Fringing beaches are sandy strands at the edge of the land where it meets the sea. When they occur at the heads of bays and coves,

Wave action and beach building. As waves approach a shore, they undergo a transformation when the water depth becomes about one-half the wavelength. The wave height and steepness increase until the wave becomes unstable, falls forward, and breaks. The water then flows across the beach to the wash zone. Redrawn from B. W. Nelson and L. Kenneth Fink, Jr., Geological and Botanical Features of Sand Beach Systems in Maine, Maine Sea Grant Publications Bulletin 14 (Augusta: Maine Critical Areas Program, State Planning Office, 1980).

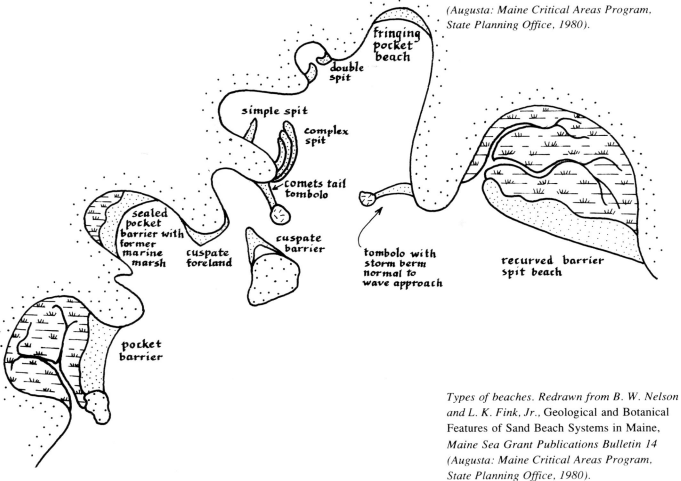

fringing pocket beach
double spit
simple spit
complex spit
comets tail tombolo
sealed pocket barrier with former marine marsh
cuspate foreland
cuspate barrier
tombolo with storm berm normal to wave approach
recurved barrier spit beach
pocket barrier

Types of beaches. Redrawn from B. W. Nelson and L. K. Fink, Jr., Geological and Botanical Features of Sand Beach Systems in Maine, Maine Sea Grant Publications Bulletin 14 (Augusta: Maine Critical Areas Program, State Planning Office, 1980).

they are called fringing pocket beaches—a type common in Maine. Crescent Beach in Cape Elizabeth is one example.

A barrier beach is attached to the mainland at both ends and forms a protective barrier for a present or former lagoon behind it. Examples include Mile Beach, at Reid State Park, and Pemaquid Beach. A tombolo beach is

Mile Beach, at Reid State Park, is a classic barrier beach. L. Kenneth Fink, Jr., photo.

Another barrier beach, this one at Roque Bluffs State Park. L. Kenneth Fink, Jr., photo.

Little River, at the Wells National Estuarine Reserve. L. Kenneth Fink, Jr., photo.

attached at both ends to islands or to an island at one end and the mainland at the other. Examples exist at Fox and Wood islands in the Popham Beach system.

Cuspate forelands are formed where two wave trains or currents come together in the lee of an island. The best examples are found at Popham Beach in the lee of Fox and Wood islands. Spits are beaches attached to the land at one end and free at the other. The best remaining example of a double barrier spit exists at Little River by Laudholm Beach in Wells.

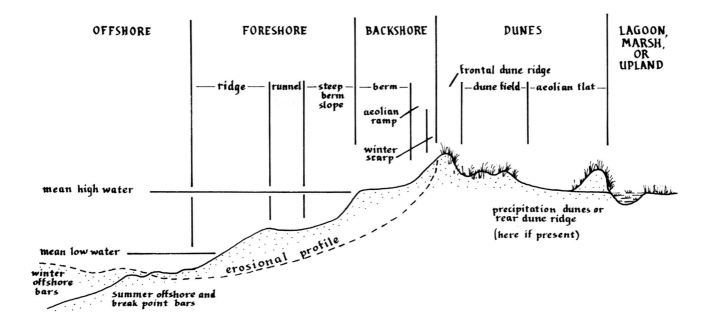

In profile, a beach is divided into offshore, foreshore, backshore, and dunes. The offshore is always submerged and often contains bars formed of sand removed from the foreshore and backshore. The foreshore is the zone between high and low tides. Here, above a ridge, is a low tide terrace containing a runnel, or shallow channel of rivulets. During the summer, as sand is transported from the offshore bars to the steep berm slope and berm, the ridge and runnel system migrates up the beach. The berm, a built-up terrace, is the major feature of the backshore.

Dunes occur between the backshore and the lagoon, marsh, or land area behind the beach. On most undeveloped beaches, the frontal ridge is the most outstanding feature of the dunes. It is also the most important, for this ridge buffers the backdunes and marshes during storms and stores sand for rebuilding beaches depleted by wind and wave.

Dune formation is itself the result of a reciprocal interaction between sand, blown landward from the berm, and vegetation, primarily American beach grass. This is a dune plant par excellence, capable of enduring major stress from salt spray and extreme changes in soil and air moisture levels, temperature, and chemistry. It can survive sand burial to a depth of three feet or more. Water-saving devices such as sunken stomates (openings that allow leaves to breathe) and curled leaves allow it to survive the desertlike dune conditions.

Once a beach grass plant gets a foothold, it begins to trap windblown sand. More sand is trapped as the plant grows until a balance between sand, plant, and wind is reached. The vegetation stabilizes the sand and establishes conditions for the formation of dune fields. Back dune fields generally reach a state of equilibrium where sand is no longer added to them in significant amounts by the wind. Instead, the sand accumulates on the frontal dune ridge. The wind continues shaping the dunes, however, as well as creating aeolian (wind-developed) flats—sparsely vegetated, level, sandy areas—behind them.

Parabolic dunes are U-shaped features carved in the sand by strong offshore winds. In Maine, the best examples of parabolic dunes stabilized by vegetation are in Phippsburg, at Seawall Beach. Others can be found at Popham, Reid, and Ogunquit beaches.

Profile of a beach. Redrawn from B. W. Nelson and L. K. Fink, Jr., Geological and Botanical Features of Sand Beach Systems in Maine, Maine Sea Grant Publications Bulletin 14 (Augusta: Maine Critical Areas Program, State Planning Office, 1980).

Today, only three of the state's beaches have large undisturbed dune fields: Popham and Seawall, in Phippsburg, and Reid (Georgetown). Together, these account for almost five and a half miles of coastline. Almost two-thirds of the original major dune fields are now heavily developed or altered. Beaches that have been changed drastically by human impact include Ogunquit, Moody, Wells, Goose Rocks, Old Orchard, and Higgins.

Seawall Beach is the largest undeveloped barrier spit beach in Maine. The beach and back dune area is well over a mile long and protects an extensive salt marsh and tidal river system behind. The dune fields contain the largest area of stabilized parabolic dunes in the state and the largest active parabolic dune. By the mouth of the Morse River, the beach forms one side of a double spit. Because of its natural condition, Seawall Beach provides a good site for studies of the development and maintenance of sand beach features.

Adjacent to Seawall Beach on the opposite side of the Morse River is the Popham Beach area, one of the largest and most complex sand beach systems in Maine. A number of significant features make up the system. At the mouth of the Morse River, which is at the southwest end of Popham's State Park Beach, is an example of a complex spit. At Fox Island and Wood Island lie the only two large sandy tombolos in Maine, spanning the distance from the islands to the mainland. Off Hunnewell Point, in an area between the mainland and Wood Island, is a large cuspate foreland beach. The Popham Beach system also contains two very large near-shore sand bars, the only ones of this size in Maine. These are migrating onshore at the western end of Hunnewell Beach and west of the Fox Island tombolo. And behind Popham Village, in a small salt marsh, are two probable old shorelines, possibly twenty-nine hundred years old. The wave-deposited sand of these relict beaches is now buried by encroaching salt marsh peat—a result of rising sea level.

Reid State Park contains two notable sand beaches: Mile Beach and Half Mile Beach. Long, straight Mile Beach is a closed barrier beach connecting Todd's and Griffith's heads, with a salt marsh behind. The beach itself is straight because it is located at the mouth of the bay and receives waves directly rather than at an oblique angle. Other features include a high and broad frontal dune ridge, numerous stablized parabolic dunes, and a continuous baymouth shoreline (the lack of a tidal exit through the beach is unique among Maine's large barrier beach systems).

Half Mile Beach, to the west of Todd's Head, is an open barrier spit. The sand here is finer than that at Mile Beach. Half Mile is at the downdrift end of the Reid Beach system, and since the finest sands are the ones carried furthest from the source by the currents, they are the ones deposited here. A few stabilized parabolic dunes are located in the back dune area.

Gravel and Cobble Beaches

Gravel and cobble beaches occur where material of coarse size (eroded outcroppings of bedrock and glacial deposits) can be worked by the waves.[2] Along the eastern shore of the United States, they are limited to the New England coast, becoming more prevalent as one proceeds northeastward. Maine has more than any other New England state, and over 450 of these occur east of the Penobscot River.

Although subject to the same beach-forming processes, gravel and cobble beaches differ from sand beaches in a number of ways. They are composed of materials in a wide range of sizes, including pebbles (from one-eighth inch to 2.5 inches) and cobbles (2.5 to 10 inches). Generally, the larger cobbles and pebbles—rounded into rods or spheres from rolling with each retreating wave—are found on the lower beach face. Proceeding landward, the large materials are gradually replaced by finer gravel until the midbeach point; then, on the berm surfaces and storm ridges of the upper beachface, larger materials (now disc-shaped) are found.

The profile of gravel and cobble beaches also differs from that of the typical sand beach. Unlike the wind-whipped dune ridge that rises twenty feet or more above the sand beach berm, the highest point of gravel and cobble beaches is a ridge, four to twelve feet in height, created by storm waves. The face of gravel and cobble beaches is also steeper than that of sand beaches and may contain three or four berms. Cusps, projections separating scooped-out

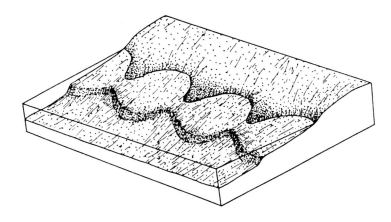

Cusps. These patterns of scooped-out depressions are common on gravel and cobble beaches and form a scalloped beachface. From B.S. Timson, Maine Critical Areas Program (1981).

depressions to form a scalloped beach face, are more common on gravel and cobble beaches.

Jasper Beach, a gravel and cobble beach at the head of Howard Cove in Machiasport, Washington County, is a notable barrier spit about twenty-six hundred feet long and more than two hundred feet wide at its broadest point.

Jasper Beach, Washington County, shows a typical cobble and pebble beach profile. Hank Tyler photo.

Its eastern half fronts a small tidal marsh that is connected to Howard Cove by an inlet channel flowing by the eastern end of the spit. Beyond the inlet channel are cliffs of fractured metamorphosed volcanic rocks. The western half of the beach is backed by glacial deposits. Materials for the beach come from some of these deposits, as well as from the ledge rock of the cliffs and from glacial till underlying the beach.

The attractive features of Jasper Beach include its accessibility, unaltered natural condition, and unusual aesthetic qualities due to the presence of highly polished volcanic rocks. They contain jasper—an opaque quartz mineral that occurs here as bright red veins in the pebbles. It is relatively rare in Maine and almost unique in such quantities in Maine's gravel and cobble beaches. Even this relatively high concentration of jasper amounts to only about 2 percent of the material at Jasper Beach. About 85 percent is composed of volcanic rocks, including red rhyolites, dark green basalt, and other, lighter-colored, volcanics. A few granitic cobbles are also found at this beach.

Volcanic rhyolite cobble makes up much of Jasper Beach. Some of the pebbles display bright red veins of the opaque quartz mineral jasper, contributing to the esthetic qualities of the beach. Hank Tyler photo.

Features of Coastal Bedrock[3]

Sea caves are excavations produced by wave action in weaker zones of bedrock at the bases of sea cliffs. There are only a few sea caves on the eastern Atlantic coast, and most of them are in Maine.

Anemone Cave, on the east shore of Mt. Desert Island, is an excellent example. Here, at the base of the cliffy slopes of Champlain Mountain, the ledges are composed of breccia, a rock produced when sharp, angular fragments broken by movement of the earth's crust are fused by pressure into a solid mass. The cave is in an area where the ledges are severely cracked and subject to wave and frost action. At low tide one may enter the large opening of the cave and observe beautiful clear tidal pools in which flowerlike sea anemones live.

The Ovens are domed, kilnlike caves in the face of a cliff at the northern end of Mt. Desert Island. Here, wave action and weathering have produced several caves up to twelve feet high, and one is about thirty feet deep. The floors of the caves are near the high-tide level.

A spouting hole, or blow hole, is a nearly vertical fissure or natural chimney extending from the inner end of a sea cave to the surface above. As sea water is forced into the cave by the rising tide and waves, air and water are compressed and rush upward through the passage, spouting intermittently. One such spouting hole is located in Englishman Bay. Another example, Blowing Cave, is at Kennebunkport, on the west shore of Sandy Cove between Walker Point and Cape Arundel.[4] When the tide is right (usually just prior to high water), and depending on wave height, the waves that enter the cave temporarily block the opening and compress the air inside. When the waves recede, the pressure decreases and the compressed air inside blows a spray of mist out the cave's entrance.

Anemone Cave on Mt. Desert Island is an excellent example of a sea cave. Dean Bennett photo.

The few rock bridges along the Maine
coast occur in the volcanic rocks
of Washington County. William Reed
photo, courtesy of Down East Magazine.

Marine arches are also features excavated by wave action. One is located at the Ovens on Mt. Desert Island—a tall, narrow arch through which a person can walk. Several others are found in the volcanic rock along the Washington County coastline.

Islands

Known for their exceptional beauty and relative inaccessibility, Maine's islands number about three thousand, each with its unique character and history.

Their diversity is due to their varied geology, which, besides contributing to the islands' scenic qualities, also provides special plant and animal habitats. The generally northeast-southwest alignment of some islands, such as those in Casco Bay, is the result of upheaval and folding during the mountain-building periods of Maine's geologic past. Other island groups, including the Porcu-

Jordan's Delight, a designated Critical Area in
Narraguagus Bay, is a unique island. Its rare
plants, nesting sites, and unusual geological
features make it especially valuable. Hank
Tyler photo. Courtesy of Down East Magazine.

Granitic rocks, like these at Hurricane Island, form many of the islands in Penobscot Bay. Hank Tyler photo.

pines in Frenchman's Bay, demonstrate a humped profile shaped by the rising and plucking action of glaciers.

Although ancient forces were responsible for their existence, it is the sea that continues to shape the islands, imparting an individual identity to each. Hidden among the cliffs on Long Porcupine, for example, a sea arch spans a ten-foot opening forty feet above the sea. A sea cliff is also visible here at low tide.

The humped profile of Bald Porcupine Island, Frenchman's Bay, was shaped by glacial action. All the Porcupine Islands show a similar profile: northern end gradually sloping, higher southern end steep and abrupt. Hank Tyler photo.

The layered volcanic-rock cliffs of Shipstern Island, at the outer reaches of Pleasant Bay in Washington County, resemble the overhanging transom of a Spanish galleon. Hank Tyler photo.

Further east, at the outer reaches of Pleasant Bay in Washington County, the sculpted cliffs of Shipstern Island resemble the overhanging transom of a Spanish galleon. Also "down east" lies Rogue Island. Here is another beautiful example of a fringing pocket beach: Great South Beach.

In this section we've explored some of Maine's most unusual geologic features, but as we shall see in Sections II and III, the state's land and waters provide settings for an even more diverse collection of plants and animals, some of them extremely rare and unusual.

Rare and Unusual Plant Life

Perspective

To our minds this is the most exquisitely beautiful of all single-flowered orchids. . . . What draws us so strongly to it is not the color or size of the flower, but rather the form—its wonderful poise and the sense it conveys of a living personality. We shall never forget the moment when our eyes first fell on its blossom in the lonely depths of a sphagnum bog. The feeling was irresistible that we had surprised some strange sentient creature in its secret bower of moss; that it was alert and listening intently with pricked-up ears.

— F. Morris and E. A. Eames, 1929[1]

The amazing little arethusa is also called dragon's mouth orchid, and the name is apt.[2] Rising out of mossy hummocks in Maine's misty peatlands and wet meadows, its pointed pink earlike sepals, gaping mouth, and fiery "tongue" (formed by a wavy-edged lower petal having pink and purple veins and yellow hairs) do resemble a tiny dragon's head. Like all plants with flowers, dragon's mouth is a vascular plant, meaning that it contains vessels that conduct water and transport nutrients and manufactured sugars throughout its body.

Maine has about fifteen hundred native species of vascular plants. Some, like arethusa, capture our attention because of their unusual or aesthetic features; others arouse our curiosity and take on special value because they are rare and seldom seen. Both qualities appeal to our human nature. In this section we are interested in both the unusual and the rare.

Why does Maine have such a large variety of vascular plants? A number of factors are responsible. Climate is a major influence on plant life, and in Maine the climate varies considerably from region to region and from one season to the next. Converging air masses, as well as differences in elevation and land forms, proximity to the Atlantic Ocean, and latitude, create three rather distinct climatological divisions. In addition, supplies of ground and surface water, though generally plentiful, are inconsistent, following an intricate network of glacially influenced drainage patterns.

Also, the thin blanket of nutrient- and root-holding material that covers the

Arethusa bulbosa, *an unusual orchid found in a few Maine peatlands. Greig Cranna photo, courtesy of* Maine Fish and Wildlife *Magazine.*

bedrock is a complex mosaic of soil types. In eastern Aroostook County, for example, the soils are derived from limestone and tend to be more alkaline than in other areas. On the upper parts of ridges and mountains, the soils are often shallow and coarse-textured, while in the valleys and on the lowlands they are deeper and finer.

It is little wonder that, faced with the challenges of maintaining life in a variable and uncertain environment, species develop unique characteristics and specialties to insure their survival. A Maine backyard, for example, might easily contain more than a hundred kinds of vascular plants, each competing for light, water, and nutrients.

Some adaptations are truly amazing. Most plants, when they burst forth from the seed, rely on food stored within the seed until they can make it on their own. However, arethusa and other orchids do not have such reserves. Instead, a fungus provides sugars and vitamins to the growing seedling, its filaments establishing a vital link between the young orchid and the soil. The plant, in turn, supplies certain vitamins to the fungus.

Even more remarkable is arethusa's method of pollination. Only the queen bumblebee is large enough to pollinate the flower, and in a marvelous example of nature's intricate relationships, she emerges from her underground nest precisely during the one to two weeks in late spring and early summer when arethusa is in bloom. Attracted by the pink flowers and arethusa's weak but inviting scent, a queen bumblebee heads for the gaping mouth of a flower. The elaborate lower lip, or petal, serves as the landing platform, guiding the bee into the flower by rows of "brushes" on its surface. These reflect ultraviolet light, visible to bees but not to humans, and guarantee that the bee will be in the proper position to brush against the flower's stamens and pick up a mass of pollen as she enters for nectar. Moving on to the next flower, she will leave behind some of the pollen from the first blossom and pick up more from the second. This cross-pollination promotes a varied gene pool, which increases the likelihood of the species' survival.

Later in the summer, arethusa's seed capsules mature. In the fall they burst forth, and the tiny seeds, clad in air-filled coats, are dispersed by the wind in numbers great enough to ensure continuation of the species. Wind is not the only means of travel; arethusa's seeds float, so streams also distribute seeds to new locations. Favorite habitats of arethusa are open peatlands, the shores of ponds, and wet meadows. It shares these habitats with sedges and other plants, including bog-rosemary, leatherleaf, small cranberry, sweet-gale, and alder. Such a collection of plants living together under similar conditions is called a community.

Communities and their constituent species vary across the landscape according to the type of habitats available. Communities also change due to natural succession—the gradual replacement of one community by another— but other changes are the result of human activities. Land developments, for example, replace natural habitats with human-engineered ones designed for our own convenience and comfort. It is not surprising, then, that in any given place communities and populations of species will vary and that some species will be rare.

About three hundred—one fifth—of Maine's approximately fifteen hundred native vascular plants are rare in the state.[3] Most of these are common somewhere else, however, and very few are actually endangered. One factor determining whether a species is considered rare in Maine is the number of locations in which it has been found—ten or fewer townships. Another factor is the actual abundance of a species. For example, a certain plant might be found in more than ten townships, but in such small numbers that it still qualifies as "rare."

Bird's-eye primrose, Primula laurentiana, *is a rare perennial that reaches the southern limit of its range in east coastal Maine. Hank Tyler photo.*

Plants may be rare for a number of reasons. Almost one third of Maine's three hundred or so rare plant species are at the northern edge of their range limit; Atlantic white cedar is one. Another third, which includes bird's-eye primrose, a coastal subarctic plant, occur at the southern edge of their range. Some species that are more common to the north or south find only a smattering of their preferred habitats in Maine. These isolated pockets and fringe populations are one means by which new species evolve, for differences in climate, soil, and other conditions may subject plants to greater stress, thus increasing the probability of mutations, which also may spread more rapidly through small populations.

Some rare species have a very restricted range. These endemics, as they are called, are scientifically valuable in studies of plant evolution, classification, and geography. Unlike California, Hawaii, or the tropics, for example, which have many local endemics, Maine has only a few. One obscure sedge, *Carex oronensis*, might be considered an endemic plant, for it is found in fields, meadows, and clearings in the Penobscot Valley and nowhere else in the world. But like many endemics, there is some question about its being a separate species. A very few plants are endemic to New England, such as *Calamagrostis fernaldii*, a little-known member of the grass family growing on a deciduous-wooded mountain slope in Piscataquis County. (However, the taxonomic status of this plant is also under dispute.)

Slender cliff-brake, Cryptogramma stelleri, *a small fern rare in Maine, favors cool, shaded ledges of limy rock.*

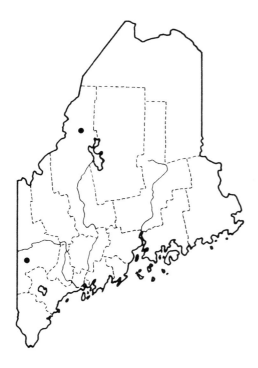

Distribution of slender cliff-brake in Maine. From New England Botanical Club (1976).

Ram's-head lady's-slipper, Cypripedium arietinum, *is a very rare orchid that occurs in only three Maine sites. Fred Bavendam photo.*

Other species may be classified as rare because they require habitats scarce in Maine, though common elsewhere. A good example is slender cliff-brake, which may be observed, among other places, high on shaded shelves and in cool crevices of a dripping-wet calcareous ledge in Oxford County.[4] This frail little fern is restricted to limestone or other calcareous rock. The most extensive deposits of such rocks and the limy soils derived from them occur in Aroostook County. More isolated areas are scattered throughout the state, especially in Oxford County and along the Kennebec, Piscataquis, and Penobscot rivers. Here live other rare lime-loving plants, including wide-leaved ladies' tresses, pale green orchid, purple clematis, and showy orchis. The moonwort fern is associated with limestone areas in Knox County and with coastal shell deposits.

Another interesting example of the influence of minerals in producing unusual habitats can be found among the igneous outcrops in northwestern Maine. Here, along the Canadian borders of Oxford, Franklin, and Somerset counties, are deposits of serpentine—a relatively soft, greasy-feeling mineral, dark green and glossy. Aleutian maidenhair fern is always found associated with this unusual mineral, whether in Newfoundland, Maine, or Vermont.

For reasons not clearly known, a few species of plants occur in Maine that are rare throughout their range. Ram's head lady's slipper is one such plant. Yellow jewelweed is another that has a wide range but is sparsely distributed within that range. These and other species about which we have little biological understanding are always subjects of interest for further investigation—and subjects of concern when they are found to be declining.

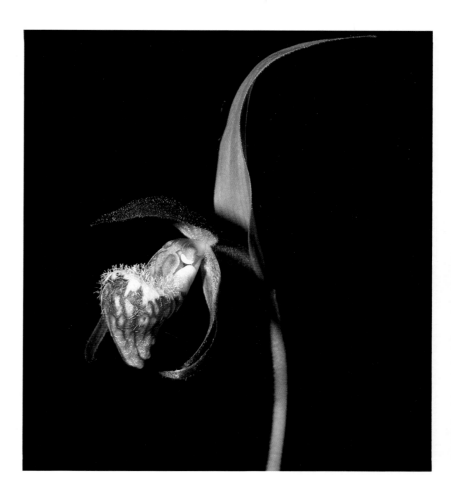

Human disturbance further affects the numbers of some rare plants. Modification of habitat is the most frequent and devastating disruption, brought about by activities that include: (1) land development for industrial, commercial, and residential purposes; (2) forestry and agricultural practices; (3) alteration of waterways for drainage, hydroelectric power, and other uses; and (4) recreation.

In most cases, the damage has been the result of too little knowledge, understanding, or appreciation of the value of these species. Sometimes the developers did not even know that the rare plants were there. A few examples of habitat destruction include the following: In the 1940s the only known native stand of flowering dogwood on Mt. Agamenticus in York County was almost completely destroyed by road construction; Kate Furbish's favorite collecting ground, the sand plains in Brunswick, is now the site of an air base; the only known stand of the great white trillium was destroyed by a logging operation; several areas of rare plants have been lost to the damming of rivers and streams; and it's possible that fragile alpine areas harboring some of Maine's most unusual species may be lost to increased recreational use. Of special concern is the increasing use of off-road vehicles, which provide access to areas formerly protected by their isolation.

It seems ironic that the decline of some species can be traced to overpicking or digging by would-be propagators. Especially vulnerable are the rare orchids. Their remarkably intricate and delicate forms, extraordinary patterns and varied hues, and relative scarcity make them special targets for overenthusiastic collectors. Showy lady's slipper is one species thought to have suffered a decline due to picking and to digging up the plants.

Great rhododendron and mountain laurel are two rare shrubs in Main that are attractive to horticulturists and gardeners as transplanted ornamentals. Great rhododendron, which can reach thirteen feet in height, is a woody shrub with thick, leathery, evergreen leaves and large, showy pink flowers.[5] In Maine, where it exists at the northern border of its range in scattered and isolated populations, this beautiful plant leads a precarious existence, experiencing natural fluctuations that affect its vigor and health. Only a few stands are known to exist in Maine, most in southern sections. The digging up and removal of shrubs and picking of flowers can pose a threat to its future in the state. Four stands are now on Maine's Register of Critical Areas.

Another beautiful shrub having wide appeal as an ornamental is mountain

Showy lady's-slipper, Cypripedium reginae, *an uncommon orchid in Maine, occurs primarily in damp calcareous areas. Hank Tyler photo.*

Mountain laurel, Kalmia latifolia, *is an example of a shrub that reaches the northern extent of its range in southern Maine. Mountain laurel occurs in only fifteen Maine locations but is very common south of the state. Hank Tyler photo.*

laurel.[6] It is an enchanting multibranched evergreen with clusters of striking rosy or pale pink flowers. It, too, is at the northern border of its range in Maine. Of the forty or so natural stands once reported in the state, only fifteen can be located today, primarily along the southern coast. Eight stands are now recognized as Critical Areas.

Some rare plants are, of course, more "rare" than others. Those rare in Maine but common elsewhere are said to be of state significance. About 120 species are rare at the state level; most of these reach the northern limit of their range in Maine. Examples are sassafras and flowering dogwood.

Sassafras albidum, *the sassafras tree, is found in extreme southern Maine, where it reaches the northern limit of its range. Hank Tyler photo.*

Well over a third of Maine's three hundred or so rare plants are of New England significance (rare in the New England region but common elsewhere in the United States). Several of Maine's rare orchids are in this category, including showy lady's slipper and showy orchis.

Over sixty species of Maine's rare vascular plants are seldom found *anywhere* in the country. Two of these plants of national significance, Furbish's lousewort and small whorled pogonia, are classified as endangered by the federal government. Maine's most famous endemic, Furbish's lousewort, grows along the bank of the St. John River and nowhere else in the world. Small whorled pogonia, a small yellowish-green orchid of mixed hardwood and second growth forests, is so rare that few botanists have ever seen it.

As one can easily imagine, determining the rarity of a particular plant is not always easy, and the problems in identifying some species can become especially complicated. The many varieties of grasses, sedges, and willows, for example, pose problems for even the professional botanist. The Critical Areas Program is compiling the official list of Maine's endangered and threatened plants.

Those who traverse Maine's countryside seeking out natural communities of living things might be said to share the curiosity of those who explore large cities. Whether it be through alleys or along a forest path, around the next corner or over the ridge, past the intersection or by the meeting of streams, one moves with all senses alert for the unexpected, the different, the distinctive. And, as in a city's neighborhoods, there is often an ethnic character to plant communities: each reflects its own special patterns of living, the characteristics of its inhabitants, and evolved customs of capturing energy and matter. In the following chapters some of Maine's most interesting natural communities and their unusual and rare botanical inhabitants will be examined.

The Furbish lousewort, Pedicularis furbishiae, *is on the Federal Endangered Species List. It grows only along a sixty-mile section of the south bank of the St. John River in Maine and New Brunswick. Kate Furbish, an amateur botanist and artist from Brunswick, Maine, discovered the plant in 1880. Hank Tyler photo, courtesy of* Maine Fish and Wildlife *Magazine.*

The small whorled pogonia, Isotria medeoloides, *another species on the Federal Endangered Species List, occurs in a few scattered locations in southern and central Maine. Most of the world's populations of small whorled pogonia are found in southern Maine and central New Hampshire. Greig Cranna photo, courtesy of* Maine Fish and Wildlife *Magazine.*

5

Alpine Plant Communities

At one time the mountains of Maine's Longfellow, Boundary, and Katahdin groups lay beneath a sea of glacial ice. Then the climate warmed, and their tops, naked and scarred, emerged as islands from the melting ice sheet. Slowly the ice disappeared and plants became established in the valleys below, creating a new sea of green. Over the centuries, waves of forest responded to slow climatic fluctuations and lapped at the mountains, surging northward until they broke against the cold arctic slopes and retreated, leaving stunted remnants in their wake.

Today, twelve mountaintops remain unforested: Katahdin, Sugarloaf, Bigelow, North Brother, Saddleback, Abraham, Goose Eye, Fort, Baldpate,

Bigelow Mountain in Franklin County, with about 135 acres of alpine plant habitat, is one of Maine's few mountains supporting alpine tundra plant species. The Friends of Bigelow in 1975 initiated a successful referendum vote directing the state to purchase and protect the Bigelow Range, and now the Bureau of Public Lands and Bureau of Parks and Recreation jointly manage the 40,000-acre Bigelow Preserve. L.M. Eastman photo.

Coe, Whitecap, and Traveler. Lying protected in the depressions and between the boulders of the cold, windy, rock-strewn peaks of many of these mountains are communities of some of our most distinctive and rare plants—the alpine tundra species.[1]

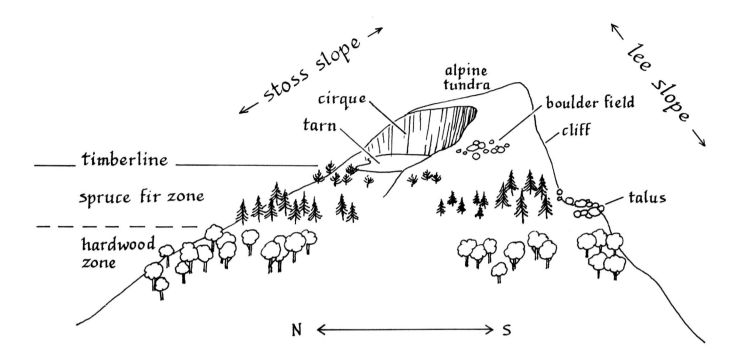

Mountain features.
Redrawn from Thomas Hanstedt,
Maine Critical Areas Program (1975).

Many of these alpine tundra plants occur widely in the vast tundra of the Arctic, but in Maine most are near the southern edge of their range. Like the Arctic, the Maine mountaintop environment can be harsh; frequent heavy fog, strong winds, high winter snowfall, and low mean annual temperatures limit the plants' active growth period.

Alpine tundra plants are small. They combat the chilling and drying effects of wind by growing in crevices between rocks or forming low, ground hugging mats. Other adaptations include tough stems and branches, small leathery leaves, and the tendency to grow in dense, self-protective tufts or clumps. Many have delicate, attractive flowers, which have brightened the landscape for more than one weary hiker.

About thirty species of alpine plants grow on Maine's mountain summits above 3500 feet. These include Bigelow's sedge, dwarf willow, bearberry willow, dwarf birch, alpine bearberry, moss plant, alpine azalea, mountain heath, lapland rosebay, and diapensia. Not all plants in these alpine communities are true tundra plants; that is, not all are widely distributed in the Arctic. Pale laurel and alpine goldenrod, for example, survive in a harsh mountaintop habitat in Maine but do not live throughout the tundra of the far north.

There are at least six different alpine tundra communities: dwarf shrub heath, sedge or rush meadow, diapensia, fellfield, snowbank, and alpine bog. These communities cover a very small total area in Maine—only about fifteen hundred acres—and are of national significance from the standpoint that only a relatively few alpine areas are to be found east of the Mississippi.

For hardy climbers and hikers, Maine's isolated alpine areas offer unique opportunities to visit an arctic environment. Because they are considered to be

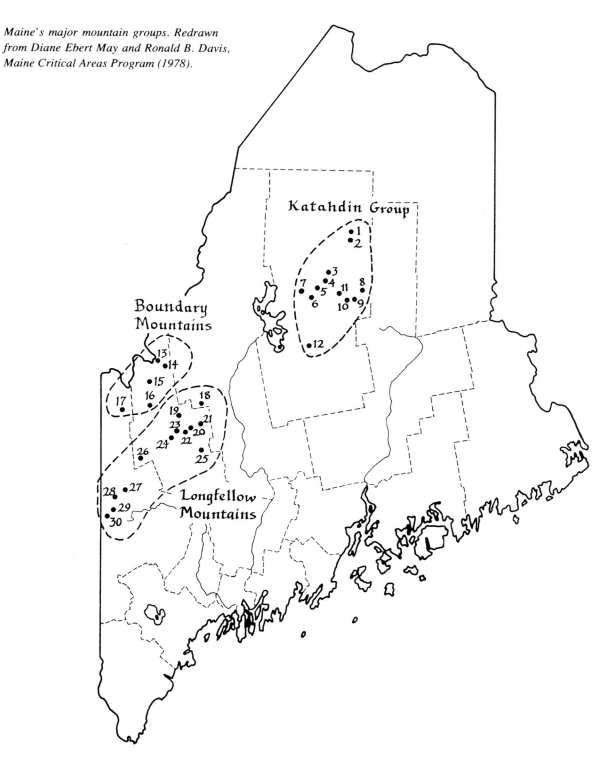

Maine's major mountain groups. Redrawn from Diane Ebert May and Ronald B. Davis, Maine Critical Areas Program (1978).

Katahdin Group
1. North Traveler
2. Traveler Mt.
3. Fort Mt.
4. North Brother
5. South Brother
6. Mt. Coe
7. Doubletop Mt.
8. North Turner
9. Mt. Katahdin
10. The Owl
11. Barren Mt.
12. White Cap Mt.

Boundary Mountain Group
13. Caribou Mt.
14. Kibby Mt.
15. Snow Mt.
16. East Kennebago Mt.
17. West Kennebago Mt.

Longfellow Mountain Group
18. Bigelow Mt.
19. Crocker Mt.
20. Sugarloaf Mt.
21. Burnt Hill
22. Spaulding Mt.
23. Saddleback Jr.
24. Saddleback Mt.
25. Mt. Abraham
26. Elephant Mt.
27. Baldpate Mt.
28. Old Speck Mt.
29. Goose Eye Mt.
30. Mt. Carlo

of national significance, seven of the twelve arctic-alpine areas were added to Maine's Register of Critical Areas between 1977 and 1981. These areas are found on Mt. Katahdin and Traveler Mountain in the Katahdin Group, and on Bigelow Mountain, Mt. Abraham, Baldpate, Goose Eye, and Saddleback mountains in the Longfellow Group. Bigelow, Katahdin, Baldpate, Goose Eye, and Traveler are protected by state ownership.

The Katahdin Group

Maine's highest mountain, Katahdin, supports the greatest number of alpine species—about thirty—on the extensive plateau known as the Tableland. Many of these plants—dwarf willow, bearberry willow, Lapland rosebay, alpine bearberry, moss plant, alpine azalea, and mountain heath—are found nowhere else in Maine. The Tableland is the largest alpine habitat in the state, sustaining examples of most of the alpine tundra communities.

Lapland rosebay, Rhododendron lapponicum, *in Maine, lives only in the alpine Tableland of Mt. Katahdin. Hank Tyler photo.*

Mt. Katahdin, in Baxter State Park, contains the greatest concentration of rare plants in Maine. Its Tableland, shown here, is the largest expanse of alpine habitat in the state and supports about thirty species of alpine plants—one of the rarest plant communities in the Northeast. Diane May photo.

Just above the krummholz—an area of stunted and deformed trees on the edge of the treeline—the dwarf shrub heath community is the most prevalent. Here, despite nutrient-poor soils, the heaths are successful. Although some of the woody heath species can reach tree height at lower elevations, low, shrubby species such as lapland rosebay and pale laurel dominate the shrub heath community above treeline. Also common is an alpine tundra species, mountain heath.

At the upper edge of Katahdin's dwarf shrub heath communities, sedges and rushes invade the heaths to share their dominance. To the casual observer these combined communities would probably seem meadowlike, for the sedges and rushes are grassy in appearance. But closer examination would reveal that many of the sedges have solid stems that are triangular in cross-section, as opposed to the the round and sometimes hollow stems of grasses and rushes. Other differences between flower and seed structures are less apparent.

Generally the sedge-rush/dwarf shrub heath communities occupy moist to dry slopes above the krummholz. Lichens and mosses, especially alpine reindeer lichen and haircap moss, form the most extensive ground cover.

Bearberry Willow, Salix uva-ursi, *is found only on Mt. Katahdin. Susan C. Gawler photo.*

Protruding dark purple spikes indicate the dominance of Bigelow's sedge. Depending on the micro-environment, dense tufts of highland rush might predominate instead. In some of these communities dwarf shrubs occur. One of these, dwarf willow, is a low, matted shrub only a few inches high. Its trunk and main branches grow in the soil, and above ground, its tiny branchlets support two to four rounded leaves about one-half to one inch in diameter. Another such shrub is dwarf birch, which grows either erect or in mats close to the ground. Its leaves, up to one inch long, vary from oval to almost circular.

Just north of the Tableland, on the ascent to Hamlin Peak, is a true meadow community where highland rush prevails, although mountain sandwort is also present. A meadow community not found on Katahdin is the sedge meadow community, which differs to the extent that Bigelow's sedge rather than highland rush is the dominant plant. Both communities often occur on the highest slopes and merge into the sedge-rush/dwarf shrub heath community.

In several areas on Katahdin's exposed Tableland one can find patches where diapensia is the predominant plant in the community. This is a dwarf

Right: *Diapensia,* Diapensia lapponica, *is a rare plant found in the alpine areas of Maine's highest mountains. It grows in very dense clumps, and its white flowers appear during the second and third weeks in June. Fred Bavendam photo, courtesy of* Maine Fish and Wildlife *Magazine.*

Alpine azalea, Louiseleuria procumbens, *a very minute plant that is found only on Mt. Katahdin. Hank Tyler photo.*

Dwarf white birch, Betula minor, *is one of nine rare plants in Maine that occur only on Mt. Katahdin. Susan C. Gawler photo.*

evergreen, cushionlike in appearance, adapted to rocky, windswept slopes. It flowers during the second week of June. Also identified with diapensia communities on Katahdin are alpine bearberry and alpine azalea. Only 50 percent or less of the ground in diapensia communities is covered by vascular plants, and few lichens and mosses grow there. The remainder of the surface is usually bare gravel.

Fellfield communities fill the crevices between boulders and rocks on the mountain's dry, rocky sites. Fellfield, from the Danish *fjoeld-mark,* means rock desert. Crustose (crusty) lichens grow on the rocks, and mosses are found on the soil between the rocks. Patches of dwarfed trees, including dwarf birch, dwarf willow, dwarf black spruce, and balsam fir, are also found.

Snowbank communities are found in depressions and on the leeward side of rocks where winter snows accumulate and do not melt until late May or June. The snow insulates the plants from the most severe winter weather but also delays their growth come spring. A snowbank community can be found on Katahdin just east of the summit of Hamlin Peak. Some of the most delicate and handsome alpine flowering plants exist in these communities, including

Laborador tea, alpine bilberry, and two rare tundra plants—moss plant and mountain heath.

A curious phenomenon that can be observed from the slopes of Katahdin and the Tableland is the striped pattern of spruce and fir forest on nearby Owl and Brother mountains. Although these "fir waves" have not been fully explained, Dabney Caldwell, a geologist and naturalist who has studied the phenomenon, has observed that when the trees on these slopes reach a certain height or age, they die.[2] Eventually the dead trees are blown over and are replaced by new growth. The process apparently is repeated with each new generation. This cycle of death and replacement is possibly related to underlying formations of rock and soil debris on the mountain slopes, which may affect moisture and rooting conditions.

Traveler Mountain is Maine's northernmost peak over thirty-five hundred feet. The upper slopes are barren, probably due in part to several fires, the last in 1903. The terrain above treeline is strewn with large rocks and boulders, and only two alpine plant communities have been identified: dwarf shrub heath and rush dwarf shrub heath.

Moss plant, Cassiope hypnoides, *an alpine member of the heath family, occurs in Maine only on Mt. Katahdin. Fred Bavendam photo.*

Fir waves on The Brothers in Baxter State Park. The natural phenomenon of alternating patterns of live and dead subalpine fir trees, called fir waves, is known only in Maine's Baxter State Park and in two other locations in northern New England. W. Donald Hudson, Jr., photo.

The Longfellow Group

Bigelow Mountain, in the townships of Bigelow and Dead River in Somerset County and Wyman in Franklin County, consists of a long wind-swept ridge with two high treeless peaks, Avery Peak and West Peak. Although tundra vegetation is less extensive in this arctic-alpine area due to the relatively dry, exposed terrain, several alpine communities exist. Dwarf shrub heath is the predominant one.

The arctic-alpine area on Mt. Abraham in Franklin County is an extensive treeless ridge about 2.5 miles long covered by boulder fields. Dry, windy conditions limit the three alpine tundra communities to protected areas. Bigelow's sedge and diapensia are the only tundra plants identified among the species of mountain vegetation here.

Examples of the alpine bog community—one of the few alpine communities not occurring above treeline on Katahdin—can be found on Baldpate, Goose Eye, and Saddleback mountains. It is dominated by sphagnum moss and

The Appalachian Trail crosses this alpine peatland in the Mahoosuc Mountains in Oxford County. This bog is on State Public Reserved Land, which is managed by the Maine Bureau of Public Lands. Hank Tyler photo.

occurs in very wet areas where moisture accumulates in hollows in the ledgy bedrock. It often contains such plants as sundew, baked-apple berry, and mountain cranberry.

Baldpate Mountain's arctic-alpine area is located in Grafton, Oxford County. Two alpine bog communities containing baked-apple berry exist in the col between West and East peaks.

Goose Eye Mountain in Riley, Oxford County, contains a long, narrow, treeless arctic-alpine area where the major alpine plant community is dwarf shrub heath. In addition to the several alpine bogs found on the mountain, two tundra plant species have been identified: Bigelow's sedge and diapensia.

Saddleback Mountain, in the towns of Sandy River and Madrid, Franklin County, has an extensive treeless arctic-alpine area along a 2.5-mile ridge. Several alpine bog and tundra plant communities exist on and around the rock slabs and boulder fields that dominate the area. Again, Bigelow's sedge and diapensia are the only alpine tundra species present.

Designation of these seven alpine sites as Critical Areas (between 1977 and 1981) was a positive step toward the management and protection of some of Maine's most fragile and unusual plant communities, which may also hold the distinction of being the state's oldest plant communities, the first to get a foothold when the tops of the mountains appeared above the shrinking glacier. In a sense, they were the pioneers of postglacial plant life—colonizers foreshadowing the lush woodland communities that developed in the valleys below.

Woodland Plant Communities

Maine is the "green thumb" of the United States—a forested projection at the northern tip of New England. Woodlands, composed of many forest types and three distinguishable forest zones, dominate the landscape; but why isn't Maine covered with a uniform forest? Two factors are primarily responsible. First is the climate, which varies considerably from place to place, depending on latitude, elevation, and proximity to the ocean. These variables affect precipitation, temperature, wind, and other factors. Second is the character of the soil, varying from thin to deep and from well-drained sands and gravels to impervious clays.

Additionally, trees and other plants may themselves alter their living conditions. Gradual changes in amounts of shade, nutrients, and moisture may create an environment more suitable for different species, which succeed the original plants. But providing that climate and soils remain stable and no other influences intrude, one type of forest may eventually prevail on a site, maintaining a dynamic equilibrium with its environment.

However, most of Maine's forests *are* subject to periodic disturbances. Fire and wind are especially destructive, but human activities have an even greater effect on trees and where they grow. Timber and pulpwood harvesting are major businesses in Maine, and as a result the normal path of forest succession has been interrupted. For these reasons, perhaps the forest should be viewed as a shifting mosaic of types rather than as an orderly progression to any one type.

As well as trees, woodlands also contain many species of shrubs (woody plants less than twenty-five feet in height, usually having more than one main stem) and non-woody herbaceous plants. A great many herbs are flowering plants while others, such as the ferns, club mosses, and horsetails, are nonflowering.

At least three major forest zones may be identified in Maine: the boreal or

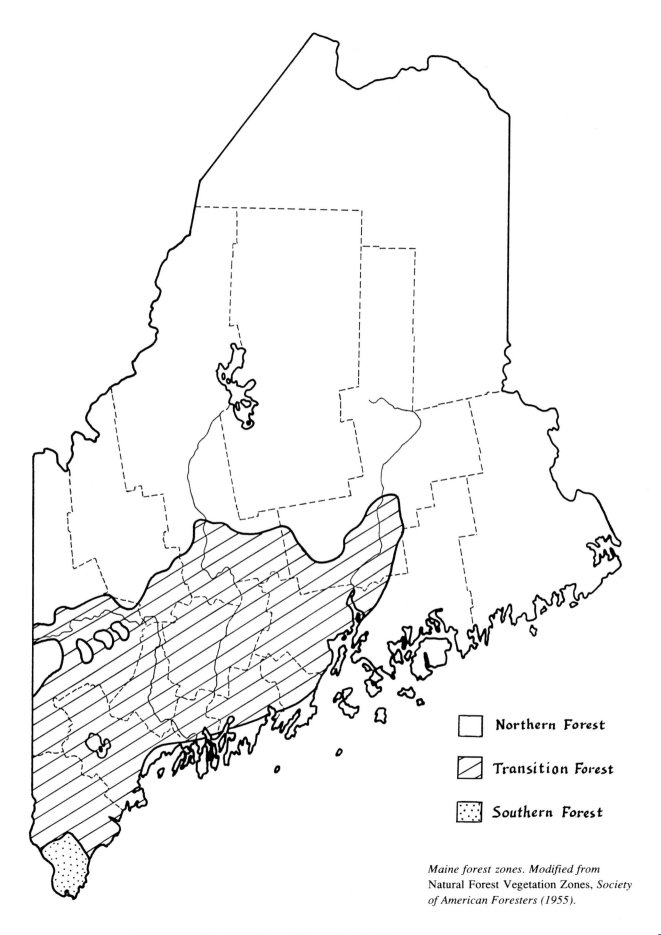

Northern Forest

Transition Forest

Southern Forest

Maine forest zones. Modified from
Natural Forest Vegetation Zones, *Society*
of American Foresters (1955).

northern zone, the transition zone, and the southern deciduous zone (characterized by hardwood native to the central eastern United States).[1] Because climate, soils, and human influences do not change abruptly from place to place, the exact boundaries of these zones are only approximate. Nevertheless, they are distinct enough to add another dimension to the variability of Maine's natural environment.

One of the most interesting aspects of these forest zones is that each harbors, often in remote and difficult-to-reach areas, some of the state's most unusual communities: old-growth forests.[2] As much as three or four hundred

Old-growth white pines tower above spruces in a northern Maine forest. Hank Tyler photo.

Old-growth trees are used by scientists to study growth patterns by tree-ring analysis, which indicates past climatological events. Dr. Laura E. Conkey has studied the old-growth red spruce on Elephant Mountain in Franklin County. From M.M. Harris and A.M. Spearing, eds., Research in Forest Productivity, Use, and Pest Control, *USDA Forest Service Gen. Tech. Rep. NE-90, 1984.*

years old (even more in the case of cedars), these stands are usually small, isolated, undisturbed remnants of virgin forests that, surprisingly, have survived centuries of logging. These precious few sites are more than simply aesthetic amenities; they are literally a contact with our past. Core samples from these trees are a centuries-long record of climatic changes, forest fires, insect infestations, and even the effects of human-caused pollution. In addition, the old-growth forests appear to favor certain animal species not found in younger woodlands, such as eagles, pine warblers, and winter wrens.

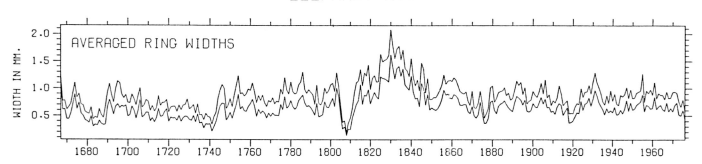

ELEPHANT MT.

AVERAGED RING WIDTHS

Northern Forest

When one thinks of Maine, two distinct images flash to mind: a sweep of open, rugged coastline, and a dark northwoods forest of spruce and fir. Thoreau wrote of these woods in 1857:

> It is all mossy and moosey. In some of those dense fir and spruce woods there is hardly room for the smoke to go up. The trees are a standing night, and every fir and spruce which you fell is a plume plucked from night's raven wing. Then at night the general stillness is more impressive than any sound, but occasionally you hear the note of an owl farther or nearer in the woods, and if near a lake, the semi-human cry of the loons at their unearthly revels.[3]

There can be a chill in the air in this northern area, even on a July night. Here winters get good marks for attendance, but also a late detention in spring for their unruly behavior. The cool climate and prevalence of poorly drained soils give the advantage to conifers, which are more numerous than their deciduous cohabitants. Spruces—red, black, and white—and balsam fir are dominant, making up an estimated 70 percent of the evergreens. Other conifers include northern white cedar, tamarack, pines (white, red, and jack), and eastern hemlock. Scattered throughout, especially on warmer, well-drained ridges, are the northern hardwoods, predominantly sugar maple, beech, and yellow birch. Associated with these species are American basswood, aspen, pin cherry, and paper birch.

From the air, this dark green forest of conical shapes is the leading edge of a vast boreal coniferous forest stretching across Canada. To the south, the cool, moist climate of Maine's coastal region draws the northern forest around the eastern tip of the transition forest of hardwoods that dominates central Maine. This maritime spruce-fir forest is most prominent on the outer peninsulas of Washington County, but also occurs in scattered areas down the rocky coastline to Casco Bay.

Today, extensive lumbering has diminished the dominance of the spruce and fir that, to many, give the northwoods its wild and primitive character. However, these beautiful trees still remain the prevalent species in large areas, especially in the north and west. Conifers are well suited to the harshness of the northern environment. When temperatures drop and the cold, dry winds of winter break off the all-too-short summers, each tree reacts to combat the crippling effects of freezing: millions of tiny cells reduce their water content and increase their sugar concentration, creating an "antifreeze" of resinous fluid. The narrow, needlelike leaves continue to live, staying, as their name suggests, ever green. And as blankets of snow envelop the spruces and firs, their flexible branches bend under the accumulating weight without breaking.

With spring comes an amazing resurgence of life on the forest floor. The only plants able to exist under the densest stands of spruce and fir are shade-tolerant species, primarily lichens and mosses, but wherever the sun's rays can penetrate—beneath the pines and occasional deciduous trees, in the scattered clearings, and along the edges of streams—many plants common to all of Maine forests appear. In his journals Thoreau reported seeing many common plants, including bunchberry, wild sarsaparilla, large-leaved aster, checkerberry, Indian cucumber, clintonia, starflower, bracken fern, self heal, and false solomon's-seal. However, rare species and communities of trees and other plants are also found in this northern forest.[4]

Giant, or green-leaved, rattlesnake plantain is an evergreen perennial similar to the more common rattlesnake plantains. This member of the orchid

Giant rattlesnake plantain, Goodyera oblongifolia, *is a plant of New England significance growing in the northern forest. Philip C. Keenan photo.*

family is a plant of New England significance. Its leaves, growing from a basal rosette, are up to four inches long and marked by a broad whitish stripe in the middle. A flower stalk bears several small, creamy-white flowers, which are pollinated by queen bumblebees. Giant rattlesnake plantain grows in coniferous woods from Alaska east to New Brunswick, Canada, and Maine. It is found in Aroostook County in forests of spruce-fir, old-growth cedar, and mixed hardwood, all on shady slopes.

Calypso, or fairy slipper, is an orchid of national significance. It prefers the deep shade of mature cedar woods, mostly on well-drained slopes with

Calypso bulbosa, *a rare boreal orchid associated with old-growth cedar forests, flowers in mid-May. Greig Cranna photo, courtesy of* Maine Fish and Wildlife *Magazine.*

limy soils. Its beautiful white flower has a large, purple-dotted, slipper-shaped lip and is supported on a stem usually less than four inches high. One prominently veined, bluish-green leaf grows from its base. Although it has no nectar, the flower is believed to attract several species of bumblebees with its faintly sweet odor and the yellow hairs on its lip that resemble pollen. Its rarity in the United States is attributed to scarcity of appropriate habitat, to its vulnerability to disturbance by logging, and to the fact that it is at the southern limit of its range.

Male fern is a showy large plant with rich green leaves up to four feet high. Because of its striking appearance, collectors have gathered it extensively for transplanting, and it is now declining over much of its American range. Though common in Europe, male fern is very rare in New England and is known from only one Maine location.

The male fern, Dryopteris felix-mas, *is known from only one location in Maine. This view shows the spore-bearing bodies on the underside of the fronds. Hank Tyler photo.*

A number of rare plants found in the northern forest zone are cliff dwellers, living in scattered communities on rock outcrops and relatively unaffected by the forests around them. Their presence is much more dependent on the nature of the ledges on which they grow. These plants include smooth woodsia, northern woodsia, green spleenwort, and arctic sandwort—all of national significance.

Smooth woodsia is a small, delicate fern that grows two to five inches high in small tufts. It lacks the reddish-brown hairs on the stalk and under the fronds of its more common relative, rusty woodsia. Found living among rocks and cliffs in the Arctic and in subarctic regions, in Maine it is at the southern limit of its range. Northern woodsia is a relative of smooth woodsia, distinguished by its brown, chaffy stalk and smooth leaves. It too is known from only a few locations in the state.

Green spleenwort is another small, delicate fern, with fronds up to six inches long. It seems to prefer limy rocks in cool, moist areas, but its ecological

Smooth woodsia, Woodsia glabella, *a small, delicate fern known from only a few locations in Maine. Laurel Smith, artist.*

Moonwort, Botrychium lunaria, *a very rare and primitive fern, grows on limestone outcrops and is found in only a few coastal locations.*

Natural jack pine stands in Maine. Redrawn from Maine Critical Areas Program (1983).

Jack pine, Pinus banksiana, *is an uncommon boreal tree that grows on about 3300 acres in northern and eastern Maine. The two main populations are along the coast of Washington and Hancock counties and in the Moose River valley in Somerset County. Hank Tyler photo.*

relationships are largely unknown. Only one location for this rare fern is known in Maine. Arctic sandwort is also known from only one place in the state. Plants of this tiny, delicate, white-flowered species form dense mats of ground foliage.

Moonwort, another northern plant of national significance, also has special requirements of the open, gravelly slopes and shores where it grows. It is a calciphile, meaning that it requires calcium, or lime. A succulent (fleshy) plant, three to six inches high, with expanded fan-shaped leaf segments, moonwort may also be identified by its fertile frond of golden brown, globular spore cases, which give it the name grape fern. Moonwort is sporadic over much of its range, which extends from Alaska to Greenland and south to the northernmost United States. In Maine, it occurs only in a few coastal areas.

A flowering plant requiring wet woods and calcareous soils is pale touch-me-not. It is of state significance in Maine, and is widely distributed from Georgia, Tennessee, Missouri, and Kansas north to Newfoundland and Saskatchewan, where it is more abundant. It can be distinguished from its common relative, orange-flowered jewelweed, by its canary-yellow flowers, which are also slightly different in shape.

Among the interesting trees of the northern forest is jack pine.[5] Superstition says that it poisons the very soil on which it grows. In reality, the scrubby and shade-intolerant jack pine is forced by taller competitors to seek the sunnier but less nutritious soils of sandy, sterile, glacial outwash plains, acid bogs, and rocky fields of granite. Perhaps even more remarkable is the jack pine's penchant for mineral-poor, fire-ravaged areas. Fire encourages its cones to open, and its dispersed seeds germinate better on a burned-over forest floor.

The jack pine prefers the cooler climate of the north. However, fossil pollen and cones indicate that when the climate cooled during glacial times, its range shifted as far south as parts of the Carolinas and the Blue Ridge Mountains. With the retreat of the giant ice sheet some twelve thousand years ago, the jack pine reestablished itself in the boreal forest to achieve its present distribution throughout a large part of Canada. Today, its southern boundary runs through central Maine.

In other states—such as Michigan, Wisconsin, and Minnesota—jack pine is a common forest tree, but in Maine it is relatively uncommon: only twenty-four stands of jack pine have been located, covering about thirty-three hundred acres. One dense old stand of two thousand acres is in the Moose River Valley, near Jackman. Other stands on the Schoodic peninsula and at Schoodic Point, exposed to harsher coastal conditions, contain fine examples of stunted, wind-blown trees.

Another conifer, the red pine, is more common throughout Maine, but old-growth forests of this reddish-barked, straight tree are rare. Only seven stands thus far meet the old-growth criteria of Maine's Critical Areas Program for age, composition, and amount of human disturbance. These stands of red pine contain trees from 100 to 250 years old, ranging up to 25 inches in diameter and 100 feet tall.

The largest and most impressive pure stand of red pine is the Cathedral Pines in Eustis. This stand extends over 220 acres and contains trees of superlative height and form, between 180 and 200 years old. These old-growth red pines are easily visited, since a public campground off Route 27 lies within the stand.

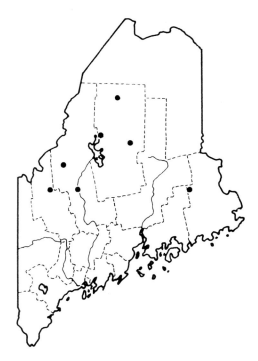

Significant old-growth red pine, Pinus resinosa, *stands in Maine. Redrawn from Maine Critical Areas Program (1983).*

A Critical Areas Program forester takes an increment boring from an old-growth red pine. Hank Tyler photo.

This old-growth stand of red spruce, Picea rubens, with trees in excess of two feet in diameter and two hundred years old, was voluntarily set aside as a preserve by the Dunn Heirs of Aroostook County. Hank Tyler photo.

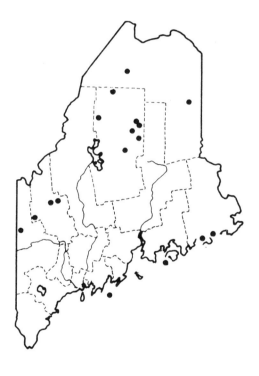

Significant old-growth red spruce stands in Maine. Redrawn from Maine Critical Areas Program (1983).

Red spruce is also found in all parts of Maine, although it is particularly associated with the northern spruce-fir forest. This tall, narrow, conical tree is one of the state's most valuable commercial species and has been heavily logged. Only twenty or so notable stands of old-growth red spruce have been identified in Maine. Most are on steep mountain slopes at elevations greater than fifteen hundred feet and thus relatively inaccesible for harvesting. Average age ranges from 150 to 250 years, but some specimens are between 300 and 400 years old.

One of the state's oldest and best developed stands of old-growth red spruce lies above the Basin Ponds, just below North Basin on the eastern side of Mt. Katahdin in Baxter State Park. It may be reached by taking the North Basin Cutoff Trail from the Chimney Pond Trail. Here, growing on rugged, ledgy terrain strewn with boulders and rocks at an elevation of 2700 feet, are trees well over three hundred years in age. One is more than 380 years old. Windblown crowns and broken tops reflect the severe environmental conditions of the site.

Another notable stand lies further south, in Franklin County. Near the junction of the Appalachian Trail and the Clearwater Brook Trail, south of Elephant Mountain, is a stand of balsam fir and old-growth red spruce. Some of the spruce are over three hundred years old and are more than twenty-one inches in diameter at breast height. The stand is maintained as a climax forest in a protected location between two peaks, which enables the long-lived red spruce to reach such age and size.

A number of stands of very old hardwood trees are also found in the northern forest zone; several, averaging about one hundred to two hundred years old, meet criteria classifying them as old-growth forests. One notable old-growth hardwood forest is a ten-acre stand of large beech, sugar maple, and yellow birch growing on a gentle southwest slope in the remote Big Reed Pond Preserve north of Baxter State Park. Many of the trees are more than two feet in diameter. The understory, consisting of a rich assortment of herbaceous plants, shows no evidence of previous cutting or fire. The preserve itself, 3800 acres around Big Reed Pond, represents nearly two-thirds of the known old-growth forest acreage in Maine that is protected by The Nature Conservancy.

On a steep, rocky slope in Penobscot County east of Baxter State Park is another prime, though small, example of a northern hardwood forest in original condition. Beech and sugar maple predominate, with some yellow birch. The stand also includes large basswood trees up to twenty-four inches in diameter at breast height, here at the very northern limit of their range. All these large trees are more than 150 years old, and a few of the sugar maples are between 190 and 240 years old. The stand's sheltered location under cliffs probably allowed it to escape severe fires in 1805 and 1825, and the steep slope prevented its being harvested for timber.

All told, some fourteen hardwood stands have been either recommended for designation or actually registered as Critical Areas of old-growth forest. These range across the state, from northern Aroostook County to Kennebec and Knox counties in the south.

Transition Forest

Between the northern forest and Maine's southern deciduous forest, the range limits of many trees overlap: oaks and hickories of the central United States grow alongside the more northern beech, birch, and maple. The mixture of hardwoods also includes aspen, pin cherry, white ash, and basswood. Among the softwoods, or coniferous trees, are white pine and hemlock.

If any one element in nature has come to symbolize Maine, it is the white pine—an imposing tree of great stature and aesthetic appeal, stimulating poets and lumbermen alike.[6] In Maine the tree is well established and widely distributed, inspiring the nickname Pine Tree State.

After the glacier had cleared the way, a succession of spruces, jack pine, and red pine appeared, followed by white pine. Its scientific name is *Pinus strobus*; *strobus* comes from the Greek and Latin and means cone—the source of its seed. Once it takes root, the white pine is the fastest growing tree in the northern forest. Widespread in southern Canada and the northern United States and along the Appalachians, it prefers the well-drained sandy and gravelly soils of glacial deposits. Some of the best pine land in eastern North America is in western Maine, where a broad apron of sandy outwash spills out from the White Mountains.

For over 350 years, this symbol of Maine has figured in the state's history.

The story of these long-lived trees is primarily an economic one. Growing undisturbed in small, pure stands along rivers and as scattered individuals in hardwood forests, white pines attained extraordinary size. (The record tree in Maine, cut in 1904, was 90 inches in diameter and 225 feet tall.) When reports of these giants reached England in the early 1600s, their fate was sealed, and by 1670 thousands were feeding the mast-starved Royal Navy. But the "pumpkin" pine, with its clear, creamy, straight-grained wood, was also prized for making boards, planks, staves, clapboards, shingles, and a host of other products of the Colonial economy. It became *the* major commercial tree, a title it held well into the nineteenth century.

Today, precious few remnants of old-growth white pine forest remain. Fewer than a dozen stands, some over three hundred years old, now warrant inclusion on Maine's Register of Critical Areas. Among them is a stand in the Allagash wilderness near Eagle Lake, which boasts a tree 130 feet in height. In Acadia National Park a four-acre site contains pines up to 185 years old, unusual in their adaptation to the stresses of the marine environment. An exceptionally dense stand in Corinna took root a century and a half ago on land

Old-growth white pine, Pinus strobus, *stands on the Register of Critical Areas. Redrawn from Maine Critical Areas Program (1983).*

Very few stands of old-growth white pine, which may attain a diameter of four feet and age of 350 years, remain. This stand is in the southern part of the state. Hank Tyler photo.

cleared by one of the region's most catastrophic hurricanes. (The Corinna stand illustrates well that white pine, which does not reproduce in its own shade, requires a disturbance of the forest canopy for regeneration.) Another site, on Pennesseewassee Lake in Oxford County, has trees up to 205 years old. And on the steep-sided, thin soiled, ledgy banks of the Presumpscot River is an assemblage of pines not unlike those encountered by the early explorers of Maine's uncharted rivers. Among these stands of old-growth white pine, one can capture the spirit of the early forest —and study it in search of better silvicultural methods.

Like white pine, eastern hemlock is scattered in both the northern and southern forest zones, sometimes occurring in a mixture of transition species. An Appalachian native, the wide-ranging eastern hemlock is found from Nova Scotia to Indiana and from southern Quebec to Alabama. It usually grows on moist soils in sheltered areas, such as in ravines and along damp river banks.

Almost a dozen old-growth stands of this long-lived tree have been discovered thus far on slopes, saddles (flat areas between hills), and along river banks and lake shores. Ages range from about 150 to 300 years old. The oldest hemlock tree in Maine (326 years old) was discovered in 1980 in an unorganized township in Penobscot County.

The woodland floor of the transition forest also contains a number of interesting rare plants. One is small whorled pogonia (shown in Section II Perspective), a diminutive green orchid with five or six leaves in a whorl at the top of its stem, just beneath its flower.[7] This nationally significant endangered plant grows in woodlands of mixed deciduous trees in the central hardwoods forest. In 1980 the total known U.S. population was about two hundred plants. Since then, discoveries of new sites have increased that figure to over 3400 plants, with nearly a quarter of them in Maine. Exact numbers are difficult to obtain, however, because small whorled pogonia may lie dormant underground for ten to twenty years.

Another of Maine's most unusual orchids is ram's-head lady's-slipper (pictured in the Section II Perspective).[8] Its single flower, supported on a slender stem four to ten inches high, is similar to a ram's head in shape. Its small conical pouch is veined in crimson and lined with silky white hairs. As soon as the plant is fertilized, the overarching sepal lowers to close the opening, preventing the entrance of other insects.

Ram's head has an interesting pattern of distribution: it grows in both the eastern United States and China. In that far-eastern country, it is a rare mountain plant growing in a dry, oak forested region at an elevation of nearly sixty-six hundred feet. Populations in the United States are widely distributed, though the species is very rare throughout its range. In Maine it is known to grow in three localities in York, Kennebec, and Somerset counties.

A species of New England significance is nodding pogonia.[9] One of northern New England's rarest orchids, this little plant is one of approximately fifty orchid species in Maine. Nodding pogonia is also known as three-bird orchid, because it usually produces three blossoms. These beautiful, delicate flowers range from pale pink to white, tinged with purple and green. The plant grows from four to twelve inches tall, with small oval leaves partly sheathing its stem.

The development and flowering of nodding pogonia is interesting. Believed to be partly saprophytic (living on dead organic matter), the plants spend several inactive years as waxy white tubers lying underground in rich, damp leaf mold. Then one year, in late July or early August, the sprouts poke through the leafy mat of the forest floor, often beside decaying logs. At first the plants

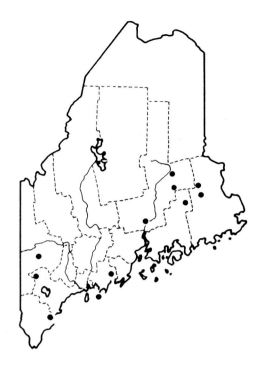

Significant old-growth hemlock, Tsuga canadensis, *stands in Maine. Redrawn from Maine Critical Areas Program (1983).*

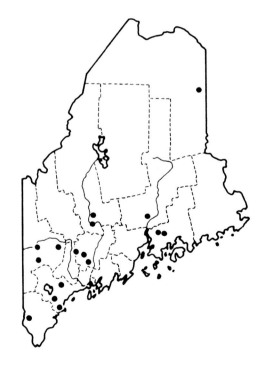

Historical and known locations of ram's-head lady's-slipper, Cypripedium arietinum, *in Maine. Redrawn from A.E. Brower, Maine Critical Areas Program (1977).*

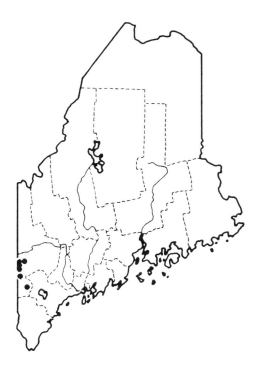

Distribution of nodding pogonia in Maine.
Redrawn from L.M. Eastman, Maine
Critical Areas Program (1976).

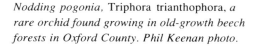

Nodding pogonia, Triphora trianthophora, a
rare orchid found growing in old-growth beech
forests in Oxford County. Phil Keenan photo.

develop rapidly, but soon their growth rate appears to slow. Then, usually
following the first chilly night of late summer, all the plants bloom simultane-
ously in one magnificent flowering. The visual crescendo builds to a spectacular peak at noon; by evening the blossoms have collapsed, fading away like the
last echoing strains of a beautiful symphony. But during the height of this
orchestrated production, large numbers of pollinators have been attracted,
guaranteeing the continuance of the species.

Maine is the northern edge of nodding pogonia's range, which extends
over much of the eastern United States in transition and central hardwood
forests. The first person to report seeing nodding pogonia in the state was
LeRoy Harvey, who in the fall of 1899 discovered four specimens growing in
a bed of leaf mold under a stand of beech in Brownfield, Oxford County. Since
then, sporadic discoveries have been made in scattered locations. Six stands
are known to exist in Maine today, all in the southwestern corner and in pure
stands of beech. In 1977 three of these stands of nodding pogonia were added
to Maine's Register of Critical Areas.

A number of other plants, though common south of Maine in the central hardwoods forest, only occasionally extend into the state's transition forest zone. These plants of state significance include Goldie's fern, smooth winterberry, and wild ginger. Another, barren strawberry is a low plant similar in apperance to the common wild strawberry, with the exception of its dry, inedible fruit and bright yellow flowers, which bloom in May and June. Associated with woods, thickets, and clearings, this state significant plant is known from only two locations in Maine, both along roadsides in Benton and Monmouth.

Barren strawberry, Waldsteinia fragarioides, *is at the northern limit of its range in Maine, where it grows in only two known locations. Hank Tyler photo, courtesy of* Maine Fish and Wildlife *Magazine.*

Southern Deciduous Forest

Near the southern tip of Maine, the winter climate is milder than elsewhere in the state. The glacial outwash soils are also deeper, and (where sands and gravels predominate) well drained. Here, at the northern edge of a vast hardwood forest extending south and west through the mid-Atlantic states, many deciduous trees compete successfully with the hardier conifers that dominate the northern two thirds of the state. In this zone, various oaks are dominant: white, northern red, black, chestnut, and scarlet. Other hardwood trees include shagbark hickory, tupelo (black gum), gray birch, red maple, black ash, and American elm. Although the American chestnut is still present, the large magnificent specimens that were once so common are gone—victims of a chestnut blight, *Endothia parasitica.* Common coniferous trees include the white pine, hemlock, and pitch pine.

The changing beauty of the deciduous forest can be appreciated throughout the year. In winter the trees' delicate gray skeletal frameworks cast a mosaic of shadows on snow and landscape. In spring, as life-giving fluids flow into limbs and twigs, their bark and buds take on brighter, livelier hues of green, yellow, red, and brown; the colors intensify with the emergence of flowers and leaves. During the dry late summer the leaves lose their luster, but as cold autumn weather slows life processes, the foliage produces one last show of unforgettable beauty. Throughout the winter, soil organisms in the duff of the forest floor disassemble the fallen leaves and remains of dead plants for reuse. When spring returns, grasses, ferns, and wildflowers emerge, sustained by the rich humus of the forest floor and the sunlight filtered by the protective canopy above.

No less interesting than the colorful changes in this forest are the rare and unusual trees and other plant life it shelters. One of these is tupelo, also known as black gum, sour gum, or pepperidge tree.[10] Tupelo can grow as tall as one hundred feet and prefers deep, rich, moist soils along streams and in swamps. Its elliptical leathery leaves, dark green above and pale below, grow on short branches perpendicular to the trunk. The bark, light brown and often tinged with red, is thick and corky and may have fissures as deep as four inches— enough to put a hand into.

Tupelo is rare in Maine; the thirteen known stands (mostly in southern and central sections) represent the northernmost excursion of a population extending south to Florida and west to Michigan, Texas, and Mexico. One stand, particularly unusual because of its location, was discovered in the 1970s, hidden in the shadow of the White Mountains in western Maine. Here the tupelo trees live in the seclusion of a small tablelike valley. At an elevation of 500 feet, these tupelos are the highest above sea level of any in northern New

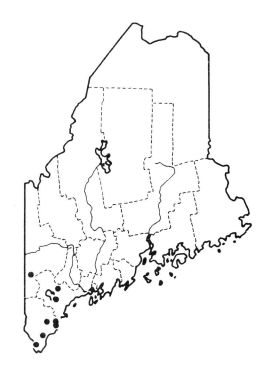

Distribution of tupelo in Maine. Redrawn from L.M. Eastman, Maine Critical Areas Program (1982).

The thick, corky bark of tupelo, or black gum, Nyssa sylvatica, *a southern hardwood bottomland tree that grows in several small perched (elevated) wetlands in southern Maine. Extraordinarily old trees may be seen at Ferry Beach State Park in Saco. Hank Tyler photo.*

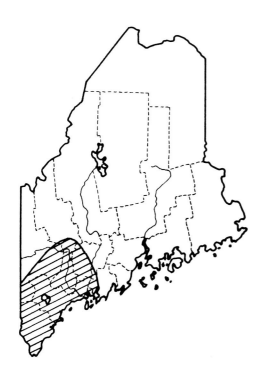

Distribution of shagbark hickory in Maine. Redrawn from Roger J. Stern, Maine Critical Areas Program (1982).

England. A walk through this unusual forest is a journey back five thousand years. The trees, up to two feet in diameter, stand on a floor of sphagnum—the moss of bogs—with large grassy hummocks protecting their bases. The conditions suggest a watery environment of the distant past when the climate was warmer. Now this stand is an isolated northern outpost of a once prevalent species.

One easily viewed stand is located at Ferry Beach State Park, near the mouth of the Saco River. Twenty or more mature trees can be found a little over a mile from the ocean in wet, swampy woods on the west side of Long Pond, off Route 9.

Another rare stand of tupelo exists in a hummocky swamp in Cumberland County. Each fall the trees distinguish themselves by being the first in the area to change color, a characteristic of tupelo. It is an amazing thought that these very trees may have displayed their striking crimson reds well before Maine's first white settler arrived, for some of them are estimated to have been living as long ago as 1575.

There are other forests of the southern deciduous zone where one can experience the woods as did the Indian, the explorer, or the early settler. Such a feeling can still be captured in a pristine sixty-acre forest in York County where old worn-out fields, abandoned in the mid-1700s, reverted to forest. Here, shagbark hickory and white oak of impressive size have re-created the open, parklike forest of pre-Colonial New England. Today this is one of the most unusual forests in the region.

Those who see shagbark hickory will not forget its name.[11] Its bark is perhaps the most unusual of any tree: ashy gray strips up to eight feet long curl away from the trunk at both ends, to be cast off onto the forest floor like a worn and tattered coat. By some estimates, shagbark hickory moved into Maine less than five thousand years ago—a relatively late entry into the white oak/ hickory/chestnut forest community that once dominated the East Coast.

Shagbark Hickory, Carya ovata, *a southern tree of the walnut family, grows in only a few southern Maine locations. Hank Tyler photo.*

Preferring a warmer climate, this forest type did not extend northward beyond southern Maine. Today, facing competition from hemlock and northern hardwoods, a cooling climate, and the detrimental effects of human activities, the shagbark hickory is declining in the state.

In the early 1980s, three important stands of shagbark hickory were placed on the Register of Critical Areas. One was in York, and another existed in nearby South Berwick—until it was cut over in the 1980s. There, above a deep ravine on ledgy soils grew an almost pure grove, some exceeding twenty inches in diameter at breast height. This was also one of the best habitats for southern herbaceous species in Maine.

To the northeast, in Woolwich, is the third designated Critical Area of shagbark hickory. The hickories are large here, diameters of twenty inches being common. Several large white oaks are also present, one twenty-three inches in diameter.

White oak is an uncommon tree of Maine's forests and occurs primarily in the southern part of the state.

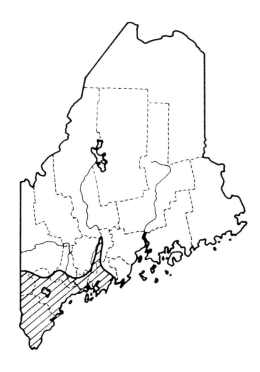

Distribution of white oak in Maine. Redrawn from Roger J. Stern, Maine Critical Areas Program (1974).

Bear oak, Quercus ilicifolia, also called scrub oak, occurs in southern Maine on sandy outwash plains generally associated with pitch pine.

White oak arrived in southern Maine as the climate shifted into a relatively warm, dry period beginning about eight thousand years ago.[12] Here, on the fringe of its range, were ideal conditions for white oak: deep glacial soils of eskers, kames, and outwash plains, and a climate tempered by the proximity of a large body of water. But beginning about five thousand years ago, with the onset of cooler and moister conditions, white oak began to decline in Maine. Changing soil conditions also may have hastened its decline and encouraged the subsequent advance of northern hardwoods. Only a few centuries ago, however, white oak still grew in numbers sufficient to attract shipbuilders in search of lumber. Supreme in strength, resilience, and durability, and of landmark beauty in form and size, the white oak made its place in human history.

Hundreds of years of feeding the voracious appetite of shipyards greatly diminished white oak in the eastern limits of its range, and in this century, unusually dry conditions in 1947 led to wildfires that devastated large areas of Maine's woodlands. In southern Maine, fires swept from Fryeburg through most of York County, destroying much of the remaining inland populations of white oak.

Today, although groves of this stately forest tree are scattered throughout Maine's southernmost counties, only a small number of old-growth stands of special significance have been identified. In them, one can still capture the flavor of the forest as encountered by the early settlers. It's a grassland forest—open, spacious, and parklike beneath the oaks' massive crowns. Some of the trees exceed two hundred years in age. Once this open forest was the domain of the wild turkey, and today's unusual vestiges still harbor other rare and interesting species, such as black gum, mountain laurel, and rhododendron.

An oak that receives scant attention is the scrub, or bear, oak. Together with pitch pine, it forms several neglected communities—the pitch pine / scrub oak barrens of southern Maine. These are considered wasteland by many Mainers because they support so little popular wildlife. What is generally not known, however, is that uniquely associated with the barrens are many extremely rare butterflies and moths, as well as one of Maine's rarest snakes, the black racer. Due to land development and effective fire prevention (occasional burning favors the growth of pitch pine over other species) only a few of these communities are left. Fortunately, two are Inland Fisheries and Wildlife Management areas.

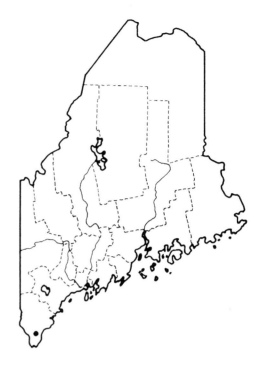

Another oak, chestnut oak, is rare in Maine, occurring only in the town of York, which is the northernmost tip of its range. Here, on Mt. Agamenticus, in a forest resembling those of eastern Massachusetts, grows Maine's major stand of chestnut oak.[13] This is a medium-size species, growing fifty to sixty feet tall and up to two feet in diameter, with long, coarsely toothed leaves similar to those of the American chestnut.

Since the thick, dark reddish-brown bark of the chestnut oak contains more tannin than most oaks, as much as 11 percent, its chief use was for tanning fine leathers—a task for which it was deemed the best. In Maine, however, records indicate that it was used only for rough lumber and firewood.

Scarlet oak is still another tree historically rare in Maine but widely distributed in the mid-Atlantic states.[14] For years this handsome medium-sized tree hung on precariously at this northern edge of its range in only seven natural stands, but in spite of a careful search none of the seven could be relocated in

Distribution of chestnut oak in Maine. Redrawn from L.M. Eastman, Maine Critical Areas Program (1976).

Scarlet oak, Quercus coccinea, *is no longer found in Maine.*

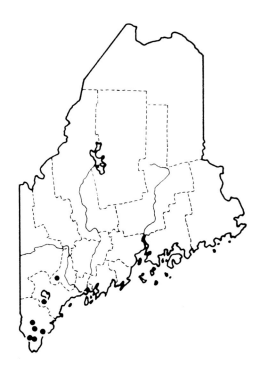

Historically known stands of scarlet oak in Maine. Redrawn from L.M. Eastman, Maine Critical Areas Program (1976).

the mid-1970s, so it must be assumed that the "lively red tint" of scarlet oak in autumn (as described in 1848 by Aaron Young, Maine's first botanist) no longer graces the dry sandy-gravelly areas of southern Maine. The forest fires of 1947, highway development, and commercial mining of sand and gravel all appear to be involved in the disappearance of this rare tree. The lesson is clear: small, isolated populations of plants are apt to be driven back from the edge of their range limits if they are not protected.

One that *is* still clinging to the edge, but barely so, is flowering dogwood.[15] It's been a long struggle for this beautiful tree, one more famous for its flowers than any other species in eastern United States. Preferring a mild climate, its ancestors spread thoughout the warmer states of the east and south, and probably the flowering dogwood established itself in Maine during one or two periods when the climate became warmer and drier.

Flowering dogwood, Cornus florida, *is a southern tree that occurs in only one Maine location, on Mt. Agamenticus. Unfortunately, most of that population has been inadvertently destroyed. This specimen was photographed by Arthur H. Norton on Mt. Agamenticus in 1937.*

In spite of its known presence, few stands of flowering dogwood have ever been recorded in the state. Botanist Kate Furbish reported in 1874 that Fayette Ridge "is my only station for this plant." In 1936, two stations were found on

Mt. Agamenticus in southern Maine. Unfortunately, construction of a road to the summit during World War II destroyed both stands. Subsequent efforts to locate other living trees were to no avail until 1973, when an eight-foot tree was discovered on the mountain. On July 15, 1976, in recognition of its value, the area was included on Maine's Register of Critical Areas, thus ensuring its continued monitoring.

Sassafras is another widely distributed tree that barely reaches into southern Maine.[16] Only five stands are now known in the state. This is an aromatic tree of the laurel family. Its bark is reddish brown and deeply furrowed. Leaves are three-lobed, yellow-green above and chalky white below, glossy and thick, with a smooth margin. In autumn the deep-blue fruits ripen on bright red stalks.

Once prized for the oil derived from the bark of its roots, sassafras was sought after by early English explorers. Tea brewed from its bark was thought to have numerous medicinal benefits, but today the Food and Drug Administration no longer allows the use of oil of sassafras in food and beverages.

Also rare in Maine but widely distributed throughout the eastern and southern United States, spicebush is known from only twelve locations in the state.[17] This handsome shrub is highly tolerant to shade and is almost always found in low, wet woods under a forest canopy that often includes eastern hemlock, red maple, yellow birch, and white ash.

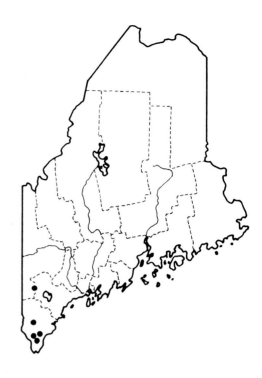

Significant sassafras, Sassafras albidum, *stands in Maine. Redrawn from L.M. Eastman,* Maine Critical Areas Program *(1976).*

Spicebush, Lindera benzoin, *is an aromatic shrub rare in Maine but widely distributed in other areas. Reprinted from D.W. Magee,* Freshwater Wetlands *(Amherst: Univ. of Massachusetts Press, 1981). Abigail Rorer, artist.*

For centuries, several unusual qualities of this fascinating plant have captured attention and interest. Perhaps most distinctive is the strongly aromatic bark. Its twigs and leaves, also pleasing to smell, make a very fragrant tea and, along with the bark, were once used as medicine for the treatment of dysentery, coughs, and colds. To early surveyors, spicebush was an indicator of good agricultural land. Woodsmen used it to build fires, recognizing it as one of the few plants that will burn well while still green. For many insects and

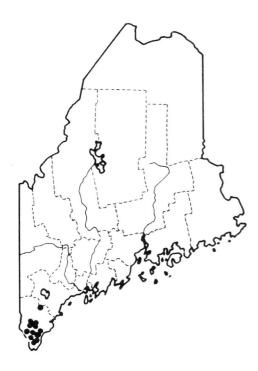

Distribution of spicebush in Maine. Redrawn from L.M. Eastman, Maine Critical Areas Program (1976).

Spotted wintergreen, Chimaphila maculata. *Fewer than a half-dozen locations are known in Maine.*

mammals, it is a source of food. So, due to its many useful qualities, spicebush, holds its own as a valued member of human as well as plant communities.

Autumn coralroot is an orchid of New England significance. Its brownish color and reduced, scalelike leaves suggest its habit of living on decaying organic matter rather than manufacturing its own food with sunlight. This plant is usually four to six inches high with a typically orchid-shaped flower. Only two locations are known in Maine, and the plant has not been observed at one of these since 1895.

A number of plants in the southern deciduous forest zone are rare in Maine but not elsewhere. One is spotted wintergreen, an attractive little evergreen occurring in dry woodlands.[18] Fewer than a half-dozen stations are known in the state, all in the southwest counties.

Northern blazing star is a showy perennial with numerous purple thistlelike flowers supported on stems up to three feet tall. Blooms occur during July and August. Its most extensive Maine location is on the Kennebunk Plains, where it finds the dry, sandy soils it prefers.

Northern blazing-star, Liatris borealis, *is a rare plant of dry, open fields and clearings. Maine's major population, at the Kennebunk Plains, was acquired by The Nature Conservancy. E.T. Richardson, Jr., photo.*

RARE AND UNUSUAL PLANT LIFE

Blunt-lobed woodsia is the largest of the four species of woodsia ferns found in Maine. It is found in dry, rocky woods and banks, usually in partial shade. Another plant found in rocky woods is early buttercup. Until 1974, it was not known to occur in Maine. Missouri rock-cress, of the mustard family, prefers a similar environment.

Blunt-lobed woodsia, Woodsia obtusa, *was first discovered in Maine in 1892, then rediscovered in 1974.*

Summer grape also was not known in Maine until discovered in Oxford County in 1974. It can be distinguished from most other grapes by the white undersides of its leaves. Still another plant reaching its northern limit in Maine (York County) is wild indigo. It grows one to three feet high, flowering in July with cluster of yellow, pea-like blossoms. Its name comes from the bluish-black dye that can be extracted from it.

Summer grape, Vitis aestivalis, *is a rare plant in Maine, where it reaches its northern limit.*

For those who enjoy plants, Maine's woodland communities provide endless opportunities for exploration. And with a little luck and a measure of persistence, perhaps one may encounter an unusual or rare species not previously reported—adding a little bit more to our growing knowledge and understanding of Maine's fascinating plant life.

7

Freshwater Wetland Plant Communities

When the last glacier disappeared from Maine, it left behind a land pock-marked with thousands of water-filled depressions and seamed by tens of thousands of miles of flowing waters. Over the next ten thousand years, glacial debris and soil washed off the land to settle along the banks and at the mouths of rivers and streams and on the quiet bottoms of lakes and ponds. Today Maine is covered by several hundred thousand acres of wetlands—freshwater marshes, peatlands, swamps, and lowlands along rivers and streams—that provide habitats for an amazing diversity of plants.[1]

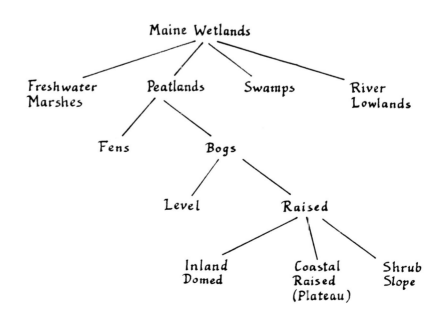

Types of Maine wetlands.

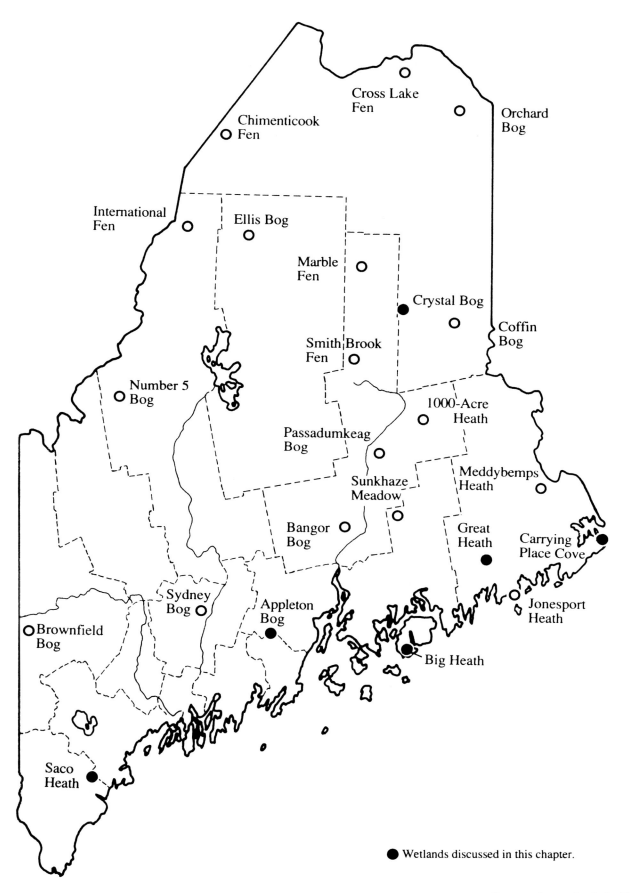

Cross Lake
Fen

Orchard
Bog

Chimenticook
Fen

International
Fen

Ellis Bog

Marble
Fen

Crystal Bog

Coffin
Bog

Smith Brook
Fen

Number 5
Bog

1000-Acre
Heath

Passadumkeag
Bog

Meddybemps
Heath

Sunkhaze
Meadow

Bangor
Bog

Great
Heath

Carrying
Place Cove

Jonesport
Heath

Sydney
Bog

Appleton
Bog

Brownfield
Bog

Big Heath

Saco
Heath

● Wetlands discussed in this chapter.

Some major wetlands in Maine.

Freshwater Marshes

Two generalized patterns of wetland development. Redrawn from S.S. Fafer and P.A. Schettig, An Ecological Characterization of Coastal Maine, 2 *(Newton, Mass.: Dept. of Interior, U.S. Fish and Wildlife Serv., Northeast Region, 1980). Originally adapted from R.G. Wetzel and from P. Dansereau and F. Segadas-Vianna.*

It is a common notion that lakes and ponds develop through a number of stages: from open water to marshes with emergent plants, then to mossy bogs, to wooded swamps, and finally to forests and dry uplands. Actually there appear to be many patterns; every situation is different, depending upon location, climate, land contour, water flow and quality, and other factors (including the influence of humans).

Freshwater marshes are likely to develop in shallow moving water where the soils are predominantly mineral rather than organic. Under these condi-

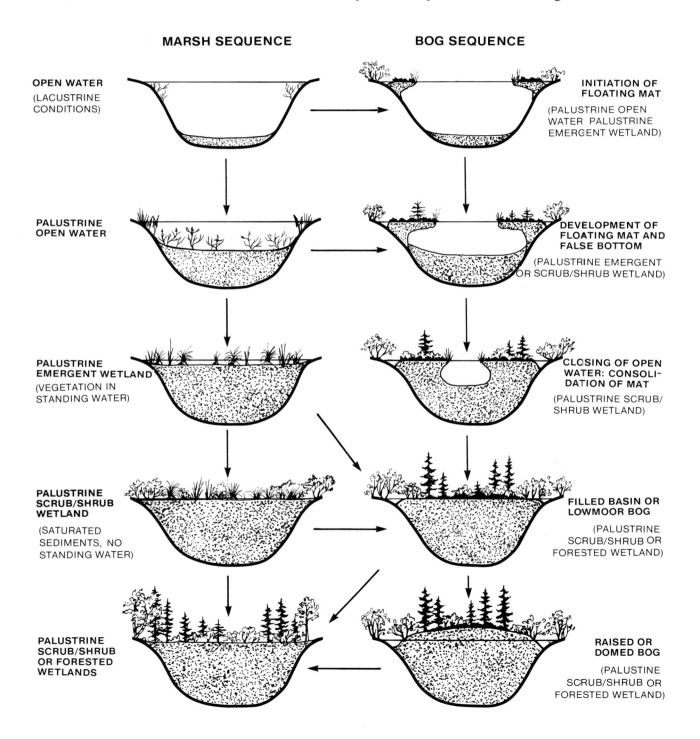

MARSH SEQUENCE

BOG SEQUENCE

OPEN WATER (LACUSTRINE CONDITIONS)

INITIATION OF FLOATING MAT (PALUSTRINE OPEN WATER PALUSTRINE EMERGENT WETLAND)

PALUSTRINE OPEN WATER

DEVELOPMENT OF FLOATING MAT AND FALSE BOTTOM (PALUSTRINE EMERGENT OR SCRUB/SHRUB WETLAND)

PALUSTRINE EMERGENT WETLAND (VEGETATION IN STANDING WATER)

CLOSING OF OPEN WATER: CONSOLIDATION OF MAT (PALUSTRINE SCRUB/SHRUB WETLAND)

PALUSTRINE SCRUB/SHRUB WETLAND (SATURATED SEDIMENTS, NO STANDING WATER)

FILLED BASIN OR LOWMOOR BOG (PALUSTRINE SCRUB/SHRUB OR FORESTED WETLAND)

PALUSTRINE SCRUB/SHRUB OR FORESTED WETLANDS

RAISED OR DOMED BOG (PALUSTINE SCRUB/SHRUB OR FORESTED WETLAND)

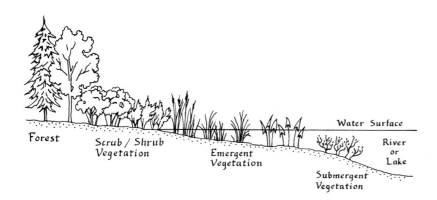

Forest

Scrub / Shrub
Vegetation

Emergent
Vegetation

Submergent
Vegetation

Water Surface

River
or
Lake

tions, emergent plants—cattails, sedges, rushes, and grasses—can get a foothold along the shores of lakes and ponds. As detritus and sediment deposits build up around their roots, the plant communities spread outward, covering larger areas and forming marshes. Marshes also develop in sediments deposited on the banks of slow-moving streams and rivers. These marshes, which have standing water only during wet seasons, are called wet meadows.

Life in a marsh often favors plants with special adaptations. For example, two-thirds of a cattail is underground, where it has an extensive food storage capacity in a horizontally branching, starchy rootstock, two to three inches thick. Many plants have special adaptations to obtain oxygen since their roots cannot absorb it from the oxygen-deficient muck. For example, air sacs and large spaces between cells allow some plants to store their oxygen; others have stems and leaves that are able to absorb oxygen from the surrounding water. The lack of oxygen on the marsh floor also limits decompostion, which results in deficiencies of plant nutrients. To overcome this problem, some plants are carnivorous—that is, they eat animals.

The bladderworts are the most common carnivorous plants in Maine. More than a dozen species exist in the Northeast; among them is the common bladderwort. Its bright yellow flowers float on the surface of open water, while the rootless plant body dangles beneath. Little sacs, or bladders, cover its narrow, branching leaves. Each sac is a miniature vacuum chamber with a door surrounded by several bristly "triggers" (actually leaves). If an unlucky water flea or other passing prey accidentally touches one of the triggers, the door opens instantaneously and the victim is sucked in as water rushes into the sac. Once inside, the victim is digested by the plant.

The purple bladderwort, on the other hand, is rare in Maine.[2] It is currently known from only one location in the state, where its small lavender flower, poking up through the water along the margin of a pond in Oxford County, is probably all that will be seen of this inconspicuous plant. Like its more common yellow-flowered relative, purple bladderwort captures insect prey with a lightning-fast water trap.

Freshwater marshes help prevent floods by slowing down runoff, and they keep water tables high during dry spells. They are also important habitats for many wildlife species, such as black and wood ducks, for which they offer abundant food and shelter.

Marshes favor plants with special adaptations, such as the large food-storage capacity of cattail rootstocks. Reprinted from D.W. Magee, Freshwater Wetlands *(Amherst: Univ. of Massachusetts Press, 1981). Abigail Rorer, artist.*

Common bladderwort, Utricularia vulgaris, *an abundant aquatic carnivorous plant in Maine. Reprinted from D.W. Magee,* Freshwater Wetlands *(Amherst: Univ. of Massachusetts Press, 1981). Abigail Rorer, artist.*

Peatland: Fens and Bogs

Due to its glaciated topography, varied soils, and—most important—its cool climate, Maine boasts the greatest number and diversity of peatland types of the northeastern states.[3] There are some ten thousand peatlands over one acre in size, covering up to seven hundred and fifty thousand acres. In all of the contiguous United States, with the possible exceptions of Minnesota and Washington, Maine has the greatest variety of peatlands.

Unlike marshes, peatlands have organic soils. This peat is made up of the partially decomposed remains of dead plants, principally sphagnum moss. A second key difference, which determines whether a body of water will become a peatland or a marsh, is the amount of water movement and exchange. The oxygen in standing water is quickly used up, and when this happens, the bacterial "scavengers" that break down dead plant and animal tissues cannot function, so the detritus accumulates to form peat.

The term *bog*, though commonly used in New England to describe peatlands in general, refers more accurately to a type of mineral-poor, acidic

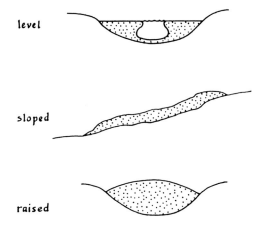

level

sloped

raised

Types of peatland based on form.

General location of peatlands. Level peatlands occur throughout the state. Raised peatlands are absent from southern Maine, the Great Sidney Bog being the most southwestern of the prominent raised bogs. Coastal plateau bogs and shrub slope heathlands are all very near the sea. Peatlands with "ladder-rung" linear patterns, called ribbed fens, are found in extreme northern Maine. Redrawn from Ian A. Worley, Maine Critical Areas Program (1981).

peatland with low water flow and nutrients obtained primarily from the atmosphere. Species diversity is lower here than in a fen, another type of peatland. The bog's principal source of peat is sphagnum moss. Fens, on the other hand, receive greater amounts of mineral-enriched surface- and ground-water, since they are often on a slight slope and nourished by nutrients replenished by the slowly moving water. They are thus less acidic than bogs, have greater species diversity, and derive their peat more from sedges and woody plants.

Of particular interest are patterned fens, found inland in the northern half

Aerial view of a ribbed fen, a very rare peatland type, in northern Maine. Only fifty ribbed fens are known in the state. The ribbed pattern is formed by alternating areas of vegetation and water. Ronald B. Davis photo.

of Maine and adjacent Canada.[4] These wetlands display unusual patterns of alternating ponds or pools and vegetated ridges. The ponds may form concentric rings, parallel ladders, eccentric arcs, or other shapes, interspersed with

Crystal Bog, in Aroostook County, displays one of the most outstanding arrangements of concentric pools in the continental United States. Thomas H. Arter photo, courtesy of Maine Fish and Wildlife *Magazine.*

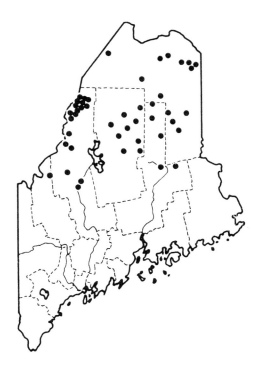

*Distribution of ribbed fens in Maine.
Redrawn from Eric R. Sorensen,
Maine Critical Areas Program (1986).*

*Differences between ribbed fens and
eccentric and concentric patterned bogs.
Redrawn from Eric. R. Sorensen,
Maine Critical Areas Program (1986).*

*English sundew, Drosera anglica,
was discovered in Crystal Bog.
Fred Bavendam photo, courtesy of
Maine Fish and Wildlife Magazine.*

ribs and bands of vegetation, all tending to form at right angles to the flow of water. Although there is no generally accepted explanation of the development of the patterns, a number of hypotheses have been advanced, involving the influence of plant growth, water-table fluctuation, ice and frost, and gravity. It is also interesting to note that patterned fens contain almost every kind of wetland plant.

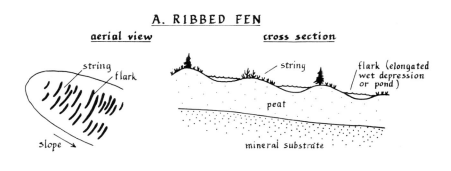

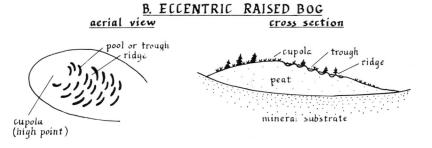

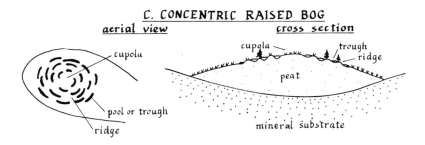

Particularly common to fens are the sedges, which in many cases can be distinguished from grasses and rushes by the triangular cross-section of their solid stems (the stems of grasses and rushes are usually round and sometimes hollow). Some sedges are rare—for example, the scantily flowered sedge, which is known to occur in only two Maine towns. A number of other rare plants also are associated with Maine's fens: English sundew, linear-leaf sundew, showy lady's-slipper, grass-of-Parnassus, northern valerian, and, perhaps the rarest of all, prairie white fringed orchid.

As far as is known, the single location of prairie white fringed orchid in Maine is also the only one in New England.[5] Plant geographers have taken a special interest in this site because it indicates an interesting disjunction of a prairie species. The orchid grows from about eight inches to over three feet high. Its flowers are creamy white and fragrant, and the deeply fringed lobes of its lip account for its common name.

English sundew and linear-leaf sundew are two of Maine's rarest carnivorous plants. Like other sundews, their leaves are covered with sticky glandular hairs, or tentacles. Once an insect gets stuck on them, the longer, outer tentacles extend (rapidly if the insect is active) and fold around the victim. Shorter hairs anesthetize the prey and produce enzymes that extract protein and other nutrients from the insect's tissues. These nutrients appear to enhance the plant's survival and reproductive functions. About two weeks later, the sundew leaf unfolds to eject the desiccated remains, and the trap is reset.

The two sundew plants may be distinguished by their leaves. English sundew has elongated oval leaves; the linear-leaf sundew's are longer and narrower. Both plants occur in Aroostook County and are of national significance.

Showy lady's-slipper (shown in the Section II Perspective) is the largest and, according to some, the most beautiful of all lady's-slippers. Its tall leafy stems, one to two feet high, bear one or two large flowers having white petals and a contrasting magenta pink pouch. The hairs on its leaves and stems are poisonous to many people, causing blisters and inflammation similar to poison ivy.

This orchid grows along the edges of wetlands and in the sunlit openings of mossy woods, but prefers neutral-to-alkaline soils and waters influenced by the presence of limestone. In bogs, its roots penetrate beneath the acid sphagnum moss to more neutral conditions below. In clearings and along woodland edges, colonies may be very large, with abundant flowers. It is interesting to note that dense colonies are sometimes found in deer yards. Some speculate that the deers' hooves push the seeds into the earth to the right depth for germination; others suggest that there is more sunlight in deer yards, thus favoring showy lady's-slipper's proclivity for edge habitats.

Showy lady's-slipper is rare in New England and appears to be declining in many parts of its range. Timber harvesting and collecting have taken their toll, especially since it takes about fifteen years for the plant to reach flowering size.

Bogs are classed as level or raised. The most common type in the Northeast is the level bog, usually occupying a glacially formed basin, such as a kettlehole. The bog may fill the basin just to the level of the existing water

Scantily flowered sedge, Carex rariflora, *is a rare plant in Maine, found growing in fens.*

Prairie white fringed orchid, Platanthera leucophaea, *a rare orchid of midwestern fens and wetlands, occurs in New England in only one Maine wetland. Mary Droege photo, courtesy of* Maine Fish and Wildlife *Magazine.*

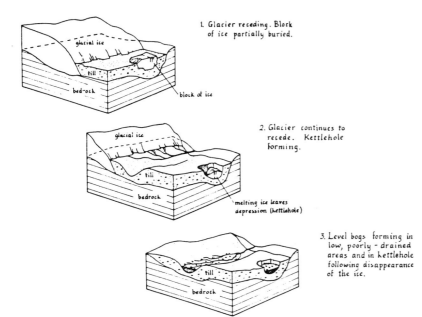

1. Glacier receding. Block of ice partially buried.

2. Glacier continues to recede. Kettlehole forming.

melting ice leaves depression (kettlehole)

3. Level bogs forming in low, poorly-drained areas and in kettlehole following disappearance of the ice.

Formation of kettlehole bogs on glacial terrain. Redrawn from S.L. Fefer and P.A. Schettig, An Ecological Characterization of Coastal Maine, 2 *(Newton, Mass.: Dept. of Interior, U.S. Fish and Wildlife Serv., Northeast Region, 1980). Originally adapted from R.W. Heeley and W.S. Motts.*

Sphagnum mosses are among the dominant plants of peatlands. The mosses release acid into the soil and water of the peatland, creating a highly acidic environment. Naomi Edelson photo, courtesy of Maine Fish and Wildlife *Magazine.*

Mountain cranberry, Vaccinium vitis-idaea, *Bog rosemary,* Andromeda glaucophylla, *and Leather-leaf,* Chamaedaphne calyculata, *are common heath plants found in Maine bogs. Bog rosemary and leather-leaf reprinted from D.W. Magee,* Freshwater Wetlands *(Amherst: Univ. of Massachusetts Press, 1981). Artist, Abigail Rorer.*

table, or, in climates where precipitation is more plentiful, the vegetation may rise to completely fill the basin. Sphagnum mosses and heaths are typical plants of bogs.

Sphagnum moss is especially adapted to the wetland environment because of its large water-storage cells. These give the plant its exceptional ability to hold water (as much as twenty-five times the plant's own weight in some species) and its ability to capture nutrients, such as calcium and sodium. The plant lives on top of the water, and as it grows, the old dead cells fall to the bottom and die, adding to the accumulating deposits of peat.

The heath plants are particularly prevalent in bogs, and add their share to peat accumulation. These include Labrador tea, sheep laurel, bog rosemary, leatherleaf, mountain cranberry, and highbush blueberry.

Maine's raised peatlands are fascinating landscape features. Though the exact nature of their development is still being debated, it is generally thought that they result from either or both of two processes: lakefill and swamping. Lakefill involves the growth and spread of plants inward toward the center of a lake, eventually filling it with the dead remains of plant and animal matter. Swamping, also known as paludification, is a rather bizarre phenomenon in which a peatland spreads to adjacent land areas: sphagnum moss, with its decay-preventing acidity, its vigorous growth, and its unusual water-absorbing capacity, builds up rapidly, extending its range and "pulling" water with it.

Climate appears to be the major determining factor in the formation of raised bogs. Only conditions that provide unusual amounts of moisture and reduce its loss through evaporation and transpiration can provide the surplus of water that favors the development of raised bogs. The best locations are those with abundant precipitation, heavy cloud cover or dense fog, cool summer temperatures, and poor drainage. Under these conditions, raised peatlands are capable of making surprising changes in the natural environment around them: creating new landforms, rerouting streams, raising water tables, retaining ground frost into the growing season, invading other ecosystems.

There are two types of raised bogs: inland domed bogs and coastal raised bogs. The typical inland domed bog usually has a poorly developed moat, called a lagg, around its perimeter, with surface pools and trees in its center. The dome may or may not be noticeable and also may not be in the center of the bog.

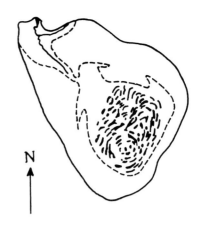

An inland domed bog in Penobscot County showing concentric patterning. Redrawn from Ian A. Worley, Maine Critical Areas Program (1981).

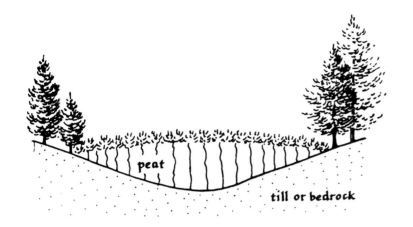

Inland domed bog.

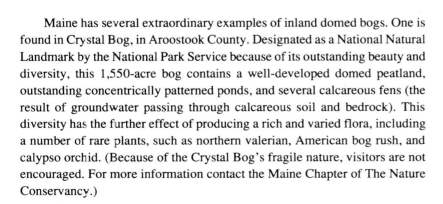

Larrabe Heath, in Machiasport, is a coastal raised peatland purchased by The Nature Conservancy as a preserve. Hank Tyler photo.

Maine has several extraordinary examples of inland domed bogs. One is found in Crystal Bog, in Aroostook County. Designated as a National Natural Landmark by the National Park Service because of its outstanding beauty and diversity, this 1,550-acre bog contains a well-developed domed peatland, outstanding concentrically patterned ponds, and several calcareous fens (the result of groundwater passing through calcareous soil and bedrock). This diversity has the further effect of producing a rich and varied flora, including a number of rare plants, such as northern valerian, American bog rush, and calypso orchid. (Because of the Crystal Bog's fragile nature, visitors are not encouraged. For more information contact the Maine Chapter of The Nature Conservancy.)

The largest peatland in Maine is the Great Heath, next to the Pleasant River above Columbia Falls in Washington County.[6] The peatland is adjacent to a significant geological feature, the glaciomarine delta of Pineo Ridge. Roughly two-thirds of this four-thousand-acre peatland is owned by the state and

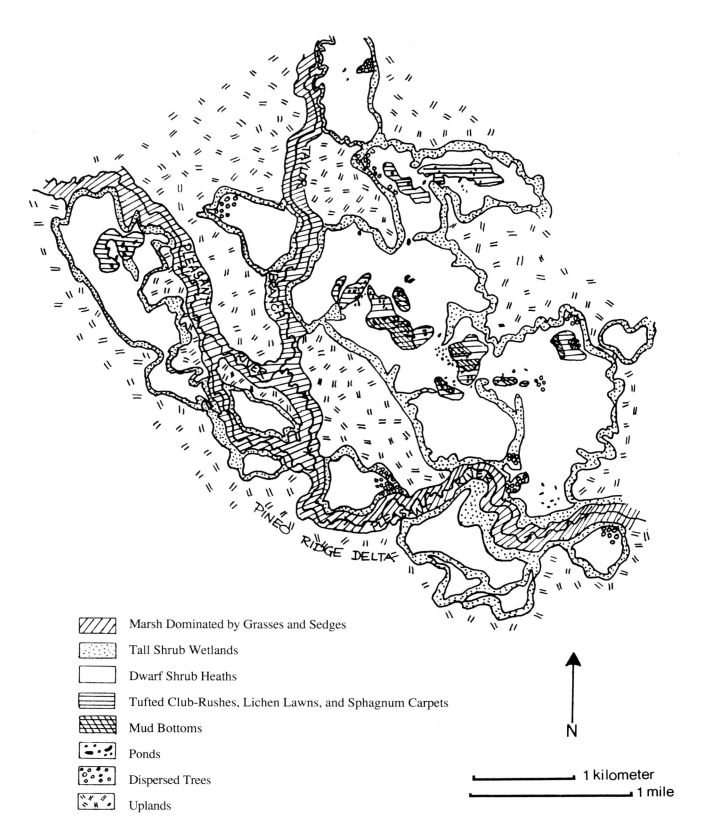

Marsh Dominated by Grasses and Sedges

Tall Shrub Wetlands

Dwarf Shrub Heaths

Tufted Club-Rushes, Lichen Lawns, and Sphagnum Carpets

Mud Bottoms

Ponds

Dispersed Trees

Uplands

N

1 kilometer

1 mile

The Great Heath, a series of coalesced domed peatlands, is Maine's largest peatland complex, covering four thousand acres and vegetated primarily by sphagnum mosses and shrubs such as huckleberry. The northern two-thirds of this exceptional peatland is owned by the State of Maine and managed as a protected resource by the Bureau of Public Lands. Janet McMahon photo.

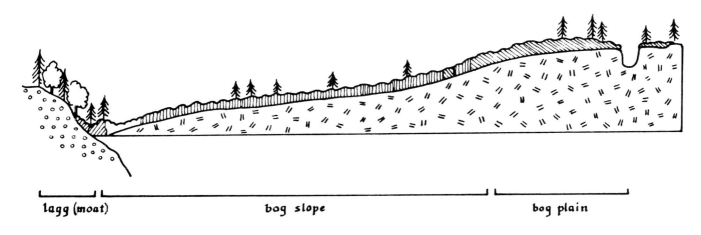

lagg (moat)   bog slope   bog plain

Tall Shrub Wetland

witherod, mountain holly, black spruce
rhodora, leatherleaf

Dwarf Shrub Heath

sheep laurel
black huckleberry

mineral soil on bedrock
peat

managed by the Bureau of Public Lands. Probably due to its proximity to the coast, the Great Heath appears to have characteristics of both inland domed and coastal raised bogs. Its numerous domes have coalesced.

The Great Heath contains the largest number of individual plants of the

Cross-section of plant communities in the Great Heath. From Caren Caljouw, Maine Critical Areas program (1982).

Cloud berry, or baked-apple berry, Rubus chamaemorus, *is a relative of the raspberry. It grows in coastal plateau peatlands along the immediate Washington County coastline. Hank Tyler photo.*

Vegetation of Number 5 Bog. Redrawn from Harry R. Tyler, Jr., and Christopher V. Davis, Maine Critical Areas Program (1982).

orchid arethusa in one place anywhere in the Northeast, estimated at over five thousand. A plant of greater rarity, found on the southern expanses of the bog plain, is baked-apple berry. A close relative of raspberries and blackberries and a member of the rose family, it grows close to the ground and has no thorns. A relatively small population of baked-apple berry occurs here, as well as on a number of coastal bogs in eastern Maine and subalpine bogs in western sections, but the plant is common farther north. In parts of Scandinavia and Canada its fruit is harvested and used fresh or made into jam or liqueur.

One hundred and sixty miles southeast of the Great Heath, within the city boundaries of Saco, is the Saco Heath, which contains probably the southernmost domed raised bog in the East. Spreading over five hundred acres, its other features include fens with slight rib patterning, a sixty- to seventy-acre stand of Atlantic white cedar, and many plant species characteristic of peatlands, such as tamarack, black spruce, heaths, sedges, and pitcher plant.

Another exceptional inland peatland, known as Number 5 Bog, lies in a remote, undeveloped area of Somerset County in northwestern Maine.[7] Covering approximately fifteen hundred acres, this is one of Maine's larger peatlands. Its undisturbed character, complex of large pools and a ribbed fen, scenic vistas, diversity of vegetation, glacial topography, and association with an unusual forest of jack pine led to its being named a National Natural Landmark.

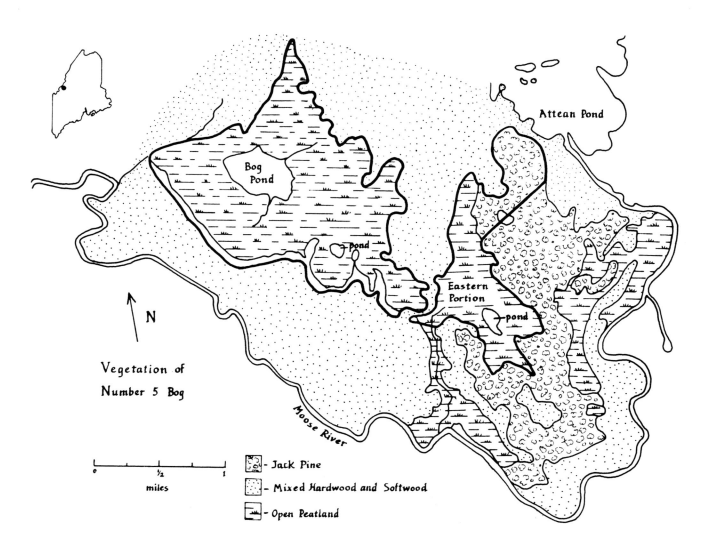

N

Vegetation of
Number 5 Bog

0   ½   1
miles

▨ - Jack Pine

▨ - Mixed Hardwood and Softwood

▨ - Open Peatland

The coastal raised bog is another rare type of peatland.[8] Although it shares many characteristics of the inland domed bog, it is distinguished by its plateau shape, which rises steeply from a well-defined moat around the bog's edge, then gradually levels off to an almost flat plain on top. (It is also known as a plateau bog.) Maine has the only well-known examples in the United States, occurring in a narrow band between Mt. Desert Island and West Quoddy Head within a mile or so of tidewater.

Carrying Place Cove Bog, in Lubec, also designated a National Natural

Number 5 Bog, a 1500-acre peatland complex in Somerset County, is located in the broad Moose River valley and surrounded by the northern Appalachian Mountains. It was recognized as a National Natural Landmark by the National Park Service in 1984. The Coburn Lands Trust donated their portion of the bog in Attean Township to the Forest Society of Maine, receiving the 1985 Critical Areas Award for their conservation action. Hank Tyler photo, courtesy of Maine Fish and Wildlife *Magazine.*

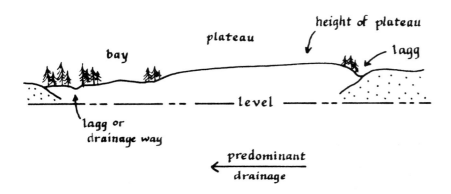

Coastal raised or plateau bog. Redrawn from Ian Worley, Maine Critical Areas Program (1980).

A cross-section of the peatland at Carrying Place Cove in West Quoddy Head State Park. Hank Tyler photo, courtesy of Maine Fish and Wildlife Magazine.

Landmark, is one of the best examples of these coastal raised peatlands. It is one of only three coastal peatlands in the United States subject to erosion by tidewater, and the exposed cross-section provides one of the finest opportunities anywhere in the world to study the history of a raised peatland.

Big Heath, in Acadia National Park, is the southernmost example of a coastal raised peatland in North America. This 420-acre peatland contains numerous ponds and is dotted with black spruce.

The shrub slope peatland, also called a "blanket bog," is another wetland type associated with the coastal raised peatland. Typical of more northern areas, shrub slope peatlands are very rare in the United States. Unlike most peatlands, which develop in depressions, they form on slopes exposed to the rain, fog, and cool temperatures of maritime climates. Examples occur on some of the outer islands of the Great Wass archipelago—Mistake Island, for instance, and the Petit Manan peninsula.

Maine's peatlands have many special qualities. There is a mysteriousness about these misty lands, an aura of the Arctic, and a freshness associated with the primitive presettlement landscape. From a scientific standpoint, they contain records of thousands of years of change in climate, vegetation, and animal life. As ecosystems, they store organic matter and water and provide habitats for wildlife, including overlooked and poorly understood species.

This classic coastal plateau peatland on Great Wass Island in Washington County is a Nature Conservancy preserve. Hank Tyler photo, courtesy of Maine Fish and Wildlife Magazine.

Peatlands have long been recognized as a natural resource for a variety of human uses, including blueberry and cranberry production. Peat is used as a soil conditioner, and in recent years, it has received considerable attention in this country as a possible source of energy.

Swamps

Swamps are wetlands overgrown with trees and shrubs. Those formed from poorly drained peatlands may be invaded first by tamaracks and black spruce, then, as the ground level is built up and drainage improves, by northern white cedar. We know less about the transition of marshes to swamps, but alders and willows are often early shrub inhabitants, along with red maples and elms. These and other plants must adapt to the wet soil and lack of oxygen if they are to survive. Many do this by spreading their roots near the surface where the soil is better aerated.

Swamps occur throughout Maine and are, for many, among the most mysterious of natural environments. A cedar swamp offers a particularly unforgettable experience. Once inside its seemingly impenetrable barricade of trees and drenched in the scent of evergreens, one is in an enchantingly beautiful world. It is dark and damp, with subdued spotlights of sun filtered and directed by the cedars above. Thick carpets of moss and sound-absorbing walls and ceilings of dense green foster an expectant silence. It's a place where animal life often remains invisible to intruders. Here one sees common plants, such as the royal fern, but it's also home to rare species.

Rooted in the cool mosses of northern swamps, capturing rays of sunlight filtered by the arbor vitae (northern white cedar), lives the rare small round-leaved orchis.[9] The flower of this beautiful little orchid has white to purple petals distinguished by a white lip spotted with magenta. Naturalist Frederick Case, after watching a colony of this orchid over a period of time, noted that the plants tend to "jump around"; that is, plants seem to disappear from some areas while "new" ones appear in other places. This may be due to the species' short life span and reseeding pattern, or perhaps individual plants lie dormant underground for several years.

Small round-leaved orchis is a subarctic plant that inhabits cold, moist

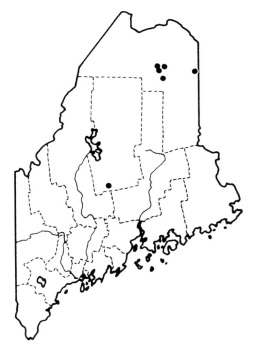

Recorded historical locations of small round-leaved orchis in Maine. Redrawn from L.M. Eastman, Maine Critical Areas Program (1977).

Small round-leaved orchis, Orchis rotundifolia, *an extremely rare species found in a few mossy calcareous swamps and wet woods in northern Maine. Susan C. Gawler photo.*

coniferous forests. It is generally found north of the Canadian border, from Greenland to Alaska. Only three active sites are currently known in Maine, all in Aroostook County.

Clammy azalea is a small to medium-sized shrub also found in swamps, as well as along the edges of streams and ponds.[10] It has many bristly or hairy

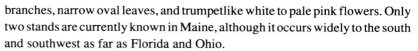

Clammy azalea, Rhododendron viscosum, *grows in swamps and damp thickets from Maine to South Carolina. It is found in two locations in Oxford County. Hank Tyler photo.*

branches, narrow oval leaves, and trumpetlike white to pale pink flowers. Only two stands are currently known in Maine, although it occurs widely to the south and southwest as far as Florida and Ohio.

Atlantic white cedar is a beautiful, strongly aromatic tree belonging to the cypress family.[11] It can reach a height of eighty feet and diameter in excess of

Atlantic white cedar.

Atlantic white cedar twig, Chamaecyparis thyoides. *Laurel Smith, artist.*

twenty inches, and may be identified by its combination of dull bluish-green, narrow, scalelike leaves, waxy bluish-gray fruits, and thin, reddish-brown and easily shredded bark. Because of the wood's rot-resistant qualities in particular, Atlantic white cedar has been cut steadily since early settlement times.

Although widely distributed in swamps and bogs on the Atlantic Gulf Coastal Plain, the cedar is now threatened by development throughout much of its range—including in Maine, its northern limit. Today only a few stands exist in scattered, isolated localities in southern sections of the state, most of which are along the coast. Several are threatened by uncontrolled logging, peat mining, and land development activities.

A large undisturbed stand of Atlantic white cedar, one of the northernmost occurrences of the tree in North America, is in Appleton Bog, in Knox County. The bog contains pure stands of virgin or near-virgin cedar, totaling over two hundred acres. (Only one other area as large exists in Maine—the Alfred-Lyman stand in the Massabesic National Forest.) In 1973, eighty-five acres of Appleton Bog were protected by the Maine Chapter of The Nature Conservancy; in 1981 it was designated a Maine Critical Area; and the U.S. Department of the Interior recognized the bog's importance by designating it a National Natural Landmark in 1984.

In addition to Atlantic white cedar swamps, the 630-acre bog contains a number of other habitats. These include a deciduous swamp of red maple, a logged-over cedar swamp, a thirty-two-acre pond, and a quaking bog with sundews, pitcher plants, heaths, Virginia chain ferns, and other plants. The pond contains a species of the alga-like pondweed, an aquatic plant with slender branching stems and delicate, tiny, flat leaves. Although this particular species is known to exist in only two other sites in Maine, it lives in cold ponds in a number of other states as well as in Newfoundland and other parts of Canada.

Rivers

Almost a hundred rare plant species grace the rocky ledges, sandy and gravelly shores, alluvial deposits, and other plant habitats of Maine's rivers and streams.[12] The two most outstanding areas for rare and threatened vascular plants are along the St. John and Aroostook rivers in northern Maine.

The seventy-three-mile stretch of the St. John River from Cross Rock Landing at Allagash to Baker Branch, high in its headwaters, is one of the most remote and primitive regions east of the Mississippi River, providing habitat for a number of rare and threatened plants significant at state, New England, and national levels. One of the reasons for this wealth of rare species is that the St. John is undammed. Winter and spring thaws cause overflowing and ice-scouring of its banks, creating a semi-open habitat where many types of plants can coexist. Without the ice, it is likely that a dense growth of shrubs would take over and exclude the rare herbs.

The St. John River is the only known location in the world for Furbish's lousewort (shown in Section II Perspective), a plant on the Federal Endangered Species list.[13] It is not a beautiful plant. The cylindrical flower head has small yellow flowers, and perhaps the plant's most attractive feature is the dense rosette of fernlike leaves at the base of the stem. Furbish's lousewort is usually found near alders and other shrubs in the shade of spruce and fir on the steepest north-facing slopes of the riverbank. Just why this plant grows only here remains a mystery.

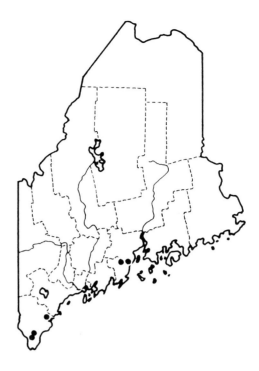

Distribution of Atlantic white cedar in Maine. Redrawn from the Maine Critical Areas Program (1982).

Pitcher plant, Sarracenia purpurea, *a spectacular insectivorous plant commonly found in many of Maine's wetlands. Naomi A. Edelson photo, courtesy of* Maine Fish and Wildlife *Magazine.*

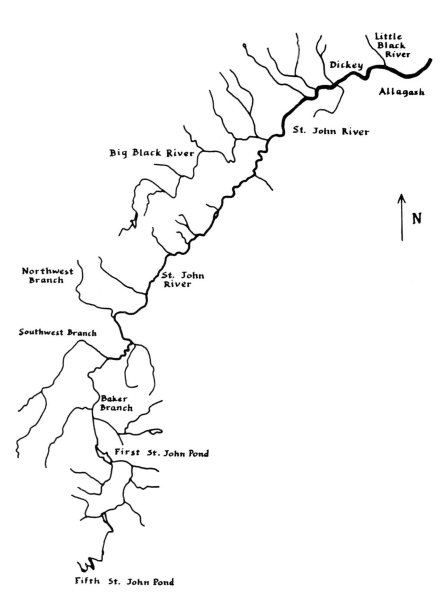

The St. John River, from Allagash
to Baker Branch, provides habitat for
a variety of rare and threatened
species of plants. Redrawn
from Maine Rivers Study, Maine
Dept. of Conservation and
National Park Service (1982).

Furbish's lousewort habitat along the
shores of the St. John River in northern
Aroostook County. Hank Tyler photo.

Three other rare plants found along the banks of the upper St. John River are being considered for the Federal Endangered Species List. Two of these—St. John oxytrope, a purplish member of the pea family, and the deep purple New England violet—are restricted to the occasional outcrops of local slate bedrock. Few plants can tolerate this difficult habitat, but the oxytrope and violet manage to find purchase for their roots in the vertical fissures of the slate.

Also being considered for the Endangered Species List is auricled twayblade, a tiny orchid that until 1984 had not been seen in Maine since 1947. Several populations are now known, widely scattered from the town of Hamlin up to the confluence of the Big Black River. However, it is an easy plant to miss, for it is usually less than four inches tall and grows concealed beneath alders on the riverbank; also, each group usually consists of fewer than twenty individual plants.

Two other very rare plants have verified locations in the upper section of the St. John. One is alpine hedysarum, a pink- or magenta-flowered perennial herb of the pea family, common in much of the Arctic. The other is St. John tansy, an Alaskan plant with many-flowered heads, which grows in sands and gravels along the shore.

St. John Oxytrope, Oxytropis campestris *var.* johannensis, *a member of the pea family, is a nationally significant plant found along the calcareous ledges and gravel shores of the St. John and Aroostook rivers. Hank Tyler photo, courtesy of* Maine Fish and Wildlife *Magazine.*

Alpine hedysarum, Hedysarum alpinum *var.* americanum, *a boreal plant and member of the pea family, and St. John Tansy,* Tanacetum huronense *var.* johannense, *a member of the composite family, are two other rare plants of national signigificance that grow on the calcareous banks of the St. John River. Hank Tyler photo.*

Cut-leaved anemone is one of at least nine plants rare to New England that have been verified as existing in this area of the upper St. John River.[14] It has a delicate air—small, with deeply cut leaves and thin, silky-haired stems having small white, yellow, or red flowers at their ends—but it displays a tenacious will to survive under the harshest conditions. Cut-leaved anemone has been found in only a few places in Maine, always in crevices in ice-scoured, upturned, vertical-layered rock along the St. John. Though rare in the state, cut-leaved anemone is a subarctic plant with a wide distribution in western North America. The relatively few individual plants in Maine represent its farthest southeastern extent.

Another New England rarity found in this location is northern painted cup.[15] Its attractive flowers, with their outer yellowish petals partially enclosed by yellow or white leaflike bracts tinged with purple, resemble hand-painted pottery. Subarctic by nature, in Canada this herb ranges from the Yukon to

Cut-leaved anemone, Anemone multifida, *is a rare plant of New England significance. This member of the buttercup family is restricted to calcareous ledges along the St. John River. Hank Tyler photo, courtesy of* Maine Fish and Wildlife *Magazine.*

Northern painted-cup, Castilleja septentrionalis, *a rare boreal plant found primarily along the St. John river shore in Aroostook County and at high elevations on Mt. Katahdin. Hank Tyler photo.*

Hudson Bay and south to the United States border. Maine is the southeastern-most extent of its range. The Aroostook River, in northern Aroostook County, is another major location, and a few individuals have been found in the North Basin of Mt. Katahdin.

Other plants of New England significance found in the upper St. John include alpine rush, St. John rose, alpine milk-vetch, bird's-eye primrose, showy arnica, pink rattlesnake root, hyssop-leaved fleabane, and anemone multiflora.

Three plants characteristic of the shores of the St. John but very rare elsewhere in the state are false asphodel, grass-of-Parnassus, and variegated horsetail. False asphodel is a member of the lily family. It displays a cylinder of delicate white flowers on a stalk usually less than one foot high and covered with sticky black hairs. This plant is especially dramatic in fruit, when the flowers give way to bright red capsules. Grass-of-Parnassus, a member of the saxifrage family, is a perennial herb with spade-shaped basal leaves and a white flower whose petals are beautifully striped with green. Variegated horsetail is almost grasslike in appearance, with slender stems four to sixteen inches tall growing in tufts.

False asphodel, Tofielda glutinosa, *found on the banks of the St. John River but rare elsewhere in Maine.*

Variegated horsetail, Equisetum variegatum, *a rare plant found on the banks of the St. John River.*

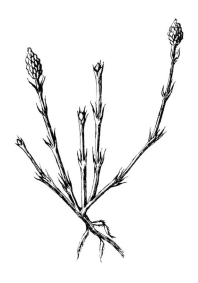

A number of rare plants, including many mentioned above, also grow along a stretch of the St. John below the Allagash / St. Francis township line. These include Furbish's lousewort, St. John oxytrope, New England violet, auricled twayblade, cut-leaved anemone, and swamp valerian.

The Aroostook River is Maine's other outstanding area for the con-

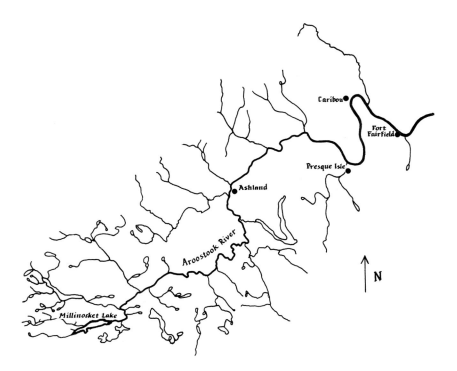

The Aroostook River is an outstanding area for rare riverine plants.

centration and variety of rare and threatened vascular plants typically associated with rivers. At least seventeen rare species have been verified by the Critical Areas Program at locations between the Canadian border and Millinocket Lake. Nationally significant species include the sandbar willow—a small tree up to eighteen feet high—and alpine hedysarum. Species of New England significance include rattlesnake root, alpine rush, Blake's milk vetch, northern painted cup, and alpine milk vetch.

Several other rivers are known to harbor rare vascular plants. The Allagash River contains one station for the New England violet. The rare long-leaved bluet grows on ledges of the Stillwater in Old Town as well as on dry ledges on the riverbank overlooking Little Spencer Stream, a tributary of the Dead River and upper Kennebec. Wet calcareous ledges and cliffs along Moxie Stream, which feeds into the upper Kennebec River, provide habitat for the nationally significant smooth woodsia fern and a number of other rare plants. Other rivers with documented rare plants include the Moose, Penobscot, Pleasant, Saco, Sheepscot, Carrabassett, Fish, Kennebec, Mattawamkeag, Piscataquis, St. Francis, St. George, and Sandy.

Those who poke around Maine's bogs and marshes or explore the edges of ponds and streams cannot help but be impressed by the profusion of plant life spawned at these meeting places of land and water. And for those who take a closer look at that "ordinary" plant, there is the possibility of discovering something so distinctive that the observer —and perhaps even the world—will find it new and wondrous.

Long-leaved bluet, Houstonia longifolia, *a rare plant found along the Stillwater River.*

8

Coastal Plant Communities

One of the pleasant surprises for anyone interested in nature is the discovery that Maine's coastline is a meeting place for two very different natural environments—where north meets south, in a manner of speaking. From Casco Bay northeastward, the cool, humid climate draws the boreal forest to the edge of the sea. Here, many photographers and painters have plied their arts to capture the misty outline of spruce and fir on a ragged, rocky coast. Southwest of Casco Bay, where the climate is warmer, one finds extensive stands of the northern hardwoods and hemlock, with white pine on the drier, sandier sites and pitch pine on similar but burned-over locations. In this area the land is more gentle, and sand beaches soften the lines where it meets the sea.

The moderating effect of the ocean on the coastal climate acts to extend the range limits of plants common to regions both north and south of Maine. Here they find a great diversity of habitats among the sand and gravel beaches, estuaries, salt marshes, and rocky shorelands and islands. It is not surprising, then, that Maine's coast harbors many interesting and rare communities and species of plants.[1]

Beach Communities

Beaches are uncommon along Maine's coast; sand beaches, for example, occupy about 2 percent, or seventy-five miles, of coastline, so plants restricted to beach habitats are naturally scarce here.[2] Few plant species inhabit beaches, for these are excessively harsh environments, where levels of temperature, solar radiation, moisture, salinity, and soil nutrients can run to extremes. In addition, their continually shifting and eroding sand and gravel do not make for a stable base upon which to grow. Storms, in particular, have catastrophic

effects on beaches and the life they support. Despite these conditions, some peculiarly adapted plants do well in these stressful environments.

American beach grass, which is the dominant plant of dunes and a key factor in their formation, can survive burial in sand to a depth of over three feet. (In fact, if it is *not* covered by sand every year, it becomes less vigorous.) Beach heather also can survive burial, although not to as great a depth.

Another key to plant survival is the prevention of water loss. Ironically, though water appears to be everywhere, the beach habitat is physiologically very dry due to exposure to wind, salt, and sun. The many methods demonstrated by beach plants to cope with the lack of water are truly innovative. Virtually all dune plants have thick cuticles —waxlike, water-repellent layers covering their outer layer of cells. In some, such as American beach grass, the stomata (pores in the protective outer layer of cells) are sunken, which permits exchange of air without loss of water. American beach grass also has curled leaves, as does broom crowberry, to prevent water loss from the leaf's under-surface. Beach heather and dusty miller are good examples of plants with hairy leaves designed to retain moisture by slowing down evaporation. A number of species have thick leaves or stems to decrease their surface-to-volume ratio so that evaporation can be reduced. This feature, called succulence, is evidenced by sea rocket, seabeach sandwort, saltwort, and others. For the same reason, some plants, such as jointweed and saltwort, have quite small leaves.

Several plant communities inhabit sandy beaches. Facing the very edge of

Saltwort, Salsola kali, *has leaves designed to reduce evaporation. From R.W. Tiner,* A Field Guide to Coastal Wetland Plants *(Amherst: Univ. of Massachusetts Press, 1987). Abigail Rorer, artist.*

Plant communities and representative species inhabiting sand beaches.

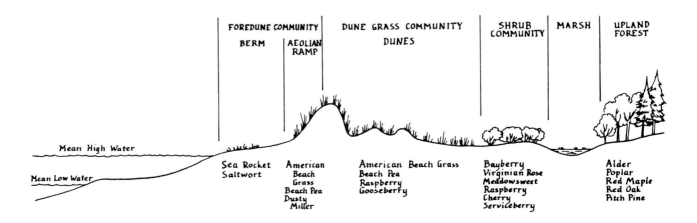

	FOREDUNE COMMUNITY		DUNE GRASS COMMUNITY	SHRUB COMMUNITY	MARSH	UPLAND FOREST
	BERM	AEOLIAN RAMP	DUNES			

Mean High Water

Mean Low Water

Sea Rocket Saltwort	American Beach Grass Beach Pea Dusty Miller	American Beach Grass Beach Pea Raspberry Gooseberry	Bayberry Virginian Rose Meadowsweet Raspberry Cherry Serviceberry	Alder Poplar Red Maple Red Oak Pitch Pine

The pitch pine forest and sand dune plant community is extremely rare in Maine and is found only in a few of the state's undisturbed sand beach systems. Hank Tyler photo.

Tall wormwood, Artemisia caudata, *an uncommon plant of Maine beaches.*

Beach heather, Hudsonia tomentosa, *grows on the sand dunes of southern coastal Maine and at a few inland sandy areas. It may be seen at Ferry Beach, Reid, and Popham Beach state parks. L. Kenneth Fink, Jr., photo. Courtesy of Maine Critical Areas Program.*

Seaside spurge, Euphorbia polygonifolia, *a common plant on beach berms south of Maine but rare on beaches in the state.*

the sea is the foredune community, where sea rocket and saltwort take up their front-line positions on the seasonal berm. These annuals are able to survive because of their rapid growth rate and great seed-production capabilities. Behind them are American beach grass, beach pea, and dusty miller. The foredune community is backed by the dune grass community, a zone with sand but no developed soil, few nutrients, and heavy salt spray. This community is dominated by American beach grass. Depending upon age, development, and other conditions, other communities may be present on the dune fields and back dune areas: the dry dune slack community, populating dry inland dunes with beach heather, sedges, rushes, and a variety of other plants; the shrub community, a dense tangle of bushes, typically including bayberry, Virginian rose, meadowsweet, and raspberry; and the dune forest community, dominated by pitch pine.

The limited amount of beach habitat in Maine also influences the rarity of plants, and several that live here are uncommon. One is tall wormwood, a rooted biennial (occasionally perennial) growing two to six feet high. Its slender and very leafy branching stems support numerous tiny flowerheads, each less than one-eighth inch in diameter. The northern coastal limit for this species of wormwood is at Reid State Park in Georgetown.

Beach heather, too, is found only as far north as Reid State Park, but it reappears on Canadian beaches. This is a densely tufted, intricately branched and matted plant, four to eight inches high. Flowers are stalked and numerous. It is found on stable sand surfaces, including the depressions of parabolic dunes.

Seaside spurge is a plant common on the berms of Massachusetts beaches but reported on only a few beaches in Maine. It is an annual with pale green, smooth, wiry stems, branching from the base and spreading radially on the sand.

Another uncommon plant is earthstar puffball, a greyish brown, spherical fungus specifically adapted to the dune environment. Its name derives from its appearance in wet weather: moisture causes the skin to split and curl away, forming starlike arms that extend down to the sand and hold it in place. When it dries, the arms draw back to release the puffball's hold on the ground and allow the mature spherical fungus to roll about and distribute its spores from an inner pouch. In Maine, it is found only on a few large baymouth barrier dune beach systems.

Gravel beaches impose even greater stress on plants; abrasion of roots and leaves is a constant threat, since most cobble beaches are exposed to considerable wave action and the stones roll around easily. Only a relatively few plants are able to colonize gravel beaches under these harsh conditions.[3]

One of these is sea lungwort, a spreading perennial that often forms large, circular mats on cobbly coastal beaches—in fact, its *only* habitat is unstable

Lungwort, Mertensia maritima, *an uncommon maritime plant found growing on gravel and cobble beaches on islands and on the mainland in Washington County. Hank Tyler photo.*

gravel beaches subject to high storm waves. Its bell-shaped flowers, rose pink to pale blue, are borne in small clusters at the end of low, spreading branches. The bluish leaves—smooth, ovate, and fleshy—inspire another of its names: oysterleaf.

Distribution of sea lungwort. Redrawn from F.C. Olday, S.C. Gawler, and B. St. John Vickery, Maine Critical Areas Program (1983).

Estuaries and Salt Marshes

Estuaries form where rivers meet the sea. The mixture of fresh and salt water produces a wide range of salinities due to fluctuations in tidal levels and amount of run-off. Only a relatively few species of plants and animals can tolerate the constant changes in salt concentration, oxygen content, temperature, and nutrient distribution. A number of the plants that inhabit estuarine

Wells National Estuarine Reserve contains extensive salt marshes, which are included in the Rachel Carson National Wildlife Refuge. Hank Tyler photo.

waters, mud bottoms, tidal flats, and emergent wetlands are particularly interesting or rare.

One is Long's bitter cress, a plant of the mustard family.[4] Its weak, curved stem, smooth at the base, supports simple, round-to-kidney-shaped leaves and petalless flowers. The first discovery of Long's bitter cress (anywhere in the world) was in the tidal estuary of the Cathance River in Bowdoinham in September 1916. In 1972, this nationally significant plant of Merrymeeting Bay was *rediscovered*, and it is now known to exist in locations along the Cathance River and around Merrymeeting Bay, growing on muck-covered ledges in the freshwater intertidal zone. It also lives in several other locations along the southern coastal plain of Chesapeake Bay and the Gulf of Mexico.

The Cathance is one of six rivers that flow together to form the Merrymeeting Bay estuary.[5] The others are the Androscoggin, Kennebec, Muddy, Abagaddasset, and Eastern. This estuary is the largest tidal bay on the eastern seaboard north of Chesapeake Bay estuary, with about one hundred miles of shoreline encompassing over four thousand acres. It is a unique natural and

Maine's largest tidal freshwater wetland and estuary, Merrymeeting Bay provides the habitat for a number of rare shoreline plants, including Parker's Pipewort, water pimpernel, and horned pondweed. Hank Tyler photo.

historic area, but unfortunately, like other estuaries in the United States, it has suffered from pollution and development.

In addition to Long's bitter cress, several other rare plants may be found here. Among them is Parker's pipewort, an aquatic plant only a few inches high that grows primarily on mudflats. Another is water pimpernel, a primrose with tiny white bell-shaped flowers that seem to bloom profusely for long periods. Horned pondweed, a submersed aquatic plant with slender threadlike branches, has also been recorded in Merrymeeting Bay. Its tiny fruits have a distinct beak. It is exposed only at full low tide, and so is difficult to spot. Pygmyweed, another tiny plant, is found growing in sprawling mats on muddy bottoms and shallow shores of the estuary. These four plants are at the northern edge of their ranges in Maine, and may be found in other estuarine habitats along the East Coast. However, all are rare throughout their ranges, for which pollution and dredging must share part of the blame.

Salt marshes are, without question, important ecosystems of estuaries, but large salt marshes are relatively uncommon in Maine. Yet the few in existence are so important to commercial fisheries, waterfowl, and other wildlife that they are now well protected.

One acre of salt marsh produces four times as much plant material as an

Left: *Parker's pipewort,* Eriocaulon parkeri, *a rare plant found in Merrymeeting Bay. From R.W. Tiner,* A Field Guide to Coastal Wetland Plants *(Amherst: Univ. of Massachusetts Press, 1987). Abigail Rorer, artist.*

Middle: *Horned pondweed,* Zannichellia palustris, *a submersed aquatic plant recorded in Merrymeeting Bay at the northern edge of its range. From R.W. Tiner,* A Field Guide to Coastal Wetland Plants *(Amherst: Univ. of Massachusetts Press, 1987). Abigail Rorer, artist.*

Right: *Pygmyweed,* Tillaea aquatica, *a rare plant throughout its range, is found in Merrymeeting Bay on muddy bottoms and shallow shores.*

acre of wheat. It is this productivity that attracts animal life to its nutrient-rich waters. Estimates suggest that two-thirds of the commercial value of fish and shellfish resources on the east coast is derived from species that live at least part of their lives in salt marshes or areas associated with them.

Since the formation of salt marshes depends upon the presence of sediment and protection from waves and currents, they are almost always found behind barrier beaches or along protected shores of estuaries. The rocky coast of Maine, therefore, does not favor salt marshes. It is not surprising that most of the state's large marshes occur, like its sandy beaches, southwest of the Kennebec River.

Three-thousand-acre Scarborough Marsh is Maine's largest. In his book about this marsh, John Snow writes: "Come with me to a unique and delicate world. The Indians called it Owascoag, the land of many grasses. It hides behind the wide sand beaches, behind the rocky inlet, behind the protective sand dunes. It begins where the last ripple of fresh water meets the ebb and flow of the tide, and ends with the crashing ocean waves. This unique and sensitive world resting between ripples and waves is the salt marsh."[6]

Like estuaries, salt marshes endure the constant mixing of salt and fresh water and exposure to harsh coastal elements, forming a rigorous environment for living things. Only a relatively few plants and animals are able to tolerate such conditions, but fortunately the cord grasses make life possible here. These grasses are called Spartina, which in Greek means cord. Spartina grasses have developed cells that can extract nearly fresh water from the briny water of their surroundings while at the same time preventing the tendency of salt water to draw out fresh water from their tissues. Any remaining salt is collected and excreted by glands in the leaves. Small tubes conduct oxygen from their leaves to their roots in the salty, oxygen-deficient mud.

The Spartina grasses quickly expand their territory by sending out underground stems. Over time a thick substrate is formed from the nutrients and silt trapped by the shoots and from the annual die-back of the shoots themselves, fertilizing the grasses and building up the marsh.

One of the rarest plants found in Maine's salt marshes is slender blue flag.[7] This beautiful, delicate plant grows from one to three feet tall and has one or two blue-veined flowers and slender, grasslike leaves. (In contrast, the common blue flag has wider leaves and several violet-blue flowers, streaked

Saltwater cord grass, Spartina alterniflora, *makes life possible in salt marshes. From R.W. Tiner,* A Field Guide to Coastal Wetland Plants *(Amherst: Univ. of Massachusetts Press, 1987). Abigail Rorer, artist.*

Slender blue-flag, Iris prismatica, *a southern iris found in a few wet meadows and marshes in York County. Naomi A. Edelson photo.*

with yellow, green, and white.) Although slender blue flag grows on the coastal plain from Nova Scotia to Georgia, historical accounts reported it growing in only four locations in Maine. In 1976, a stand of about twenty-five plants was rediscovered where Kate Furbish first found it in 1898, on the edge of a salt marsh on an island in Wells. These plants are now protected in the Wells National Estuarine Reserve, in a portion of the Rachel Carson National Wildlife Refuge.

Several other plants that are rare in Maine but common to the south inhabit emergent wetlands dominated by cord grass. These include dwarf saltwort, American sea blite, and marsh elder.

Rocky Shorelands

The ledges, headlands, and offshore islands of Maine's rocky shorelands support a number of rare plant species. Those with northern affinities are found along the Washington County coastline.[8] Here, on the exposed headlands and outer islands, a very cool, humid climate and frequent fog create an environment similar to that of Maritime and Arctic Canada.

How species of plants were able to colonize some of the outer islands is an interesting question. Water, of course, is a seed dispersal agent, but it is more likely that wind is responsible for the conifers on the islands and for most pioneer species. It is also possible that many species were carried in the digestive tracts of birds such as ducks.

One of Maine's coastal subarctic plants is beachhead iris. Although not rare (it is known from almost sixty locations), Maine is its only location in the United States. Here it lives at the extreme southern edge of its range, which extends north to Newfoundland. Although it resembles its relative, common blue-flag iris, it is usually shorter and has flowers with very short petals so that the bloom appears to have only three parts instead of the usual six. It is found along the crests of sea cliffs, in bedrock crevices, and behind sea beaches.

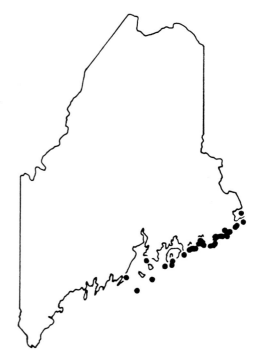

Distribution of beachhead iris along the Maine coast. Redrawn from F.C. Olday, S.C. Gawler, and B. St. John Vickery, Maine Critical Areas Program (1983).

Beachhead iris, Iris hookeri, *a subarctic maritime plant. An uncommon species in Maine, it is found along the coastline of Washington and Hancock counties. Hank Tyler photo.*

Roseroot stonecrop, Sedum rosea, *a subarctic maritime plant, grows in rocky crevices along the downeast coast. Hank Tyler photo.*

Distribution of roseroot stonecrop along the Maine coast. Redrawn from F.C. Olday, S.C. Gawler, and B. St. John Vickery, Maine Critical Areas Program (1983).

Leafy bracted aster, Aster foliaceus, *with beach head iris and roseroot stonecrop, make up one of Maine's most distinctive communities of the rocky coast.*

Roseroot stonecrop is another subarctic coastal plant. It can be recognized by its pale-green fleshy foliage, which appears to be rimmed with frost, and its thick, scaly, rootlike stem, which emits the odor of roses when bruised. Leafy bracted aster is a showy, blue-violet-flowered plant, one to two feet tall. Both leafy bracted aster and roseroot stonecrop are found along the rocky coast and offshore islands from Washington County to Lincoln County. Leafy bracted aster is also reported on the Isles of Shoals. Neither is considered rare north of

New England, being widely distributed in cold northern regions and on high mountain tops. These two plants, with beachhead iris, make up one of Maine's most distinctive floral communities.

Another subarctic plant, bird's-eye primrose, grows from Labrador south, reaching the extreme southern limit of its range on the east coast of Maine. In flower, this tiny plant appears to look up at a lucky finder with its attractive

yellow "eye," located in the center of lilac-colored flowers. Because of its rarity, being "eye-to-eye" with a bird's-eye primrose is a special experience.

Blinks is also found in Maine at its extreme southern limit in eastern North America. It is rare in New England, and like many subarctic plants, it has been discovered only on offshore islands. Blinks is a tiny annual with weak, smooth stems, four to eight inches long, and inconspicuous white flowers. Its shiny seeds give it the name blinks.

Marsh felwort, a subarctic member of the gentian family, is known to live on several islands off the coast of Washington and Hancock counties, as well as at Schoodic Point. This plant grows about ten inches high and has one-inch-diameter blue flowers, stiff branches, and fleshy, narrow leaves. Rare in New England, it is an important part of the distinctive flora of Maine's eastern coast.

Distribution of bird's-eye primrose along the Maine coast. Redrawn from F.C. Olday, S.C. Gawler, and B. St. John Vickery, Maine Critical Areas Program (1983).

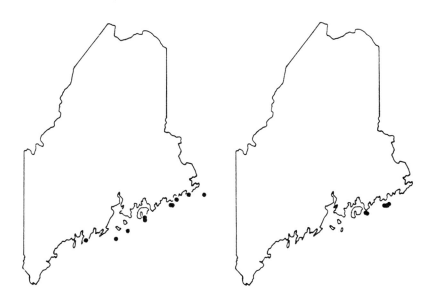

Left: *Blinks,* Montia lamprosperma, *is sparsely distributed along the Maine coast. Redrawn from F.C. Olday, S.C. Gawler, and B. St. John Vickery, Maine Critical Areas Program (1983).*

Right: *Distribution of marsh felwort,* Lomatogonium rotatum, *along the Maine coast. Redrawn from F.C. Olday, S.C. Gawler, and B. St. John Vickery, Maine Critical Areas Program (1983).*

Luminous moss and inkberry are two other plants found along the rocky shore, although luminous moss is not limited to the coast. This species of moss

Luminous moss, Schistostega pennata, *grows in caves and sometimes under buildings. Only three locations are known in Maine. Sunlight reflected through the plant's lenslike chloroplasts creates an emerald glow. Dean Bennett photo.*

Inkberry, Ilex glabra, *a member of the holly family, occurs in Maine only on one offshore island. Another colony grows at the southern tip of Nova Scotia. These isolated remnant populations of a southern species are indicative of the warmer climate five thousand years ago. Susan C. Gawler photo.*

is a curiosity because it seems to emit a glowing green light.[9] (Actually, light shining on the leaves reflects off green chloroplasts and passes back through the lenslike structure of the plant's spherical cells. The glow is similar to that produced by reflectors on roadside signs or by cat's eyes.) This little filamentous moss is usually found in cool, low-light rock crevices and boulder caves, beneath uprooted trees, and under barns. Although it is widespread in Canada and the northern United States, only three locations are known in Maine—one on a mountain in Franklin County and two on the coast in Knox and Hancock counties. The two coastal sites have been designated as Critical Areas.

Inkberry is found along the coast from Nova Scotia to Florida and Louisiana, but in Maine it is known to grow in only one locality, at the edge of a sphagnum peatland on Isle au Haut.[10] This is one of the northernmost stands in North America and is of great interest to botanists. Inkberry is a handsome evergreen shrub belonging to the holly family, growing from one and a half to six feet tall. Among its oblong, leathery, and shiny dark-green leaves are lustrous black berries that produce an inklike stain when crushed. Inkberry leaves contain caffeine and were once used as a substitute for tea. Its berries also provided fabric dyes. One shrub produces as much as five pounds of berries, which are a favorite food for birds. In 1977, the Isle au Haut inkberry stand was included on Maine's Register of Critical Areas.

Few would disagree that the spectacular beauty of the Maine coast owes much to the character of its vegetation. For the plants here, the challenge to survive is formidable; yet many do, responding to the stresses they encounter with an amazing array of adaptive devices. One has only to look closely—in rocky crevices and along sandy and gravelly shores, mud flats, and marshes—to encounter the wonder of this coast.

Uncommon Wildlife

Perspective

There are some who can live without wild things, and some who cannot. . .
Like winds and sunsets, wild things were taken for granted until progress
began to do away with them. Now we face the question whether a still higher
"standard of living" is worth the cost in things natural, wild, and free.

— Aldo Leopold, 1940[1]

It is difficult to imagine Maine without wild animals. Its diverse habitats,
ranging from mountain slopes of arctic tundra to the murky depths of the ocean
gulf, support an amazing diversity of animal life. Over a thousand species of
marine invertebrates, from relatively unknown worms to the celebrated
lobster, inhabit the state's coastal environs. Their number is exceeded only by
the insect species, estimated at an overwhelming sixteen thousand. (Still, this

Bald eagle, Haliaeetus leucocephalus,
*symbolizes conservation efforts to protect
wildlife. Maine is the only northeastern
state where this endangered species can
be seen in any significant numbers.
Mark McCullough photo.*

is not many when one considers that there are more than one million insect species in the world.)

When it comes to higher orders of animal life on the planet, the numbers drop sharply, but the boundaries of Maine still enclose an impressive assortment. According to the *Atlas of Breeding Birds in Maine, 1978-1983*, as many as four hundredspecies of birds have been sighted, of which 201 breed in the state. Other animal species include over sixty mammals, ten salamanders, nine frogs and toads, eight turtles, and eleven snakes. Many of these species exist in great numbers. For example, in a 1950 geographic study of Maine wildlife Richard Day estimated that summer bird populations may reach one hundred million, and small mammals, including shrews, moles, and mice, may number over four billion![3]

From earliest prehistory, humans and the animals with which they share the planet have lived inseparable lives. To Native Americans, who depended upon wildlife for their survival, nature was sacred, and they wasted little. It was in this context that they took moose, beaver, and ruffed grouse from the forest; from the coast, seal and waterfowl; from rivers and streams, alewives, shad, and salmon. When European settlers arrived, they too quickly came to depend upon hunting, trapping, and fishing.

Gradually there came a shift from survival to sport, from necessity to luxury, from giving ceremonial thanks to exploiting unthinkingly. Beneath these changing values, however, many people retained a fascination, a curiosity, an aesthetic appreciation for wildlife. It could be seen in the Wabanaki, who fashioned ceremonial artifacts in the images of animals, who included animals in their beadwork and adopted them as totems. Today we see it reflected in the time and money people spend photographing, painting, and otherwise enjoying wildlife. But along with this attraction to wild creatures has come a rising concern for declining numbers and species.

It is a quiet disaster, the loss of wildlife. It doesn't happen all at once, but more like the slow collecting of mists as a bank of fog settles in. Loss of species is a normal evolutionary occurrence, but in the past two centuries the rate of extinction has increased drastically. It is estimated that in prehistoric times one mammal species became extinct in the world about every 150 years and one bird species every 250 years. Since 1800, in less than two centuries, more than two hundred animal species have been lost—fifty in the United States alone. Gone forever are the passenger pigeon, the giant sea mink, the Labrador duck, and the great auk.[4] As a result, the world today is a little emptier, a little less interesting; what other effects there may be we can only guess.

The English naturalist John Josselyn, who lived in what is now Scarborough during the 1600s, wrote that flocks of the passenger pigeon number-

The passenger pigeon, Ectopistes migratorius, *now extinct, was last seen in Maine in 1896.*

ing millions were so extensive during migrations that "I could see no sun." But every barrel has a bottom, and by the mid-1850s it was rapidly coming into sight. The last passenger pigeon in Maine was reportedly shot in 1896, in Dexter. Eighteen years later, at the Cincinnati Zoo, the last passenger pigeon succumbed, lone survivor of a species that once, by its sheer numbers, turned the day into night.

The giant sea mink, Mustela vison macrodon, *once quite common in the Penobscot Bay area, became extinct in the mid 1800s.*

The giant sea mink met a similar fate. This three-foot-long mammal was once quite common in the Penobscot Bay area. Its reddish fur was sought by pelt hunters. With their guns and dogs, these hunters had completely exterminated the sea mink by about 1860.

The Labrador duck, Camptorhynchus labradorius, *probably a winter resident off the Maine coast, met its demise from over-hunting during the latter half of the nineteenth century.*

Relentless foraging for food and feathers brought about the demise of other species. In the nineteenth century, New England vessels were outfitted specifically for hunting expeditions to kill birds for their plumage. In Labrador, millions of wildfowl were killed during the breeding season. Among the unfortunate was a little sea bird, the Labrador duck, which probably had wintered off the Maine coast. The last known specimen was taken in 1875 on Long Island, New York. Another resident of the Maine coast driven to extinction was the great auk. A large, flightless, penguinlike bird, it was slaughtered wholesale to feed the coastal and island dwellers, sailors, and explorers.

Some species of animals were more fortunate—or hardier—and, though greatly reduced in numbers, managed to survive being exiled from their diminished and intruded-upon former habitats. Between the arrival of the first colonists and the early 1900s, an estimated dozen species of birds and

The extinct great auk, Pinguinus impennis, *once found along the Maine coast, suffered from wholesale slaughter to feed coastal dwellers and visitors.*

mammals were driven or extirpated from Maine. Among them were the eastern cougar, gray wolf, woodland caribou, and eastern turkey.

The eastern timber wolf, Canis lupus lycaon, *once common throughout Maine, disappeared around 1860.*

The gray, or timber, wolf was once common throughout Maine. A statewide bounty was placed on the animal in 1832 and remained in effect until 1916. As a result of killing and wilderness habitat loss, most of the wolf population apparently was gone by 1860. There are still occasional scattered reports of wolf tracks or howls in remote northern areas—an empty, lonely echo of the wolf's former presence.

The eastern mountain lion, Felis concolor cougar, *is classified as extirpated from Maine, although reports of sightings persist.*

Thoreau reported hearing a cougar scream during one of his trips to the Maine woods in the mid-1800s. In this century, one was reported to have been killed near Mt. Kineo in the Moosehead Lake area in 1906. The last reported killing of a cougar is thought to have occurred in the vicinity of Lake Umbagog about 1920. By that year the species had all but disappeared from the eastern United States, except for Florida; however, reports of tracks and sightings in Maine have persisted. Today, its existence remains a mystery and subject of much speculation.

The eastern turkey is another former year-round resident of York County and parts of Oxford and Cumberland counties. During Colonial times, parts of southern Maine were covered by virgin forests of oak, chestnut, hazel, and hickory. These open forests were suited to the large wild turkey, which eats nuts, seeds, and insects. Its habitat changed with the harvesting of the forests, and as early as 1672 turkeys reportedly were scarce in the Scarborough area. By the early 1800s, few remained. There *is* an upbeat side to this story: in the mid-1960s, the Department of Inland Fisheries and Wildlife began a turkey restocking program in southern Maine. After years of experimentation, this species lives once again within the boundaries of the state, and limited hunting is permitted.

Wild tom turkey, Meleagris gallopavo, *displaying. Thanks to a successful reintroduction program this bird can be found once again in southern Maine. Leonard Lee Rue III photo.*

The effects of the loss of wildlife can never be measured with absolute certainty. Like each strand in an aerial acrobat's safety net, every animal helps to maintain the strength and resilience of an ecosystem— whether by enriching the soil, pollinating plants, maintaining a balance among species, or serving some other function. Because we are part of the same net, we are directly or indirectly affected by what every other organism does. And because we also use animals as resources for a variety of benefits, their loss can have untold consequences to us.

In a sense, wild things are barometers of environmental health, and because we breathe the same air, drink the same water, and eat the same food, their well-being is cause for concern. We need only be reminded of the lethal connection between DDT (and other pesticide) use and the disappearance of songbirds and birds of prey. But pesticide use is only one of many causes for the decrease in numbers of wildlife species. Not surprisingly, loss and deterioration of habitat leads the list. Destroy an animal's home or living conditions and it must move or die.

Although no one knows for sure, habitat destruction, along with overhunting, is thought to have driven the woodland caribou from Maine's northern forest—its last stand in the northeastern United States. Lichens and mosses, the caribou's main food source, grow in deep beds on the floor of damp, heavily shaded spruce-fir forests or hang in thick clumps from branches and cover the trunks of the trees. Extensive lumbering of the forest altered conditions for the

Woodland caribou, Rangifer tarandus. *Efforts to reestablish this extirpated species in Maine were begun in 1986. William Cross photo, courtesy of Maine Department of Inland Fisheries and Wildlife.*

growth of this favorite food, further adding to the challenges facing the woodland caribou in Maine.

Other factors contribute to the decline of a species. Extreme specialization of some species compounds the problems of habitat loss because such animals simply are not able to utilize other food sources or habitats if their original one is destroyed. Reproductive rate is another factor; for example, butterflies multiply rapidly but whales do not.

Competition can also be a problem. Nonnative species, whether introduced by accident or deliberately (to combat pests, for example, or as sport species), frequently have forced the decline of native populations. The eastern bluebird has suffered because of the introduction of the starling and house sparrow in the latter half of the nineteenth century. Starlings were introduced by a Shakespeare fan who decided that the people in the United States should see and know all the birds mentioned in Shakespeare's plays. English sparrows were widely stocked by American towns and cities in the hope that they would eliminate troublesome cankerworms and spanworms (Portland, Maine, for example, got a shipment in 1854). The resulting competition for nest holes is a primary factor in the decline of the beautiful bluebird.

Aldo Leopold wrote, in reference to the conservation of plants and animals: "To keep every cog and wheel is the first precaution of intelligent tinkering."[5] We would do well to heed this bit of wisdom, for we are indeed parts of an intricate mechanism, with each organism having a place and a function. Does one disassemble a clock and discard some of its parts and still expect it to work as well as ever once it is put back together? Obviously not; one is careful to save all the parts.

We know relatively little about the functions of our plants and animals, but isn't it prudent to assume that they have a crucial role on our planet? And if they do, should not their conservation be a concern of all? In Maine, the Endangered and Nongame Wildlife Project of the Maine Department of Inland Fisheries and Wildlife judged the relative endangerment of Maine's vertebrate wildlife species according to current knowledge of their rarity or declining numbers.[6] (These include native species breeding in Maine as well as those living a significant part of their annual or life cycles in the state.) Six categories were identified: (1) endangered, (2) threatened, (3) special concern, (4) indeterminate, (5) extirpated, and (6) watch.

The first two classifications, endangered and threatened, hold legal bearing; by law, it is the policy of the state to conserve species in these categories by protecting their numbers and the ecosystems upon which they depend. Species of wildlife categorized as state endangered are those in immediate danger of extirpation or extinction and for which we have documentation of critically low or declining populations due to loss or destruction of habitat, overexploitation, pollution, disease, or other serious disturbances. This group also includes ones listed on the Federal Endangered Species List. State threatened species are those which will probably become endangered if population levels decline any further. Species on the Federal Threatened Species List are also included on the state list.

The remaining four categories, while not having the weight of law behind them, nevertheless warrant extraordinary attention. The "special concern" category includes species that could easily become threatened or endangered because of unusual population declines, precariously small numbers, restricted distributions, or specialized habitat requirements. Species of indeterminate status are ones that may qualify for one of the first three categories, but more data is needed before that is known for certain. The fifth category includes extirpated species—those which were at one time native to Maine but have not been documented as indigenous to the state for the past fifty years. The final class is a watch list that includes species not currently endangered or threatened, or likely to become so in the near future, but considered vulnerable due to their small numbers, existence in only a few locations, dependence on critical habitats, or declining or unstable populations.

In the chapters that follow, Maine's uncommon wildlife species are identified and described. Invertebrates were selected on the basis of studies by the Maine Critical Areas Program. The selection of vertebrates—fish, amphibians, reptiles, birds, and mammals—was based on the Maine Department of Inland Fisheries and Wildlife's official Maine Endangered Species List and (in the case of some fishes) on information from the Maine Department of Marine Resources.

Invertebrates

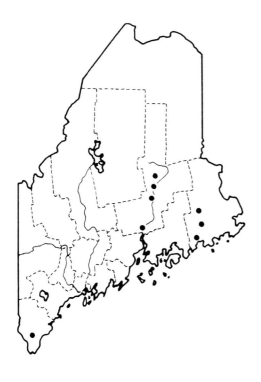

9

Distribution of the bog elfin.
Redrawn from A.E. Brower, Maine
Critical Areas Program (1978).

Homo sapiens shares this planet with more than a million known animal species, and over 90 percent of them are different from us in a very major way: they don't have a backbone. These are the invertebrates. And that difference is just the beginning; invertebrate species—which were among the earliest organisms to emerge from seas of the past—have evolved into an astonishing diversity of creatures, peculiar (by our standards) in both the way they look and the way they act.

Anyone who spends time poking around woods and fields and the edges of ponds, streams, and tidal areas will never cease to be surprised by the unexpected shapes, forms, and behavior of invertebrate creatures. Some can be seen easily by the naked eye, while others are so tiny they are barely visible. They may be wormlike, gelatinous, with or without a shell, smooth, spiny, round, long, oval, crawling, walking, flying, floating, or swimming. This amazing array is the product of hundreds of millions of years of evolution.

The class Insecta is largest group of invertebrates in the world. They have evolved in an incredible diversity of forms and habits, and each plays out its role in an intricate web of associations so overwhelmingly complex that our understanding barely scratches the surface. Our knowledge is growing, however. We know, for example, that even the irritating black fly serves a purpose, for its larvae are the main source of food for young Atlantic salmon.

Not all species of insects are as common and as well known as the black fly, and these rare forms are of special interest to scientists patiently unraveling the mysteries of the world. Of the more than sixteen thousand insect species in Maine, two of the rarest are the bog elfin and the Katahdin arctic butterfly.

The bog elfin is a small and sprightly butterfly.[1] At full wingspread, the adult insect is less than an inch across, and in the larval stage of its life cycle it is so small that it can burrow inside a spruce needle to feed. Found primarily in eastern Canada and Maine, it was first reported in Maine in the 1920s.

Today, the best habitats in the state for this rare and interesting local species appear to be bogs in Lincoln, the Enfield-Passadumkeag area, and Berwick. Here, on warm, sunny, quiet days in early June, the little butterfly may be seen flitting about in the sun high up among black spruces—a jerky, erratic flight. Or it might be resting and feeding on the beautiful pink blossoms of rhodora plants, its small, delicate wings fluttering gently, first one, then the other.

The survival of these small, isolated, and vulnerable colonies of bog elfin is yet another argument for the protection of certain wetlands. As with other rare species, the temptation to collect specimens unnecessarily must be resisted, for we do not know which bog elfin taken might be the last, pushing the species over the brink into extinction.

The Katahdin arctic butterfly lives high on Mt. Katahdin's great wind-swept plateau.[2] Bearing a remarkable resemblance to the lichen-clad, glacially strewn rocks on which it rests, the insect can be difficult to spot. When approached, it often launches itself up into the wind and is blown over the edge of the plateau, but gradually it works its way back.

Thousands of years ago, this butterfly species was caught here on the mountain during the massive glacial retreat. Outflanked by the advancing warmth, it retreated to the bleak tundra highland where temperatures were more to its liking and remained there, cut off from its Arctic parent species, *Oeneis polixenes,* which is found on the open tundra from Labrador to Alaska. Isolated on Mt. Katahdin, it evolved into a subspecies of *Oeneis polixenes.*

Due to the remoteness and harsh climate of its location and the strenuous climb required to gain access to its home, the Katahdin arctic butterfly wasn't discovered until 1901. For the same reasons, it also has been difficult to study. Nevertheless, some of the details of its two-year life cycle are now known.

Normally the flying adult emerges in July. During a short period of about a month, it lays its eggs. These hatch, and the young larvae, stout-bodied and hairy, feed on grasses and sedges. With the coming of cold weather, they hibernate in the tundra, and the following spring they feed again, reaching full growth by the end of the warm summer season. Then the larvae pupate, a complex stage during which they transform into adults. The following year the adult butterflies emerge.

Not only is the rare Katahdin arctic butterfly one of the few arctic subspecies of butterflies found in the contiguous United States, it is unique to Katahdin. Therefore, this isolated population is internationally significant.

Many of Maine's invertebrates find water more to their liking than tundra. A close look along the edge of a pond or stream, where sunshine warms the shallows and stimulates the growth of green plants, will reveal a busy world of aquatic insects, snails, mussels, and crayfish. Below the surface, beyond the limit of rooted plants, exist bloodworms, mollusks, midges, and other varieties of invertebrates. Further from the shore, but still within the penetration range of the sun's rays, drift great numbers of microscopic animals, such as the segmented, semitransparent shelled copepods and the strange, wheellike rotifers. But it's along the coast that one can see the most amazing and fascinating of these creatures—particularly in a narrow band along the rocky edge, where twice daily the sea engulfs the weathered bedrock and is caught and subdued in quiet tidepools among cracks and crevices. Here, in the strangely beautiful, complicated world of the intertidal zone, live the marine invertebrates.[3]

Well over a hundred species, representing eleven of the twenty-two common groups of marine invertebrates, inhabit this stressful environment. Over thousands of years each species has evolved to fill its paricular niche, combining to form the beautiful tapestries of intricate designs and textures

Bog elfin, Incisalia lanoraieensis, *an uncommon butterfly discovered in Maine in the 1920s.*

Katahdin arctic butterfly, Oeneis polixenes katahdin, *a variety of subarctic butterfly found only on the Tableland of Mt. Katahdin.*

Northern lampshell brachiopod, Terebratulina septentrionalis, *an ancient marine invertebrate found in offshore subtidal waters and in a very few intertidal areas in Cobscook Bay, Washington County. Fred Bavendam photo.*

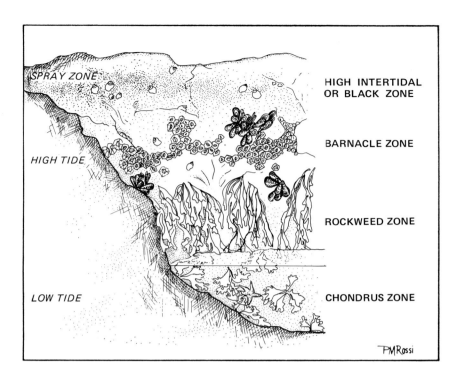

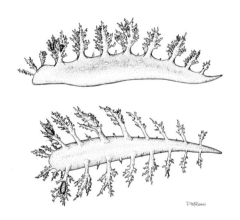

Intertidal zonation. From Maine Critical Areas Program (1982). Patrice M. Rossi, artist.

The bushy-backed nudibranch, Dendronotus frondosus, *is a noteworthy species on the rocky shore of West Quoddy Head. Patrice M. Rossi, artist.*

characteristic of this area between land and water. In those places where the waves and high tides have worked the rocky shores, distinct zones are apparent: the high intertidal, or black, zone; the barnacle zone; the rockweed zone; and the Irish moss, or chondrus, zone.

The black zone is the home for dark marine lichens and microscopic blue-green algae. Here, in scattered pools where the only source of sea water is salt spray, live the hardiest of the marine invertebrates. They include periwinkles, springtails, and other creatures.

A lighter, gray-white zone of barnacles appears below the black zone. Sometimes these small, pale-shelled animals are so numerous that there is no room for other species. In the damper areas live mussels, small worms (some segmented and some not), and small crustaceans called amphipods. Limpets, mussels, and predatory dry whelks inhabit tidepools and watery crevices.

Below the barnacle zone is a zone of brown algae, known as rockweed. Great numbers of mussels cluster around the holdfasts of the algae, feeding on plankton filtered from the water. Other bottom-feeders often found associated with the mussels, are species of nematodes (unsegmented worms) and oligochaetes, which are segmented. Under the protective cover of the rockweed, periwinkles and limpets browse on the algae growing on the bedrock surface. Large horse mussels, which feed on phytoplankton—microscopic floating plants—filtered from seawater, lie wedged into crevices. Occasionally sea urchins and green crabs can be seen in the tidepools.

Exposed at only the lowest tides is a dark red zone. The color is attributed to the dominance of the red alga *Chondrus crispus,* commonly called Irish moss. Covered with water most of the time, this colorful band supports more species than any other, although the number of species found in this zone can vary greatly depending on the availablity of suitable habitat, such as protected crevices. Characteristic species found in this zone include the green sponge, horse mussel, green crab, scale worm, northern starfish, arctic clam, and chiton.

One may well ask of what value is such a group of creatures, most of which lead secretive lives confined to a relatively small area. The fact is, these seemingly unimportant, inconspicuous little animals are of critical importance to higher order animals that we depend upon for food and other benefits. At the lower end of the food chain, these invertebrates eat microscopic plants and the larger phytoplankton and algae and convert them into animal protein to be eaten by fish, mammals, and birds.

Some marine invertebrates, such as the filter feeders, are also indicators of environmental health, since they are long-lived and generally confined to one area, unable to escape the effects of pollutants. Mollusks, for example, have feeding habits that concentrate and magnify the presence of human-produced poisons (or naturally occuring toxins, as in Red Tide) in the environment.

From scientific and educational viewpoints, areas of abundance and high diversity, such as the intertidal zone, provide special opportunities for study and teaching. But it's their secretive nature and myriad unusual forms, luring even the most casual visitor to squint and poke among the rocks and seaweed, that may be the marine invertebrates' greatest values to humans.

Maine has more miles of rocky intertidal habitat than any other state on the east coast. North of Cape Elizabeth lies a coastline of rocky headlands and seaward islands, unsurpassed in its variety of colorful and interesting species. Here in the intertidal zone, at the extreme limits of their range, live species found nowhere else in the United States.

A number of Maine's intertidal areas are particularly noted for their high species diversity. One of these, West Quoddy Head, is located in South Lubec, Washington County. Quoddy Head State Park is easily accessible and is a favorite of marine scientists and students. Steep slopes and cobble beaches with conical bedrock projections characterize the site. The chondrus zone contains a mixture of red and green algae and kelp as well as sponges and starfish. A number of small, shallow puddles can be found in the rockweed zone. Characteristic species of the site include periwinkles, whelks, limpets, horse mussels, and anemones. There is no barnacle zone as such. The high intertidal zone is ledgy and full of crevices, providing homes for periwinkles.

Schoodic Point in Acadia National Park is in Winter Harbor, Hancock County. Although the site's slope is generally moderate, the blocky granite

A few of Maine's intertidal bedrock areas with a high diversity of marine invertebrates. Redrawn from L.F. Doggett, P.F. Larsen, and S.C. Sykes, Maine Critical Areas Program (1978).

An intertidal zone in Cobscook Bay, Washington County, where the tidal range is as much as twenty feet. The bay supports a rich diversity of northern marine invertebrates. Hank Tyler and Fred Bavendam photos.

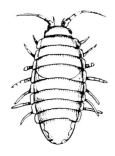

The isopod Idotea balthica *is one of approximately thirty species of invertebrates found at Two Lights State Park.*

Crumb of bread sponge, Halichondria panicea, *and the daisy brittle star,* Ophiopholis aculeata, *are found in the chondrus zone. Patrice M. Rossi, artist.*

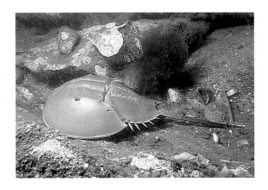

The Horseshoe crab, Limulus polyphemus, *is a very ancient marine invertebrate, dating back 200 million years to Triassic times. Horseshoe crabs inhabit and breed in a few of the warm-water bays along southern and mid-coast Maine. Fred Bavendam photo.*

creates a complex surface that results in a somewhat patchy zonation. One of the most interesting characteristics of the area is the profusion of tide pools. Above the high intertidal zone, a thick spruce forest bounds the area.

Two Lights State Park is in Cape Elizabeth, Cumberland County. Visitors to this popular site can walk down gradually sloping, water-worn metamorphic rocks to the water's edge. At low tide, shallow tide pools can be found in all four of the easily identified zones. Among the approximately thirty species that have been identified at the site are the isopod *Idotea baltica* and the daisy brittle star. The isopod is a green creature with a flat, oval body an inch or so long and

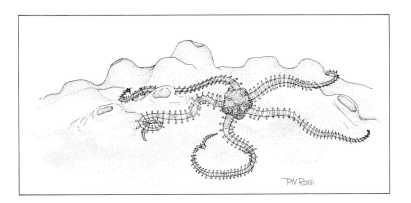

large round eyes. The brittle star differs from other starfish in that it has a distinct, flat center disk and spines on each segment of its five arms. It can be very colorful, with reddish disks and arms banded alternately red and white.

The Isles of Shoals consist of seven principal islands about six miles southeast of the coast of Maine. The Maine-New Hampshire boundary runs through the group of islands. One of the Maine islands, Appledore, is the site of the Shoals Marine Laboratory, which for many years has been used for summer programs in marine science. The island's shore areas of high species diversity are especially valued as outdoor classrooms.

Among the most interesting and rare invertebrates in Maine is the horseshoe crab.[4] Lumbering and awkward within its dark brown, tanklike armor, this creature is a prehistoric holdover—a relic of the past. It is not a true crab and is actually related to the spiders, scorpions, and ticks, though it is much larger: some specimens can reach two feet in length. Seven pairs of jointed appendages under its hard, horny covering allow it to move forward and grasp its prey, which consists primarily of worms and mollusks. A long tail spine helps it to burrow.

In June, horseshoe crabs come in from deep offshore waters on a high tide. They cruise the shoreline in breeding pairs, the male firmly clasped to and trailing behind the female. They pause at dozens of places in the shallows where sand beaches and mudflats meet, and at each site they lay, fertilize, and bury from two hundred to one thousand eggs. By midsummer tiny larvae emerge, each less than one-tenth of an inch long. Eight to ten years later the survivors reach maturity and return to repeat this ancient mating ritual.

For 200 million years, since the age of dinosaurs, the horseshoe crab has survived almost unchanged, but lately it has had to cope with ever-increasing pressure from relatively new predators: humans. Biological supply businesses and pharmaceutical firms have, in recent years, taken increasing numbers for educational research and medical applications. Chitin from the crab's exoskeleton is an accelerator of blood clotting and healing. Some are also being harvested in Maine by eel fishermen for bait. In Massachusetts, where the horseshoe crab is much more common, it is widely regarded as a pest around recreational beaches and as a predator of commercial clams, and the state has instituted a bounty program. The long-term effects of the program are still to be documented.

The species of horseshoe crab found in Maine lives in an area stretching from Central America to the Bay of Fundy. Other species are found in the East Indies, China, and Japan. Because the horseshoe crab prefers warmer waters, Maine is at the northernmost and easternmost extent of its range. Here, only a few significant breeding sites are known: several sites in Casco Bay, one in an estuary in Lincoln County, and two more in Hancock County. The horseshoe crab is susceptible to depletion in the state because of its low numbers, scattered population, and slow growth rate.

The mollusks, though not nearly as unusual in appearance as the horseshoe crab, have their own special appeal—as evidenced by the enormous mounds of shells left by early peoples in coastal regions. Some of the largest Indian shell heaps in the world are located on the upper Damariscotta River. Up to thirty feet deep, they give mute testimony to the powerful attraction of shellfish, which for thousands of years lured generations of Native Americans to the coast. Many of these middens contain large numbers of oyster shells.[5]

The Whalesback, a huge Wabenaki shell heap on the upper Damariscotta River, during an 1886 mining operation. The shells, mostly from oysters, were used for chicken "scratch," lime, and road fill. By the end of 1886 the midden was almost obliterated. Courtesy of Pictorial Studio, Newcastle, Maine.

The oysters were gathered from a nearby bed, estimated at about fourteen acres and probably located in a shallow salt pond above Newcastle and Damariscotta. The bed is calculated to have at one time produced eight to nine hundred bushels of oysters annually.

The American oyster, Crassostrea virginica, *is rare in Maine.*

Significant naturally occuring American oyster populations in Maine. Redrawn from Joel Cowger, Maine Critical Areas Program (1975).

Once abundant and distributed widely, natural beds of American oysters are rare in Maine today. Their presence here may, in fact, be an indication that the waters were warmer in the past. Maine's few oyster beds are in estuaries and bays where water temperatures are higher and salinities are lower than average. Here, oysters may spawn when temperatures reach sixty-eight degrees Fahrenheit. The larvae hatch and drift for a short time with the currents, enjoying a freedom of movement in the planktonic stage that they will never have again. It's a short-lived freedom, for in two to three weeks they settle down— literally—to a long and sedentary life cemented in one place. Here, after years of straining water through their gills to catch the minute plants and animals that make up their food source, they may reach lengths of nine inches or more.

Oysters' inability to move makes them vulnerable to more than the effects of climate and weather. Due to the combined detrimental effects of a dam, a railroad, and a match factory, a few scattered specimens are all that remain today of the Damariscotta bed that once attracted the Wabanaki to those early feasts. Only two areas in the state now have substantial natural populations of the oyster; one is on the Piscataqua River and the other on the Marsh River in Newcastle.

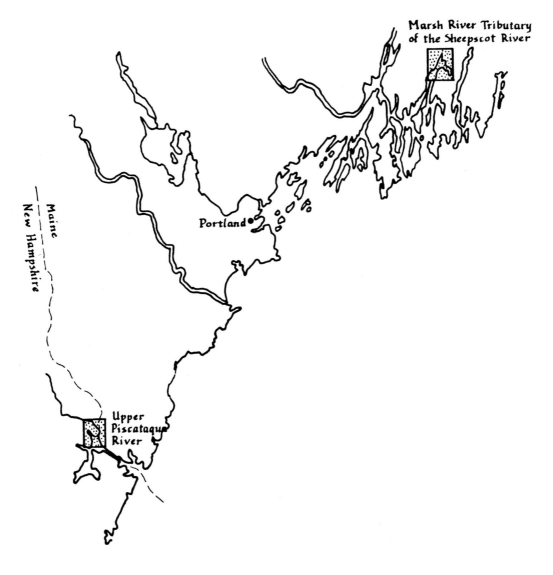

The Piscataqua River oyster bed, on the Maine-New Hampshire border five miles above Kittery, is the larger, covering sixty-six acres and containing an estimated twenty-three thousand bushels. Polluted by organic and industrial wastes and pesticides, it has not been commercially harvested since 1947.

The Marsh River oyster bed in Newcastle represents the northernmost oyster population in the United States. Lack of natural replacement prompted closing part of the river to oyster harvesting in 1968.

Although they are affected by pollution and siltation, these two beds may represent a unique gene pool of cold-water-adapted populations for commercial aquaculture ventures. To assist in their conservation, both beds were designated as Critical Areas in December 1975.

The bleached and broken shells of another mollusk, the quahog, also lie in many of Maine's coastal shell heaps.[6] Other relics of this thick, heavy bivalve are in the beads used by early coastal Indians as money, *wampum*.

The presence of the quahog, Mercenaria mercenaria, *indicates warmer coastal-water habitats than normally found in Maine.*

The first scientific reference to quahogs in Maine was made by Addison Emery Verrill, who explored Casco Bay in 1873. He noted their presence in Quahog Bay, thirty miles northeast of Portland. Over the years much has been learned about these invertebrates. Their dirty-white, rugged shells, hinged by a ligament, open to allow the large muscular foot to emerge for movement and for a pair of siphons to take in water and expel wastes. Hundreds have been observed on mudflats at times, discharging fluids like miniature geysers. When disturbed, the mollusk withdraws its soft body between the valves, which clamp shut so tightly that it is difficult to pry them open.

Quahogs may live up to eighteen years. In the planktonic stage, newly hatched young can swim but are also moved by tides and currents. Following the free-swimming stage, which lasts about a day, a six- to twelve-day shell-forming stage begins. During this time, each quahog develops a foot and crawls about the bottom, using the foot as a means of locomotion. Periodically the young quahog anchors itself to solid objects by means of a thread formed by secretions from a gland in its foot. The gland disappears as the mollusk grows and takes on adult characteristics.

Throughout its life the quahog has many predators. During the planktonic stage, it is sought after by fish, crustaceans, and other mollusks. Later it is taken by herring gulls, who have developed a surprisingly effective way to crack its hard shell. A gull will pick up a quahog, carry it high over the rocky shore, and drop it on the rocks below. Then the bird immediately dives to dine on the juicy morsel now accessible inside the broken shell. The most serious predator of the quahog, however, is the green crab. This mobile and hardy creature is capable of crushing and disposing of quahogs an inch or more in length and is particularly active against juveniles.

Significant quahog areas in Maine. Redrawn from A.H. Gustafson, Maine Critical Areas Program (1977).

Although the quahog may be found in the Gulf of St. Lawrence in the Northumberland Strait between Nova Scotia and New Brunswick, it prefers warmer waters to the south, extending its range to the Gulf of Mexico. In Maine quahogs may be found all along the coast in the warmer coves and estuaries. The major areas, however, are found between the New Meadows River in West Bath and the Harraseeket River in Freeport. With careful monitoring and management, Maine should always have populations of this interesting invertebrate.

Not so abundant in Maine, although it can be found from the Gulf of St. Lawrence to North Carolina, is the dwarf tellin.[7] Why is it relatively rare in the

The dwarf tellin, Tellina agilis, *is rare in Maine due to the scarcity of its preferred habitat, sand beaches.*

state? Because it forages for microscopic animals on grains of sand, and Maine has few intertidal sandy beaches.

This bivalve mollusk is shiny white, narrow, and only half an inch long. It prefers a clean, sandy beach, where it burrows to a depth of about an inch with its muscular foot. There, laying on its left side, it extends its two long siphons to the surface. The intake siphon sucks in large sand grains from which the mollusk "crops" minute diatoms and other animal life. Not all is ideal with this arrangement; many a dwarf tellin has lost a siphon or foot to a grazing flounder or has suddenly become a snack for a horseshoe crab, duck, or lobster.

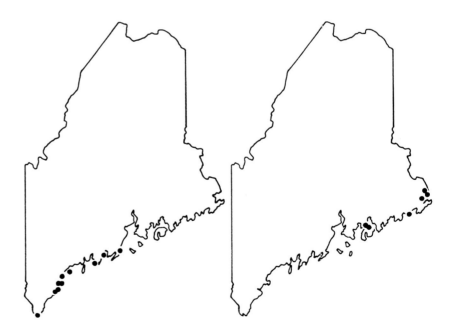

Left: *Locations of dwarf tellin in Maine. Redrawn from Mary Ann Gilbert, Maine Critical Areas Program (1977).*

Right: *Locations of the gaper clam,* Mya truncata, *in Maine. Redrawn from Mary Ann Gilbert, Maine Critical Areas Program (1977).*

Only two or three beaches in southern Maine have been identified as significant habitats for the dwarf tellin. These areas are particularly valuable for education and research, and care should be taken to control dredging or filling that might detrimentally change the sizes of particles in the sediments on which this unusual little mollusk lives.

The gaper clam is another uncommon bivalve inhabiting Maine's coastal intertidal zone.[8] Found in only a few areas in Hancock and Washington counties, this rare mollusk is one of the few Arctic species of marine invertebrates in the United States. It grows to three inches in length and has a heavy, chalky white shell sculpted with coarse growth lines. Protruding from the truncated and widely gaping rear of the clam are two long joined siphons for pumping in water, filtering out the food, and ejecting wastes.

Studies of this clam and other animals on the edge of their natural range are helpful in learning about the postglacial distribution of organisms. Knowing of their locations and maintaining them in a natural state is, therefore, of considerable importance.

On the extreme eastern coast of Washington County live two of Maine's most interesting mussels—the discordant and the little black.[9] Both species are small, rectangular to oval in shape, and dark brown in color. What makes these two bivalves unusual is their special technique for withstanding the ice and other rigors of the high Arctic shores that are their main habitat.

Instead of lying exposed on the bottom, these mussels weave nests consisting of a least a thousand threadlike filaments secreted by a byssal gland on the posterior side of the foot. Inside each nest resides a tiny mussel, suspended by a single thread attached to its foot. The foot is agile enough to weave the nest in all directions by attaching the threads to a rocky crevice or to the leaflike bodies of seaweeds, a job that takes up to two weeks. Once the nest is completed, the amazing little creature can loosen it to provide a flow of water for filter feeding or tighten it for protection—all by extending or contracting the gland in its foot. With time the nest becomes camouflaged by bits of debris entangled in the threads, and small aquatic animals take up residence on it.

The mussel is a male during the first two years of its life, but then effects a sex change to female so that it can produce eggs. The yolky eggs are laid in a mucous string in the protective nest. Because the ice-free season is extremely short in Arctic waters the young develop directly, bypassing the larval stage common to many invertebrates. Eventually, as they grow larger, they leave the nest to settle in new spots and construct their own nests.

Both the discordant mussel and the little black mussel range from the Arctic Ocean to south of New England, and both have been found in Passamaquoddy and Cobscook bays. Because those most likely to be collected are large, older females, which are necessary for successful reproduction, the few sites known to support populations of the two mussels should be protected from overcollecting.

Buried just beneath soft sand and mud in the shallow waters of northern seas, where they have adapted to withstand the stress of cold temperatures and low levels of oxygen, are species of the mollusk Astarte.[10] Six species of this filter-feeding bivalve occur in Maine. All are small, with thick brown shells. Astarte have been found in only three locations, all in Washington County.

Smooth top shell is another cold-water species, a small snail less than one-half inch in diameter.[11] Its shell is fragile and smooth and shines brightly iridescent with a bluish cast. Smooth top shell lives on seaweeds in the lower zones of the intertidal area, to a depth of about six feet below the sea's surface. Here it grazes on brown algae and kelp and is, in turn, consumed by flounder and eider ducks.

Locations of the discordant mussel, Musculus discors, *and the little black mussel,* Musculus niger, *in Maine. Redrawn from Mary Ann Gilbert, Maine Critical Areas Program (1977).*

Astarte castanea. *The Astarte species are rare marine invertebrates in Maine.*

As with other organisms, smooth top shell has evolved its own special means of survival. Its young avoid the precarious planktonic stage, during which larvae float free and are scooped up by many other animals. Instead, shiny egg masses containing one to two hundred eggs are laid on the algae and kelp, where the young develop completely into tiny snails before they leave this first home.

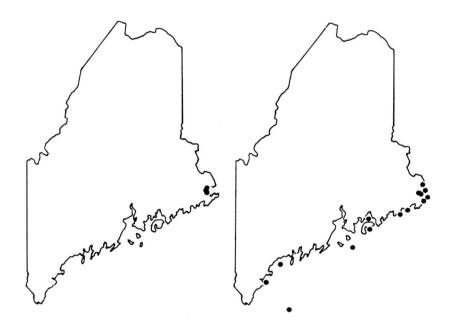

Left: *Locations of the mollusk Astarte in Maine. Redrawn from Mary Ann Gilbert, Maine Critical Areas Program (1977).*

Right: *Locations of smooth top shell in Maine. Redrawn from Mary Ann Gilbert, Maine Critical Areas Program (1977).*

As one of the few Arctic marine invertebrates that can be studied intertidally in the United States, the smooth top shell is valued for its

Smooth top shell, Margarites helicinus, *a snail, is one of the few arctic marine invertebrates that can be found intertidally in the United States.*

educational and research uses. In Maine, where it lives at the southern part of its range, only six sites are known, the two most important ones being in Cobscook Bay.

Invertebrates are among the most interesting and least known animals inhabiting the state. Though a great number are tiny and inconspicuous, their value should never be underestimated, and future studies of these creatures are certain to contribute to a growing interest, appreciation, and understanding of them.

10

Fishes

The striped bass, Morone saxatilis, *now extirpated from Maine, is being restocked in the Kennebec River with the hope that it may once more return to spawn.*

Some 400 million years ago, a new group of creatures evolved. They were the fishes, the oldest major group of vertebrates. Fifty million years later they had spawned such a variety of species that this period has been called the Age of Fishes.

They were without jaws at first, and some jawless species, including the lamprey, still survive, relatively unchanged from their prehistoric ancestors. But our best known fishes developed around 100 million years ago, during the Cretaceous Period. These are the bony fishes, which adapted to aquatic life with gills, scales, fins, and skeletons of bone (rather than just cartilage, as in sharks and rays). They total thirty to forty thousand species worldwide, outnumbering all other vertebrates combined. Some four thousand species exist in North America, of which approximately seventy are found in Maine. Forty species are native to the state; the rest have been introduced since the middle of the nineteenth century.[1]

Some fish live all of their lives in fresh water, but others migrate between fresh water and salt water to spawn. Those which live most of their lives at sea,

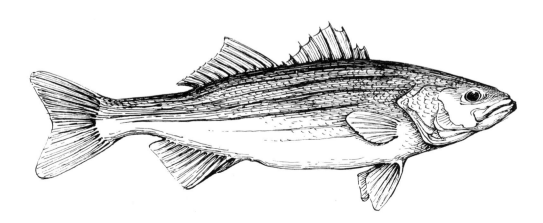

returning to spawn in their native rivers and streams, are called *anadromous.* Those which migrate downstream to breed in marine waters are *catadromous* species.

Protecting fish requires the management of delicate habitats. Our record has not been the best in this respect, and the fish have suffered for it—some more than others. For example, the striped bass is a victim of dams and pollution and no longer spawns in Maine, so in this sense it is considered extirpated.[2] Historically, the largest resident population was in the Kennebec River, but since the 1950s there has been no further evidence of spawning. However, in 1982, encouraged by improvement in the quality of the water, fisheries scientists began restocking efforts in the Kennebec. They release juvenile striped bass (fall fingerlings), hoping to imprint them to this habitat so they will return to spawn in the river.

The Atlantic sturgeon's population is so small that the species could easily become threatened. Those fortunate enough to glimpse this fish making one of

The Atlantic sturgeon, Acipenser sturio, *a primitive fish that can attain gigantic proportions, is a species with such low numbers that it could easily become threatened.*

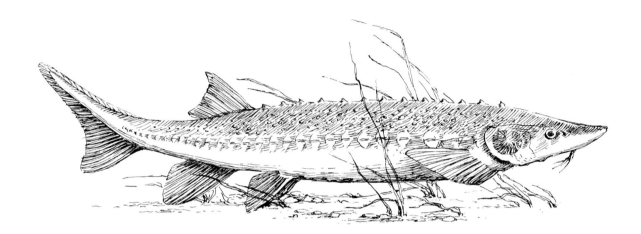

its occasional leaps will not soon forget the sight. Prehistoric in appearance, the Atlantic sturgeon can attain gigantic proportions—up to eight hundred pounds and fourteen feet long—although average weights range from sixty to two hundred pounds and lengths from six to ten feet. It is a fish of ancient lineage and one of the few jawless species still extant.

Propelled by a primitive tail and the muscular movements of a body covered with stiff bony plates, the huge Atlantic sturgeon roams the bays and rivers of the Atlantic coast from north of the St. Lawrence River to the Gulf of Mexico. As it swims along the bottom, the whiskerlike, sensitive feelers on its flat snout just touch the river bed or ocean floor and its tubular mouth sucks up any small animals encountered. An anadromous fish, it spawns for the first time at the age of twenty to thirty years, laying two to three million heavy, sticky eggs in up to ten feet of fresh running water. The young spend their first few years in lower tidal reaches of rivers and the remainder of their lives in the ocean.

Accounts from the early settlers on the Kennebec River indicate that these fish were caught by the hundreds in Colonial times and provided an excellent supply of food. In addition to their flesh, commercial interests sought the sturgeon for its roe and oil. However, as the rivers became polluted and dams barred access to gravel-bottomed spawning areas, their numbers declined. Commercial sturgeon fishing eventually ceased in Maine nearly a century ago.

Today, an estimated several hundred Atlantic sturgeon can be found in the state, chiefly in the estuary of the Kennebec River, which includes Merrymeeting Bay. Maine law now prohibits the taking of any sturgeon from the river, and requires that only those six feet or longer may be caught in other areas. Perhaps with appropriate management this species will recover, adding to the diversity of our coastal environs.

The short-nosed sturgeon, like its relative the Atlantic sturgeon, is a prehistoric holdover and one of the larger species of fish frequenting fresh

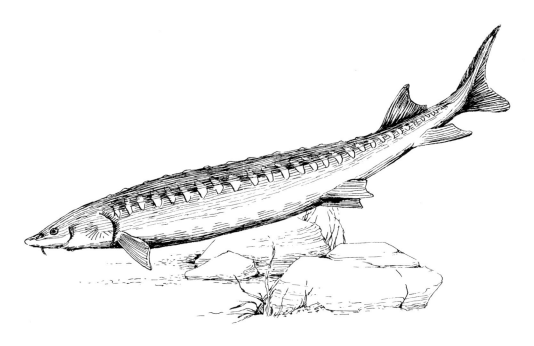

The short-nosed sturgeon, Acipenser brevirostris, *is on the Federal Endangered Species List. In Maine, it still frequents the Sheepscot and Kennebec rivers.*

waters. It too is covered with bony plates but is much smaller and has a shorter and blunter snout. Unlike the Atlantic sturgeon, which spends the greater part of its life at sea, the short-nosed sturgeon can be found in tidal river basins throughout the year. In Maine the short-nosed sturgeon is still found in the Sheepscot and Merrymeeting Bay estuaries and up the Kennebec River as far as Augusta.

After well over 100 million years of successful evolutionary history, it's unfortunate that this ancient fish, in a mere "tick" of time, finds itself in danger. Pollution, obstruction of favored spawning grounds, and overfishing have reduced its numbers to the point that it is now classified as rare by the International Union for Conservation of Nature and Natural Resources, and as endangered by the United States Department of Interior.

Another anadromous fish greatly diminished in Maine is the American shad. It is the largest member of the true herring family, and its relatively deep body can measure between eighteen and thirty inches long. It may weigh up to nine pounds. The American shad can be identified by a series of dark spots beginning near the upper back edge of its gill and extending along the upper body (and decreasing in size) toward the tail fin.

Commercial fishermen have long taken American shad for its flesh and its roe, which is sometimes processed as caviar. Both have a fine flavor. Gill netting is the most popular method of commercial fishing. Some fishermen also seek the fish for sport; on light tackle it can put up a strong and exciting fight.

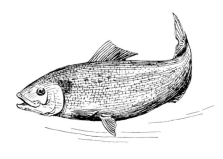

The American shad, Alosa sapidissima, *is an anadromous fish whose numbers in Maine have been greatly reduced.*

Like the Atlantic sturgeon, the American shad occurs in Maine as only a remnant of its former population. Most of its native runs were lost due to damming and pollution. During the 1970s, water quality began to improve in many of the state's polluted rivers and streams, and by the mid 1980s efforts were underway to restore the American shad to several rivers (including the Kennebec, Penobscot, and St. Croix) and it was starting to come back in the Merrymeeting Bay area of the lower Kennebec.

The landlocked arctic charr is a fish classified in the "special concern"

Landlocked arctic charr, or blueback charr, Salvelinus alpinus oquassa. *This glacial relict occurs in only ten deepwater lakes in northern Maine. William Cross photo.*

category by the Maine Endangered and Nongame Wildlife Project. The history of this fish is an interesting one. The story starts with its relative, the ocean arctic charr, which each year leaves the icy waters of its home, driven by a primeval urge to ascend chilly coastal rivers to spawn. During the last glacial period, the arctic climatic conditions of northern Canada and Greenland extended much further south, and the charr moved along with the advancing glaciers, spawning in rivers at the edge of the ice sheets. When the ice again receded, some charr populations became isolated from the sea in the region we call Maine, Vermont, New Hampshire, Quebec, and New Brunswick. Two separate landlocked populations became established in Maine: the blueback charr and the Sunapee charr.

The blueback charr (also called the blueback trout) is typically charrlike in appearance: quite slim, with a large mouth and slightly to moderately forked tail. Average size ranges from six to fourteen inches in length and from one-half to one pound in weight. In summer its color is generally pale and silvery, except for the dark blue back. During the fall breeding season, a dramatic change in coloration takes place and both males and females assume brilliant colors: yellow to red bellies, whitish-yellow spots on their sides, and orange paired fins with bright white leading edges.

The blueback charr was first discovered in 1853, inhabiting Oquossoc Lake in Rangeley, Maine. Historical accounts in the latter half of the 1800s report that bushels, and even cartloads, of bluebacks were speared and netted when the fish moved into shallow streams to spawn. By the early 1900s it was gone and thought to be extinct, its disappearance coinciding with the introduction of rainbow smelt and landlocked salmon into the Rangeley Lakes. It is believed that competition for food and predation from these species caused the demise of the blueback.

It was almost a half century later, in 1948, that the blueback was rediscovered in northern Maine. Today it is known to exist in ten ponds, all in

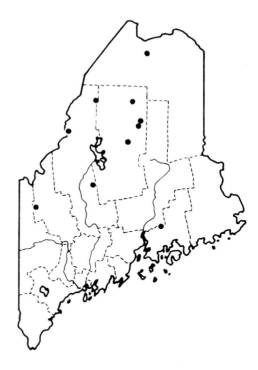

Distribution of landlocked arctic charr in Maine. Redrawn from the Maine Dept. of Inland Fisheries and Wildlife and the Maine State Planning Office (1985).

Sunapee charr, Salvelinus alpinus, *is another glacial relict. Native populations occur only in Floods Pond in Otis, Maine. A second native population, in New Hampshire's Sunapee Lake, is now extinct. Frederick W. Kircheis photo.*

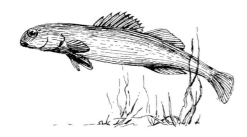

The swamp darter, Etheostoma fusiforme, *is the smallest freshwater fish in Maine.*

The grass pickerel, Esox americanus vermiculatus, *although common south of Maine, is known from only two very small streams in the state.*

the headwaters of the St. John, Penobscot, Aroostook, and Piscataquis rivers. These are cold, deep ponds, and during the warm summer months the blueback lives in their cool depths near the bottom, where it feeds on small planktonic plants and animals.

The Sunapee charr (also known as the Sunapee trout) is similar to the blueback charr. During the fall spawning season its pale summer color turns to brilliant hues of red and orange, inspiring the local name golden trout. The largest Sunapee on record weighed over five pounds and measured twenty-six inches.

The charr was first discovered in Sunapee Lake in New Hampshire; however, that lake no longer supports populations of the fish, possibly due to hybridization with lake trout. It is found today in only three locations in Maine and in two lakes in central Idaho. In Maine, Floods Pond, in Otis, contains the only native population of the Sunapee. In an effort to protect the future of the species, biologists have removed eggs from Floods Pond to rear fish for stocking. Introduced populations now exist in Coffee Pond in Cumberland County and South Branch Ponds in Piscataquis County.

Three fish species are assigned to the "indeterminate status" category: the swamp darter, grass pickerel, and brook stickleback. The swamp darter is the smallest freshwater fish found in Maine, seldom reaching more than 2.5 inches in length. Because the fish doesn't have an air bladder it has no buoyancy; it spends its life on the bottom of muddy, swampy bodies of water, often in clumps of aquatic vegetation. Here it lies in wait for small aquatic insects and other invertebrates, darting out to capture them at the slightest movement. Though abundant south of New England, along the Gulf and Atlantic coastal plains, the swamp darter has been taken in only a few waters in southern Maine.

The grass pickerel is the smallest member of the pike family. To the uninitiated it looks like the common chain pickerel. It averages from six to ten inches in length and about one-half pound in weight. As its name suggests, the grass pickerel frequents weedy beds and submerged brushy areas in isolated pools of rivers and streams. Though it is common south of Maine in a range extending to Alabama, it is known from only two very small streams in the state, both tributaries of the Kennebec River in the Merrymeeting Bay area.

The brook stickleback is a member of a family of small fishes of northern marine and fresh waters. The sticklebacks range in size from one and one-half to four inches long and are characterized by spines on their backs. The brook stickleback is strictly a freshwater species and may be identified by its five or six dorsal spines.

Sticklebacks feed on fish eggs, small fish fry, and invertebrates. Their breeding and nesting habits are especially interesting. In quiet waters during the May and June breeding season, the male builds a small round nest of grass and twigs bonded together by secreted threads of mucus. Once the nest is completed one or more females deposit their eggs in it. The male fertilizes them, then aggressively guards the eggs until they hatch, even staying around for a short time to protect the young.

The brook stickleback has been found in Oxford, Somerset, and Washington counties but is very scarce in Maine. It is much more common in southern New England and in states further south.

This chapter would not be complete without some mention of the Atlantic salmon. It's a thrilling sight when this beautiful, silvery fish explodes in graceful arcs from the broken surfaces of rapids and pools, fighting its way upstream to reach its spawning grounds. For most salmon these remarkable migrations take place in the spring, although salmon runs also occur in the fall.

After the salmon reach their upstream spawning areas, they rest in cool, deep pools until the spawning period—from October to November. Eggs are laid and fertilized in a nest dug by the female in a cool, fast-flowing riffle area, then buried about six inches deep in the gravelly bottom. Most adults then attempt to return to the ocean, but only a few fish actually survive the trip to spawn again.

The young, known as parr, hatch the next spring and remain in the rivers and streams for two to three years before migrating to the ocean in the smolt stage. At this time, they average seven inches long. When they return to spawn two years later, the average salmon is thirty inches long and weighs ten pounds. (The state record is about twenty-eight pounds.)

Today, the Atlantic salmon is the subject of one of the most concerted efforts to bring back a fish driven into serious decline by human activity. Prized by the early Wabanakis and later by the colonists as a food source, salmon was originally taken in great numbers from more than twenty Maine streams. As the industrial economy developed in the eighteenth century, dams were built to provide water power for mills, and pollution soon followed. Overharvested, barred from their spawning grounds, their waters fouled, the salmon began to disappear. By the 1950s only nine rivers in Washington County supported runs, and only a few hundred salmon were estimated in the largest migrations.

In 1947, the Atlantic Sea-Run Salmon Commission was established to bring back the salmon to Maine's rivers and regulate its harvesting. For a number of years, through the work of the commission and other agencies and organizations, the lot of this much-abused fish improved. Fishways were constructed, pollution controls implemented, and hatcheries used to supplement natural production. The salmon fishery is now partially restored, and Maine in the late 1980s is the only place in the United States with a native population of Atlantic salmon.

It's a truism that wildlife protection efforts, once underway, cannot be relaxed, and this is well illustrated in the case of the Atlantic salmon. In the late 1960s commercial fishermen discovered the secret ocean habitat of the salmon off the west coast of Greenland—and the world catch increased dramatically, exceeding more then ten thousand metric tons a year. Today, it is estimated that for every salmon returning to Maine's rivers, at least one other salmon of Maine origin is caught on the high seas. Commercial overharvesting combined with the negative effects of acidification on some rivers and streams, plus the high costs of restoration, continue to cloud the future of the Atlantic salmon. It is a problem of international dimensions, requiring the attention and cooperation of governments around the North Atlantic.

Maine is fortunate in that it still enjoys a diverse and comparatively well-protected fishery, but as the record shows, fish are vulnerable creatures. Only one thoughtless act, such as releasing an exotic species into a pond or stream, or the introduction of a single contaminant, can have severe consequences. We must be vigilant, both individually and collectively, to safeguard their future.

The brook stickleback, Culaeo inconstans, *is very uncommon in Maine, although common in states farther to the south.*

11

Amphibians
and Reptiles

Amphibians crawled out of the ooze to take up life, or at least part of it, on land more than 300 million years ago. The earliest reptiles appeared some fifty million years later. Amphibians have to return to the swamps and ponds to breed because their gelatinous eggs cannot survive in air, and so the reptiles, whose eggs are protected by a tough, waterproof shell, slowly took over the land.

Fossils record an amazing variety of reptiles. Some were like snakes, others like modern-day lizards. There were birdlike reptiles, fishlike reptiles, and some may even have been warm-blooded like the mammals that would one day take over as the dominant terrestrial vertebrates. For a time, however, the reptiles roamed over the earth, and one group of their kind, the dinosaurs, was supreme for 160 million years. Their demise, in one of the mysterious global extinctions that have punctuated the history of life on earth, cleared the way for the modern Age of Mammals.

Today, very distant relatives of those ancient creatures live on. Indeed, approximately nine thousand kinds of reptiles and amphibians (often called herptiles, or herps for short, when considered together) inhabit the earth. Climate plays a key role in determining where they live. Most of these cold-blooded animals are not active at temperatures much below fifty degrees Fahrenheit and regulate their body temperature by moving from cooler to warmer places. Maine, with only 100 to 170 frost-free days each year, has just thirty-eight species and subspecies of amphibians and reptiles—a very limited number compared with southern regions.

Many of the herptiles that do inhabit Maine are at the extreme northern edge of their range; therefore they are scarce, and, it is assumed, more susceptible to extirpation or extreme population fluctuations. And many remain enigmatic, associated with the darkness and dampness of swamps and caves. It is true that on the whole they do lead private lives—concealed, evasive, and obscure in their habits. As a result, we have little knowledge of the natural history of many species.

What we do know is that, like other inhabitants of this planet, reptiles and amphibians have made themselves important during several hundred million years of performing their special roles in the ecosystem. Many are also recognized for the way they directly benefit our own species. For example, the meat of some turtles and frogs is considered a delicacy, and venom from certain poisonous snakes is used in medicine. Reptile skins are taken, often illegally, for luxury goods such as shoes and luggage. Amphibians, because of their sensitivity, are being monitored for the effects of acid rain. And although some people look on reptiles and amphibians with repugnance, many others are fascinated by them and enjoy observing them. Unfortunately, in some states (California, for example) collectors have so depleted populations that strict regulations have been placed on their taking.

Volunteers working for the Maine Amphibian and Reptile Atlas Project are actively investigating herptiles in the state.[1] Begun in the mid 1980s, this research effort is a collaborative undertaking by the Maine Chapter of The Nature Conservancy's Natural Heritage Program, the University of Maine's Wildlife Department, the Maine Audubon Society, and the Department of Inland Fisheries and Wildlife. The project's goals are to determine the status and location of species, collect information about their life histories, and identify which ones are rare.

Amphibians

Many of Maine's amphibians are abundant and well known: the spring peeper—nature's woodwind, announcing with its musical chorus the rebirth of life in bogs and marshes at the end of winter; the warty, insect-hunting toad, welcomed by gardeners; the bullfrog, with its self-important, throat-clearing, "harumphing" call; and the secretive, red-backed salamander, hiding beneath a decaying log. This salamander is so common that it outnumbers all the birds inhabiting the forested areas it frequents—some 90 percent of the state's land area. As many as a thousand may live in a tract of just one acre.

None of the state's nineteen amphibians is currently considered endangered, threatened, or of special concern by the Endangered and Nongame Wildlife Project. Though several appear to be uncommon, only Tremblay's salamander is listed as having indeterminate status. Two others, the four-toed salamander and the northern spring salamander, are also thought to be especially uncommon, but little is known about them.

Tremblay's salamander is a slender gray to gray-black amphibian about

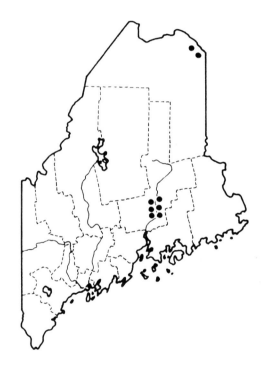

Locations of Tremblay's salamander in Maine. Redrawn from Maine Amphibian and Reptile Atlas Project, 1984–85 data.

Tremblay's salamander, Ambystoma tremblayi, is quite uncommon in Maine. Reprinted, by permission, from R.M. DeGraaf and D.D. Rudis, Amphibians and Reptiles of New England: Habitats and Natural History (Amherst: Univ. of Massachusetts Press, 1983). © 1983 by the Univ. of Massachusetts Press. Abigail Rorer, artist.

three to six inches long, with bluish-white spotty markings. It is easily confused with the blue-spotted salamander. Interestingly, only females exist in the population. Tremblay's salamander is a hybrid created by the interbreeding of the blue-spotted and Jefferson salamanders, which results in all-female offspring. Its habitat is deciduous forests near small ponds and lakes. In early spring the Tremblay's salamanders migrate to ponds to breed, where the females mate only with blue-spotted males. Later, as many as 150 eggs are laid on pond bottoms or submerged sticks. Tremblay's salamander is quite uncommon thoughout its range, which stretches from northern Wisconsin east through southern Quebec Province to the New England coastal plain. It has been identified in several Maine localities, particularly in Penobscot and Aroostook counties.

The four-toed salamander is tiny—two to four inches long. Its coloring is yellowish to reddish-brown above, with grayish sides and a white belly spotted with black. Whereas most salamanders have five toes on their hind feet, this one has four. Like a number of other amphibians, the four-toed salamander can shed its tail in order to escape a predator. A groove at the base of the tail shows where the break would occur, if needed. After shedding one tail, the salamander can regenerate another.

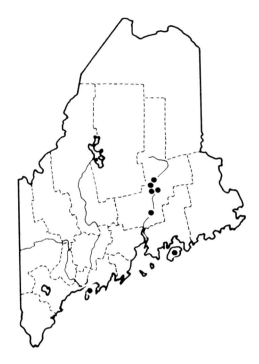

Locations of the four-toed salamander in Maine. Redrawn from Maine Amphibian and Reptile Atlas Project, 1983-85 data.

The secretive, nocturnal four-toed salamander, Hemidactylium scutatum, lives in Maine in disjunct populations at the northern periphery of its range. From A.O. Epple, The Amphibians of New England (Camden, Maine: Down East Books, 1983). Patrice M. Rossi, artist.

The four-toed salamander prefers the sphagnum moss of wet, acidic woodlands and wetlands. It is also found in hardwood forests, hiding in moist decaying wood and under stones and wet leaves, and usually hibernates among the decaying roots of trees. Breeding takes place in late summer or fall, and eggs are laid the next spring, usually in depressions of sphagnum moss. It is interesting to note that communal nests containing up to eight hundred eggs have been discovered, guarded by watchful mothers.

In Maine the four-toed salamander lives in disjunct populations at the northern periphery of its range, which extends from Nova Scotia west to Wisconsin and south to Alabama and Georgia. Secretive and nocturnal, it is difficult to find, but it may be more common than formerly suspected; more thorough searching in recent years has revealed greater numbers of this salamander in Maine.

The northern spring salamander is, at four to eight inches long, one of the largest lungless salamanders. Respiration for salamanders in this family is accomplished through the skin and the lining of the mouth. The color of this

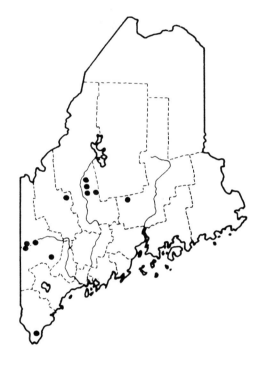

The northern spring salamander, Gyrinophilus porphyriticus porphyriticus, *is probably uncommon in Maine. From A.O. Epple,* The Amphibians of New England *(Camden, Maine: Down East Books, 1983). Patrice M. Rossi, artist.*

species varies from yellowish brown and pink to reddish brown with a mottled pattern on its darker colored back. It lives in shady wet depressions, cool springs, and mountain streams, wintering in burrows in wet soil near the water. It is a nocturnal hunter and preys on aquatic insects, crustaceans, worms, snails, spiders, small frogs, and other salamanders. Mating occurs from mid October on. Eggs are deposited from April into the summer and guarded by the female. The range of the northern spring salamander extends from west-central Maine to northern Alabama. It is probably uncommon in Maine, being restricted to local areas by its narrow habitat and niche requirements.

Locations of the northern spring salamander in Maine. Redrawn from Maine Amphibian and Reptile Atlas Project, 1984–85 data.

Reptiles

Maine has a total of nineteen species and subspecies of reptiles: eleven snakes and eight turtles. There are no lizards in the state. As a rule, turtles are regarded with curiosity but little fear; snakes, like spiders, suffer from a bad reputation. They are the most feared and least understood of Maine's animals. This is unfortunate, because snakes play important roles in ecosystems as well as directly benefiting humans by eating insects, mice, and other pests.

In Maine today there are no poisonous snakes—at least that's the general opinion in the scientific community. The only poisonous snake known in the past was the timber rattlesnake. Once thought to inhabit forested (or brushy) rocky hillsides in Oxford, Cumberland, and York counties, it has long been extirpated; the last record of a specimen was about 1860. Although this snake is uncommon to rare in the rest of New England, herpetologists are optimistic

The timber rattlesnake, Crotalus horridus, *was last recorded in Maine about 1860. Reprinted, by permission, from R.M. DeGraaf and D.D. Rudis,* Amphibians and Reptiles of New England: Habitats and Natural History *(Amherst: Univ. of Massachusetts Press, 1983). © 1983 by the Univ. of Massachusetts Press. Abigail Rorer, artist.*

that it may still exist in Maine. Suitable habitat is still available, and it is entirely possible that the timber rattlesnake could move into Maine from southern New Hampshire. Nevertheless, as of 1987, intensive searches had proved unsuccessful. The lack of sightings may be due to its isolated habitat, nocturnal hunting habits, and shy, unaggressive behavior.

Maine's snakes range in size from the black racer (up to six feet long) down to the red-bellied snake (only about ten inches long). The garter snake is the most common and has been known to reach three and a half (perhaps four) feet in length. Snakes also vary in color, from the handsome eastern milk snake, with its large reddish-brown, black-bordered blotches, to the beautiful green grass snake and the appropriately named red-bellied snake. The graceful movements of snakes are also fascinating to watch, and if one ever comes upon a snake devouring a frog or mouse, it's truly amazing to see how it can unhinge its jaw to swallow its prey whole.

Snakes can be found any time from May through September in Maine — and almost any place: one roofer was surprised to find a milk snake beneath the flashing around a chimney, high up on top of a house. Another species, the water snake, is Maine's only snake that is primarily aquatic, although it spends much of its time basking in sunny areas near water. It is also one of the few New England snakes that is nocturnal.

Not all of Maine's snakes are common. In fact, several interesting species are receiving special attention from the Maine Amphibian and Reptile Atlas Project because of their rarity and our lack of knowledge about them. These include the state endangered black racer, the ribbon snake, and the northern brown snake.

The black racer is large, slender, and agile. Except for some white under its chin, it is satiny black. The snake's habitat includes forests, old fields, roadsides, swamps, stone walls, and farms. It hunts small mammals and birds, birds' eggs, insects, frogs, toads, and other snakes. May to early June is the breeding time for the black racer. Several weeks after mating it lays seven to thirty eggs in loose soil or rotting wood and vegetation. The eggs usually hatch in late August or September.

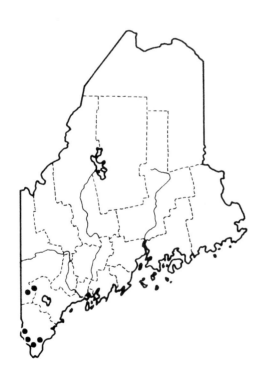

Locations of the black racer in Maine. Redrawn from Maine Amphibian and Reptile Atlas Project, 1984–86 data.

Often many snakes will gather in deep rock crevices or holes, such as old woodchuck burrows, for their winter hibernation. During other seasons, however, the black racer is territorial, ranging throughout large tracts of fields and woodlands, so land development is especially threatening to this species. Reliable sightings of the black racer have been made in only a few Maine

The black racer, Coluber constrictor, *is a large snake, up to six feet long, known from only a few locations in Maine. Reprinted, by permission, from R.M. DeGraaf and D.D. Rudis,* Amphibians and Reptiles of New England: Habitats and Natural History *(Amherst: Univ. of Massachusetts Press, 1983). © 1983 by the Univ. of Massachusetts Press. Abigail Rorer, artist.*

locations, and one of these is undergoing development. Although the northern black racer is locally abundant in its range —from southern Maine to central Alabama—the scarcity of sightings (despite concentrated studies within its known habitats) and absence of road kills are indications of its rarity in the state.

Two subspecies of ribbon snake occur in Maine: the eastern ribbon snake and the northern ribbon snake. These snakes are very slender and average from eighteen to forty inches in length. The eastern subspecies has a reddish-brown back with yellow side stripes and a yellow back stripe. The back of the northern version is black or dark brown; like the eastern, its side stripes are yellow, but

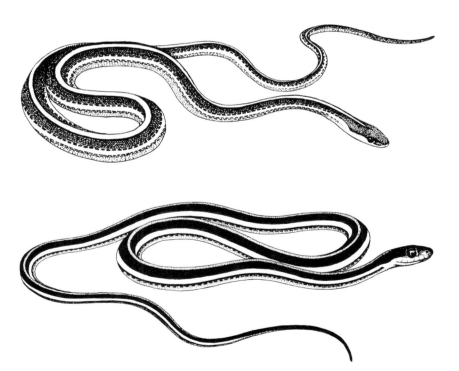

Two subspecies of ribbon snake—eastern, Thamnophis sauritus sauritus, *and northern,* T. sauritus septentrionalis—*appear to have low populations in Maine. Reprinted, by permission, from R.M. DeGraaf and D.D. Rudis,* Amphibians and Reptiles of New England: Habitats and Natural History *(Amherst: Univ. of Massachusetts Press, 1983). © 1983 by the Univ. of Massachusetts Press. Abigail Rorer, artist.*

the yellow back stripe is dulled with brown pigment. Both ribbon snakes are semiaquatic, preferring dense vegetation near the edges of streams, ponds, and wetlands. Their diet consists principally of frogs, toads, and salamanders. They hibernate during the cold season, from October to March. Warm weather brings them out again, and in the mid to late summer months they give birth to their young, which are born alive rather than hatching from eggs.

The range of the eastern ribbon snake extends from southern Maine to South Carolina and the Florida panhandle and west to southern Indiana. The northern subspecies occurs from central Maine west to Michigan and south to southeastern Illinois, Indiana, Ohio, and northern Pennsylvania. From the evidence available, it appears that Maine has fairly low populations of ribbon snakes, and their ranges are limited. Only three sightings, for example, were reported during 1985 in York and Kennebec counties. For this reason the eastern and northern ribbon snakes are listed in the "special concern" category. However, these subspecies are quick, secretive, and difficult to distinguish from garter snakes without close inspection, so it is possible that further studies will indicate that they are actually quite common in some areas.

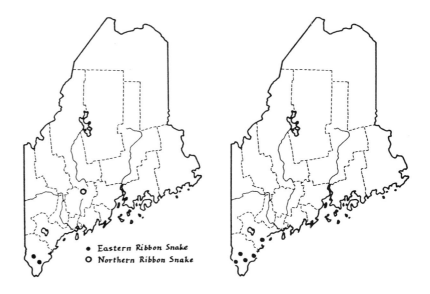

Left: *Known locations of the eastern ribbon snake and northern ribbon snake in Maine. Redrawn from Maine Amphibian and Reptile Atlas Project, 1985 data.*

Right: *Locations of the northern brown snake in Maine. Redrawn from Maine Amphibian and Reptile Atlas Project, 1984-85 data.*

Only a few sightings of the northern brown snake, Storeria dekayi dekayi, *have been made in Maine. Reprinted, by permission, from R.M. DeGraaf and D.D. Rudis,* Amphibians and Reptiles of New England: Habitats and Natural History *(Amherst: Univ. of Massachusetts Press, 1983). © 1983 by the Univ. of Massachusetts Press. Abigail Rorer, artist.*

The northern brown snake is a little creature, from ten to twenty inches long. It is yellow-brown, brown, or reddish brown, with two parallel rows of blackish spots bordering an indistinct light stripe down its back. On each side of its head is a dark downward streak.

The northern brown snake lives in both dry and moist habitats, including woods, fields, vacant lots, and trash piles. In winter it hibernates in large groups in holes and abandoned animal burrows. Breeding occurs in spring (and possibly in the fall), with an average of fourteen young born live in mid to late summer. During the hot days of summer the northern brown snake moves down into the soil, where it is cooler. Although secretive and nocturnal, it has been observed in gardens searching for slugs, worms, insects, and tiny toads.

The range of this snake covers an area from southern Maine and Canada west to Michigan and south to South Carolina. Only a few sightings have occurred in Maine. Until more information is available, the species holds indeterminate status.

Some of the most unusual reptiles are turtles. Odd and ungainly looking with their protective shells, turtles have remained relatively unchanged for 150 million years. As a group, they may live longer than any other animals—up to 150 years for certain species. In spite of their long, successful history on earth, some turtle species are today fighting for their survival.

Occasionally found wandering off the Maine coast are three marine turtles whose futures are of concern: the Atlantic leatherback and the Atlantic Ridley, both on the Federal Endangered Species List, and the Atlantic loggerhead turtle, on the Federal Threatened Species List. These are turtles of tropical seas and are much different from the pond and land species we are accustomed to seeing. Their legs and feet are flippers, designed for swimming, not for walking on land. They rarely come ashore, except when the female drags herself up onto the beach in late spring to lay her eggs. None, however, nests as far north as Maine.

The Atlantic leatherback is the largest of all turtles in the world, growing to as much as eight feet in length and nearly a ton in weight. Its carapace (upper shell) and plastron (lower shell) are covered with a smooth black to dark-brown skin, prompting the name leatherback. Seven prominent lengthwise ridges on the leatherback's carapace aid in identification, although determining the exact species of adult sea turtles can be difficult because years of life in the sea often leave them scarred and encrusted with barnacles. The Atlantic leatherback, a swimmer of open seas, is lured from its tropical environment to as far north as Nova Scotia by the warm waters of the Gulf Stream.

At the opposite end of the size spectrum is the Atlantic Ridley turtle. This smallest of the Atlantic sea turtles measures twenty to twenty-five inches long. Identifying characteristics include a keellike ridge running down the middle of the back, and four enlarged plates that form a bridge on each side of the shell, connecting the plastron with the carapace. The adults are gray and the young are black. This species also ranges from the Gulf of Mexico to Nova Scotia.

The Atlantic loggerhead is another large turtle, reaching up to seven feet and nine hundred pounds, although weights of three hundred pounds or less are more common. This reddish-brown turtle feeds on animals such as Portugese men-of-war and shellfish. Most loggerheads live in warm Atlantic waters, but occasionally strays reach as far north as Newfoundland and as far south as Argentina.

A number of land turtles are also uncommon in Maine. One is the eastern box turtle, listed as state endangered. It is known only in York, Lincoln, and (perhaps) Penobscot counties. As of the mid 1980s no sightings had been made since 1967, although the box turtle probably still occurs in southwestern Maine. It is more abundant farther south in its range, which extends to northern Florida and west to the Mississippi River and southern Illinois.

The box turtle is small, four to seven inches long. Its size gives little hint of the turtle's age, however, which for some may reach at least a hundred years. The box turtle, true to its name, can be recognized by a high, dark brown or

The Atlantic leatherback turtle, Dermochelys coriacea, *the largest of all turtles in the world, is found occasionally off the Maine coast.*

The Atlantic Ridley turtle, Lepidochelys kempi, *the smallest of the Atlantic sea turtles, ranges from the Gulf of Mexico to Nova Scotia.*

The Atlantic loggerhead turtle, Caretta caretta, *is a large sea turtle that lives in warm waters but occasionally strays as far north as Newfoundland.*

The eastern box turtle, Terrapene carolina carolina, *is very rare in Maine. Reprinted, by permission, from R.M. DeGraaf and D.D. Rudis,* Amphibians and Reptiles of New England: Habitats and Natural History *(Amherst: Univ. of Massachusetts Press, 1983). © 1983 by the Univ. of Massachusetts Press. Abigail Rorer, artist.*

black boxy carapace with yellow, orange, or olive markings. The patterns and colors are extremely variable. In situations of danger the box turtle normally can close its shell tightly, though some obese specimens have died trapped inside an outgrown shell.

The habitat of the box turtle includes moist woodlands, bogs, marshes, meadows, and stream banks, where it hunts earthworms, slugs, snails, insects, and toads. It also eats berries, fruits, and fungi, and its habit of eating poisonous mushrooms is said to have killed humans who subsequently ate the turtle's flesh. The box turtle was also popular with Indians, who not only ate them but buried them as totems with their dead and used their shells for ceremonial rattles.

The box turtle hibernates from late fall to early spring, buried up to two feet deep in loose soil, mud, or decaying vegetation. Following the winter season mating occurs, and the female is able to fertilize eggs for up to four years from stored sperm. Three to eight eggs are laid in nests; the hatchlings, born in August to September, usually live out their lives in an area from 150 to 750 feet in diameter.

Two land turtle species are listed as threatened in Maine: Blanding's turtle and the spotted turtle. Blanding's turtle can be identified by a bright yellow

Blanding's Turtle, Emydoidea blandingii, *is a threatened species in Maine. John Albright photo.*

Locations of Blanding's turtle in Maine. Redrawn from Maine Amphibian and Reptile Atlas Project, 1984–86 data.

chin and throat. It is 5 to 10.5 inches long, with a black, heavily spotted, helmet-shaped carapace. Although it prefers shallow waters of ponds, marshes, and creeks with soft, muddy bottoms and dense aquatic vegetation, Blanding's turtle frequently comes ashore to bask or hunt for food. Its diet consists of insects, crustaceans, mollusks, fish, and aquatic plants. Breeding occurs most often in early spring, followed by the laying of six to eleven eggs in nests located in sandy soils. Very tolerant of cold, this turtle can be found as far north as Nova Scotia, across the Great Lake states to Minnesota, and south to central Illinois. In Canada, where it is very rare, Blanding's turtle is an endangered species. Its range in the eastern United States is very restricted, with only scattered colonies in New York, New Hampshire, Massachusetts, and southwestern Maine. In 1985 only three specimens of Blanding's turtle were reported in the state, all in York County.

The spotted turtle, like Blanding's turtle, is aquatic, preferring small, shallow bodies of water with muddy bottoms. It is small, 3.5 to 5 inches long, with a black carapace polka-dotted with round yellow spots, which also extend to its head, neck, legs, and feet. Its food, which it takes underwater, consists of aquatic invertebrates, small fish, frogs, and vegetable matter. During the winter the turtle hibernates in muddy bottoms. Breeding occurs in early spring, followed by the laying of three to five eggs in nests in well-drained soils. The spotted turtle is uncommon to rare throughout its range, and few sightings have been recorded in Maine.

The wood turtle, another species rare in Maine, is actually a turtle of both dry land and water. Like the box turtle, it is popular as a pet, and widespread collecting has contributed to its general decline throughout its range, which extends from Nova Scotia to Minnesota and south to Virginia. Although it has been found throughout Maine, with sightings from Aroostook County to York County, and is easy to capture and identify, reports have been few and sporadic. Until more information is obtained, it has been given indeterminate status.

The spotted turtle, Clemmys outtata, *is listed as threatened in Maine. John Albright photo.*

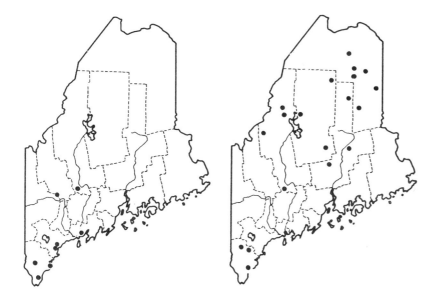

Left: *Locations of the spotted turtle in Maine. Redrawn from Maine Amphibian and Reptile Atlas Project, 1965–85 data.*

Right: *Locations of the wood turtle in Maine. Redrawn from Maine Amphibian and Reptile Atlas Project, 1978–85 data.*

The wood turtle's very rough, dark shell, sometimes exceeding seven inches in length, also gives it the name sculptured turtle. Its habitats include deciduous woodlands and slow-moving streams with sandy bottoms. An omnivorous feeder, it eats grass, moss, and fungi, as well as worms, slugs, frogs, and fish. Muddy banks and bottoms are favorite spots for hibernation, which ends in March or April. Mating occurs in water from March to October, with four to twelve eggs laid in May or June in sandy or gravelly soils. Hatchlings may winter-over in the nest.

Reptiles and amphibians add much to the diversity of Maine's natural environment, and to our enjoyment, as well. Unfortunately, as a group they are vulnerable to the negative effects of environmental alteration. Conservation organizations and agencies, through programs such as the Maine Amphibian and Reptile Atlas Project, provide opportunities for all citizens to become involved in monitoring these sensitive indicators of changing habitats.

Sightings of the wood turtle, Clemmys insculpta, *have been few and sporadic in Maine. Reprinted, by permission, from R.M. and D.D. Rudis,* Amphibians and Reptiles of New England: Habitats and Natural History *(Amherst: Univ. of Massachusetts Press, 1983). © 1983 by the Univ. of Massachusetts Press. Abigail Rorer, artist.*

12

Birds

One hundred and fifty million years ago a crow-sized creature with teeth, clawed wings, and a reptilian tail inhabited the forests. This *Archaeopteryx*, the oldest of known birds, was the first link in an evolutionary chain that has produced the graceful and beautiful species we admire today. Gradually this new addition to the planet's fauna spread, occupying thousands of ecological slots. By 60 million years ago, great flightless carnivorous species, up to ten feet tall, roamed portions of the earth. One of these was *Diatryma giganteum*, possibly the most frightening bird ever to live in North America. It was taller than a man, shaped like an ostrich, with a head larger than a horse's from which hung a large, viciously hooked beak. Today, eight thousand or more species and more than twenty-eight thousand subspecies of birds live around the world; only their scaly legs, oviparous (egg-laying) characteristics, and internal structures give hints of their reptilian ancestry.

Maine is blessed with an abundance of these fascinating creatures: raptors, seabirds, wading birds, shorebirds, songbirds—the list is long and the categories many. No other northeastern state, for example, has so many different warblers. And Maine's large areas of undeveloped seacoast, remote islands, and cool climate make it practically the only place in the eastern United States where common eiders, razorbill auks, black guillemots, puffins, and Leach's storm-petrels all come to nest every summer (although a very few storm-petrels and an eider duck colony do nest on islands off Massachusetts).

Most of Maine's birds are summer visitors, although some, such as the black-capped chickadee and ruffed grouse, stay all year. A few, like the redpoll and the harlequin duck, spend their summers farther north but travel south to winter in Maine, where the climate is comparatively warmer. Others, such as the arctic tern and the bobolink, migrate here to breed from their wintering areas in the southern hemisphere. The major migration route in Maine is along the coast; there are no significant flyways in the mountainous regions. Migrating birds of all kinds—hawks, ducks, songbirds, and others—may be seen. For example, from five to seven thousand raptors, including sharp-shinned hawks, merlins, peregrine falcons, ospreys, northern harriers, and kestrels are known to fly over the southern tip of Harpswell every fall. Mt. Agamenticus, in York County, is another popular hawk-watching site.

A number of Maine areas are traditionally used for rest and feeding by migrating birds. Waterfowl, such as grebes, ducks, and geese, stop over at inland and coastal marshes, bays, estuaries, and shores. Shorebirds—sandpipers and plovers, for example—use tidal mudflats. Especially important areas are Biddeford Pool, Scarborough Marsh, Back Bay in Portland, the Presumpscot River estuary, Merrymeeting Bay, and flats from Lubec to Quoddy Head. Migratory land-bird concentration areas are coastal peninsulas (for example, Schoodic Point and Cape Elizabeth), islands (including Matinicus and Monhegan), woods near waterfalls, and along major river valleys. The stopover islands are known as "migrant traps," functioning much as oases in the desert for traveling birds in need of food and rest.

Birds bring enjoyment to millions of Maine's tourists and thousands of year-round residents. It's estimated that one Maine household in three feeds birds. And beyond the pleasure they bring and their economic value, birds have great ecological importance in their intricate relationships with other plants and animals. These include recycling nutrients, pollinating plants, distributing seeds, and maintaining links in food chains.

Birds have not always received the best treatment from humans. They have suffered directly from pesticides, chemical wastes, and oil spills, and indirectly from vehicular accidents, towers in flight paths, overhead wires, and land developments. In the past, their eggs, feathers, and flesh have been harvested for profit. Whether through human ignorance or carelessness, some species have suffered great damage, and many, unfortunately, continue to suffer. The alteration and loss of habitat is probably the most serious problem now affecting birds. Changing practices of land use, including the harvesting and reforestation of woodlands, the development and reversion of agricultural lands, and the building of towns and cities, have had profound effects on the kinds and numbers of species inhabiting an area. Some species actually thrive in these changing habitats: the non-native pigeons, English sparrows, starlings, and grackles that proliferate in human settlements, for example. These in turn compete with some native species, such as the bluebird, to the extent that such native populations have been greatly reduced. Other species have suffered more directly; the piping plover and least tern, for example, must compete with humans for space on Maine's few sand beaches.

Today, rare or declining species are receiving the attention of several agencies and organizations, which include the state departments of Inland Fisheries and Wildlife and Marine Resources, Maine's Critical Areas Program, the Maine Audubon Society, the various state chapters of the National Audubon Society, the Maine Chapter of The Nature Conservancy, and a variety of others at federal, state, and local levels. Many of these are working with the Maine Endangered and Nongame Project to help identify and categorize species according to level of endangerment. Species listed by the project are included in this chapter.[1]

Birds of Prey: The Raptors

The raptors—hawks, eagles, falcons, and owls—have perhaps suffered most from the ignorance and carelessness of humans. They have long been regarded as pests and threats to farm and ranch animals. Hawks and eagles, in particular, have been poisoned and hunted relentlessly from the beginning of European settlement. In recent times, more perverse killers quietly menaced these carnivorous birds— debilitating chemicals that crept up food chains to accumulate in destructive dosages within their tissues. Today, with increasing environmental awareness and greater appreciation of their value, raptor populations are being protected and restored.

The bald eagle (pictured in Section III Perspective) became the national symbol of the United States by an Act of Congress in June 1782.[2] Ironically, two centuries later the eagle population had been so sharply reduced that the species was listed by the United States Department of Interior as endangered, a designation that still applies today. The decline was slow and sinister. It was first noted around 1900, and was primarily due to shooting and poisoning. In Maine, no more than one hundred pairs were estimated to exist in 1908; not over sixty pairs in 1949; and by 1974, only thirty-five active nests and a total of fifteen young were counted. The causes were many, including depletion of food supplies by pollution, disturbance and destruction of nests, and outright killing. But most devastating was contamination by pesticides, primarily DDT, and other chemicals.

In the 1960s the National Audubon Society monitored the few existing active eagles' nests in Maine, then, in 1976 the Maine Eagle Project began an extensive monitoring and data-gathering effort to determine the status of the bald eagle in the state. Some encouraging signs have been gleaned from their thousands of hours of careful field work and painstaking analysis of hundreds of reports. One such sign is an increase in the productivity index, a measure of the number of eaglets per breeding pair of birds. In 1962, for example, only about three eaglets were fledged per ten mated pairs of adults. By 1985 the number had improved to eight eaglets for every ten breeding pairs, approaching normal levels. In that year, eighty-five nesting pairs were estimated to exist in the state.

Today, Maine is the only northeastern state where the bald eagle can be seen in any numbers. Two thirds of the breeding population is located in eastern coastal sections of Washington and Hancock counties; the remaining one third is found near inland lakes and the larger river systems. The Washington County coast is also an important wintering area where many eagles from outside the state come to feed.

Lifted aloft by broad wings that span seven to eight feet, the bald eagle is magnificent in flight, easily identifiable by glints of white from its head and tail. Unlike the turkey vulture, another large soaring bird that is being seen more frequently in Maine, the bald eagle's wings are held level in flight, not uptilted. Since it feeds largely on fish, the eagle is often seen flying over bodies of water.

The bald eagle is a member of the hawk family, which possibly has the keenest eyesight of any group of living animals. It uses binocular vision to spot its prey and can judge distance and movement with uncanny accuracy. Its large size also enables it to carry fish of good size, muskrats, and rabbits, as well as traffic-killed animals and other carrion to its nest. However, contrary to many stories about the size of prey the bald eagle can take, it is unable to lift more than fifteen pounds.

Eagles are thought to mate for life—which may be for a half century or more, according to the lifespan records of captured animals. Their nests, which are often reused year after year, can measure seven to eight feet in diameter and up to twelve feet high and are thought to be the largest of all nests built by a

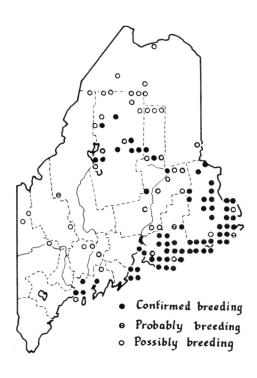

Distribution of the bald eagle, Haliaetua leucocephalus, *in Maine. Redrawn from P.R. Adamus, comp.* Atlas of Breeding Birds in Maine, 1978–1983 *(Augusta: Maine Department of Inland Fisheries and Wildlife, 1987).*

single pair of birds. In courtship, the male puts on a spectacular display of loops in the air. Following mating, in March, two dull white eggs are usually laid; about thirty-five days later, the nearly black young hatch out. When two eaglets are in the nest, competition between them can be so fierce that one frequently dies. Approximately two and a half months after hatching, the young birds join their parents in flight.

For young eagles born in the final years of the twentieth century, the opportunities for a long life and many offspring are much brighter. Due to past population declines ample unoccupied breeding areas are available; the rivers and lakes are cleaner; and public awareness that the renaissance of the bald eagle symbolizes regeneration of the environment is at an all-time high.

Another eagle, the golden eagle, is classified as an endangered species in Maine. Though populations appear more secure in the midwest and west, it has declined steadily in eastern North America. East of the Mississippi River most states have but scattered pairs, and probably few of these breed. Suspected reasons include shooting, vandalism of nests, environmental contaminants, and changing land use practices.

The golden eagle, Aquila chrysaetos, *is rare in Maine and classified as a state endangered species.*

There are few recent records of the golden eagle's presence in Maine. They include a single bird reported seen in Oxford County in 1968, a pair that lived in Baxter State Park in 1974, and one active nest spotted during an aerial survey in 1987—pitifully few sightings for a raptor thought to have bred, at one time, in Oxford, Somerset, Penobscot, Hancock, and Piscataquis counties.

The golden eagle is a large, impressive dark bird with golden feathers at the nape of its neck. Like the bald eagle, the female is larger than the male, but both sexes can attain wingspreads of seven feet or more. Beautiful in flight, the golden eagle soars and glides with great ease, but it can also dive at speeds in excess of one hundred miles per hour to capture small mammals, snakes, turtles, skunks, and owls. The prey may be carried to nests, which are located most often on cliffs. Some nests are huge: eight to ten feet across and up to four feet deep. A pair of eagles may have several nests and use some of them on a rotating basis. Commonly, two dull white, brown-freckled eggs are laid in the spring. The young hatch after approximately forty-five days of incubation.

Records kept on golden eagles in captivity indicate that life expectancy may be fifty years or more.

The peregrine falcon may eventually fare better than the golden eagle in Maine. After being absent since the 1950s or 1960s, it is back as a reintroduced raptor.[3] Nearly crow-size, it is easily identified as a falcon by its pointed wings,

Immature peregrine falcon, Falco peregrinus. *Efforts to reestablish Maine's peregrine population of this endangered species were begun in 1984. Mark Wilson photo.*

narrow tail, and rapid wing movements. Other distinguishing characteristics are a barred tail, spotted chest and belly, and black, downward-pointing bars below the eyes, conspicuously displayed against white. Although known as the duck hawk, the peregrine falcon also preys on a variety of birds and occasionally on insects and mammals. It is especially noted for its astonishing speed when in pursuit of prey. One report in 1930 told of a peregrine passing a plane going 175 miles per hour. In the wild the falcon nests mostly on cliffs, but it doesn't build its own nest, preferring to scoop out a depression in the soil or to use nests of other birds.

Once one of the most widely distributed birds in the world, the peregrine falcon began suffering a severe decline in the 1950s, especially in parts of Europe and in most of the United States. The primary cause was increased use of chemical pesticides, particularly DDT. Other factors included shooting, egg collecting, loss of nesting habitat, and human disturbance. The last confirmed record of a natural breeding pair in Maine was in 1962, although a probable nesting was documented in Acadia National Park in 1980. By 1971, most North American nesting populations were restricted to Alaska and Canada. Today, this endangered species is making a comeback through captive breeding.

The effort to reestablish the state's population of peregrine falcons was begun in 1984 by the Maine Endangered and Nongame Project. A total of nineteen chicks obtained from the Cornell University Ornithological Laboratory were released on remote mountaintops in Acadia National Park and Baxter State Park, and in the town of Amherst.

Among the criteria used in selecting sites was the absence of great horned owls, the major predator of young peregrines. To determine the owls' presence (or absence), a recorded cassette tape of calls was played at potential sites at dawn and dusk during the winter and spring before the planned falcon introduction.

The reintroduction program used a process called "hacking," a centuries-old method for gradually conditioning young birds born in captivity to their natural environment. Hacking is a labor-intensive effort, requiring project personnel to babysit the young birds around the clock. The falcons were fed dead poultry through a chute in a hack box so that the food wouldn't be associated with humans. At the end of the summer all nineteen had survived, and they migrated south. Twenty-eight more falcons were released in 1985. This time another site was added: the tall Key Bank building in Portland. (It is not uncommon for eyries to be located on high buildings in cities.) This too was a successful season, and all survived. The real success, however, will be measured by the return of nesting pairs once the young to reach breeding age—usually three years after hatching.

Two other birds of prey are watch-listed: Cooper's hawk and the red-shouldered hawk. Cooper's hawk belongs to the family of accipiters, or bird hawks. It is a raptor of forests and farmlands. The size of a crow, with a long rounded tail and short rounded wings, Cooper's hawk maneuvers easily and swiftly around trees and through brush to catch birds and small mammals in its talons. Interestingly, it will sometimes take its prey to water and drown it. Like other raptors at the top of the food chain, Cooper's hawks suffered a serious population decline in the 1970s due to pesticide accumulation in their tissues. Now uncommon throughout its range from southern Canada to northern Mexico, its status in Maine is unclear.

The red-shouldered hawk belongs to the buteo family, called buzzard hawks. These are large, thickset hawks with broad wings and wide rounded tails. Adults can be identified by wide dark bands across the tail, reddish shoulders, and pale red, brown, and white bars on the underside from throat to tail. It too is also a hawk of woodlands and swamps, where it hunts a variety of small mammals, reptiles, amphibians, birds, and insects, though it is particularly known as a mouse and small rodent hunter. In recent years declines have been noted over much of its range, and although its population in Maine seems secure at the present, monitoring is recommended by the Maine Endangered and Nongame Project.

Cooper's Hawk, Accipiter cooperi, *is uncommon throughout its range from southern Canada to northern Mexico. Its status in Maine is unclear.*

The red-shouldered hawk, Buteo lineatus, *is watch listed in Maine.*

Birds of the Sea

An unusual combination of land, water, and climate draws some of North America's most interesting birds to the coast of Maine. The climate, abnormally cold for this latitude, is influenced by strong westerly winds that create deep mixing of cold water. Strong tidal currents sweep into the Gulf of Maine twice daily, forcing cold, plankton-rich waters up through the gulf and into the confines of the Bay of Fundy, where tidal amplitude reaches fifty feet in many places. With each rising tide, nutrient-laden water mixes in the Gulf of Maine to create the very productive waters found off the Maine coast. Here, on approximately 650 of Maine's remote islands, live the alcids, the terns, eider ducks, and other fascinating birds of northern seas.

These seabird nesting islands represent a unique resource, not only to Maine but to the nation. Most are relatively small—some little more than spray-drenched ledges. Many are secluded, and it is probably this remoteness that has allowed the seabird colonies to survive, for during the nesting period (from April to July) they are extremely vulnerable to disruptions.

Petit Manan Island, in Washington County, is one of Maine's important seabird nesting islands for terns. It is owned by the U.S. Fish and Wildlife Service. Hank Tyler photo.

The story of Maine's seabirds has not always been a pleasant one. In the past, they suffered the plunder of plume hunters and egg gatherers as well as mass slaughter to feed islanders, sailors, and explorers. Later, the introduction of rats, cats, dogs, goats, and other predators and competitors upset the ecosystems of nesting islands. During the twentieth century, seabird populations made a healthy comeback. Efforts are underway to protect and monitor nesting areas and in some cases, reestablish colonies of seabirds such as the coastal terns and puffins.

Terns are small, sleek, slender seabirds, neat in appearance and graceful on the wing. Four species nest along the Maine coast: the least tern, roseate tern, common tern, and arctic tern.[4] All are mostly white with long slender wings, forked tails, black caps, and thin, pointed bills. Although the four species are similar in appearance, with practice each can be distinguished by the color of the bill and wings and the length of the tail. Summer coloration of the least tern's bill is yellow; arctic is blood red; common, red-orange; and roseate, reddish.

Terns are diving birds, hovering in midair when they see a small fish or crustacean and then plunging headfirst into the water to capture it. A common food is the sand launce, or sand eel, a small, slender, silvery fish that swims in large schools. Other favorites are shrimp and mollusks.

Terns spend most of their lives over water, coming to shore only to breed and often returning to the same nesting colonies. Courtship consists of an interesting ceremony called the "fish flight," in which a pair carry a fish aloft, exchanging it several times in flight. Sometime around the first of June, a clutch of one to three eggs is laid in a nest, often situated in the open with little protection against predation and other disturbances. For the next twenty days, both parents share incubation. Thirty days after hatching, the young are able to fly, but they continue to depend on their parents a while longer for food. In late summer the birds depart for their wintering ranges, which extend into the southern hemisphere.

Once among the most abundant nesting birds on the Atlantic coast, terns were nearly eliminated from the eastern shores of North America by plume hunters between 1880 and 1900. In Maine, large numbers were slaughtered during 1886 and 1887. Following the passage of a protective law by the Maine Legislature in 1889, the populations recovered, peaking between 1920 and 1940. Since the 1950s, however, terns have experienced a steady decline—the result of loss of habitat, human disturbance of nesting sites, and predation by increasing numbers of gulls.

It's no coincidence that the forty-year decline of Maine's common and arctic terns occurred during a period of spectacular increase in the populations of great black-backed and herring gulls. These birds not only prey on eggs and chicks but take over nesting areas as well. The herring gull population, which was reduced by 1901 to an estimated eleven thousand pairs in New England, experienced an eightfold increase by 1977. The rise of black-backed gulls was even more amazing: they were completely eliminated from New England waters in the 1880s, but by 1977 approximately twenty thousand pairs nested on islands from Long Island, New York, to the Canadian border, the result of expanded food supplies from increased inshore fishing activities and garbage dumps. Since the late 1970s, Maine's gull populations have remained high, posing a serious problem for the terns.

The small laughing gull also nests among tern colonies. Uncommon in Maine, where it is at the northern limit of its range, the laughing gull is prevalent along the rest of the Atlantic and Gulf coasts in summer. It is known to sometimes eat eggs and young of other terns as well as steal fish from them.

Today, terns nest on about thirty of the approximately three thousand Maine coastal islands. Historical records show that terns once nested on 115 islands. Only eight major colonies of three hundred or more birds are now known to exist.

The least tern is listed as state and federal endangered. Not only are its

Arctic tern, Sterna paradisea, *reaches the southern limit of its nesting range in the Gulf of Maine, where it nests on only a few islands. Kathleen Blanchard photo.*

Laughing gull, Larus atricilla, *is rarely seen in Maine, where it periodically nests on a few southern and mid-coast islands. Stephen W. Kress photo.*

The vulnerable nest of the least tern, Sterna antillarum, *is simply a hollow scraped in the sand above the high-tide line. Patrick W. Grace photo.*

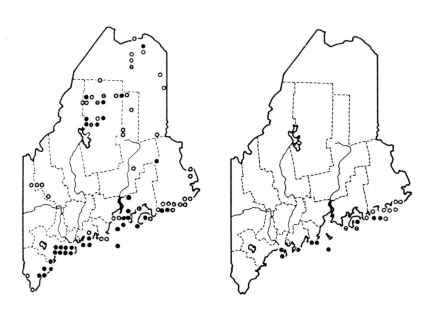

Left: *Distribution of the least tern in Maine. Redrawn from P.R. Adamus, comp.* Atlas of Breeding Birds in Maine, 1978–1983 *(Augusta: Maine Department of Inland Fisheries and Wildlife, 1987).*

Right: *Distribution of the roseate tern,* Sterna dougalli, *in Maine. Redrawn from P.R. Adamus, comp.* Atlas of Breeding Birds in Maine, 1978–1983 *(Augusta: Maine Department of Inland Fisheries and Wildlife, 1987).*

numbers low, but its habit of scraping out shallow nests on open, mainland beaches makes it especially vulnerable to human disturbance and predation. Eggs and chicks are at the mercy of gulls, crows, owls, foxes, skunks, raccoons, domestic cats, dogs, and people. By some estimates, these problems have added up to an 80 percent reduction of numbers along the Atlantic coast since the early 1940s. In order to protect the few active nesting sites, three have been designated as Critical Areas—one in Scarborough and two in Phippsburg. In the mid 1980s, however, only one site was reported in use, and along the entire coastline, nesting occurred on as few as a half dozen beaches.

The roseate tern, the rarest of the terns on a worldwide scale, is a threatened species in Maine. Here it is near the periphery of a breeding range that extends along the Atlantic seacoast from the Caribbean to Nova Scotia. In the mid 1970s most of the state's population, perhaps as many as seventy-five breeding pairs, nested on North Sugarloaf Island at the mouth of the Kennebec River in Phippsburg. A decade later, no pairs were seen nesting on the island; statewide, only about sixty pairs of nesting roseate terns were reported.

Left: *Distribution of the common tern,* Sterna hirundo, *in Maine. Redrawn from P.R. Adamus, comp.* Atlas of Breeding Birds in Maine, 1978–1983 *(Augusta: Maine Department of Inland Fisheries and Wildlife, 1987).*

Right: *Distribution of the arctic tern in Maine. Redrawn from P.R. Adamus, comp.* Atlas of Breeding Birds in Maine, 1978–1983 *(Augusta: Maine Department of Inland Fisheries and Wildlife, 1987).*

The common tern and the arctic tern are listed as species of special concern in Maine. Although several thousand pairs of each nest in the state, both have experienced severe population declines since the 1940s, and their island habitats are threatened by human disturbance and predation. The common tern nests along the Eastern Coast from North Carolina to Newfoundland and inland to central and southern Canada. Its wintering range extends into the southern hemisphere. Although common terns once nested on more than thirty Maine islands, today most nesting sites are located on just six islands. In the mid 1970s one of the largest populations lived, like the roseate tern, on North Sugarloaf Island in Phippsburg, but ten years later the common tern was also not to be found there.

The arctic tern's breeding grounds extend from Massachussets northward to the Arctic, while its wintering area is ten thousand miles south, in subantarctic seas. Most of the arctic terns off the coast of Maine are found on just three islands: Petit Manan Island, Matinicus Rock, and Machias Seal Island.

Another bird of special concern in the state is the harlequin duck. It is a relatively rare species in the eastern United States, and a large portion of the population that does winter on the western side of the Atlantic Ocean is found in Maine. True to its name, the male harlequin is stunningly marked; it has chestnut sides, and white patches of bizarre shape are scattered over its slate-colored body. In winter the duck flocks to the rough surf off rocky coastal areas, where it feeds on barnacles, crustaceans, limpets, and small fishes. In summer it moves to inland areas north of Maine. There, it haunts turbulent mountain streams in which it seemingly defies the pressures of swift currents by diving to the bottom and walking upstream in search of the larvae of mayflies and caddisflies.

Several other sea birds of Maine's coast are watch-listed. These include the razorbill, Atlantic (or common) puffin, Leach's storm-petrel, Bonaparte's gull, and Barrow's goldeneye.

The razorbill is a member of the alcids—sea birds of the auk family.[5] With its black and white plumage, large head, short tail, chunky penguinlike body, and short legs, the razorbill is a miniature of the extinct great auk. It is distinguished from other alcids by its relatively large size, bright yellow mouth, deep bill with a thin upper mandible hooked at the tip, and its tail—held uptilted while swimming. It is adept at using its short wings and large feet to swim and dive to great depths in pursuit of fishes and marine invertebrates. To the astonishment of some fishermen, razorbills have been caught in nets sixty feet below the surface.

Small colonies of razorbills, which are exceedingly rare along the coast of Maine, exist on only a very few islands; among them are Machias Seal Island and Matinicus Rock. Pairs return to the same spot every year—usually a narrow, seaward-facing ledge—where the female lays a single egg, either in a crevice or on an exposed surface. If dislodged, the pear-shaped egg will rotate in a tight circle rather than roll off the ledge. To avoid predators such as gulls, young razorbills leave the ledge about two weeks after hatching, sometimes leaping into the sea from cliffs several hundred feet above the water. Until they can fly, they swim under the watchful protection of their parents.

The common puffin, also called the sea parrot because of its large and brightly colored bill, is another intriguing sea bird. Estimates of the world population of the three subspecies of the common puffin run as high as fifteen million. The subspecies found in Maine ranges from Norway across the North Atlantic to Iceland, Greenland, eastern Canada, and south to Maine. Although it formerly nested on eight coastal islands, today colonies are found only on

The harlequin duck, Histrionicus histrionicus, *is a species of special concern in Maine.*

The common puffin, Fratercula arctica, *formerly nested on eight coastal Maine islands, but now nests naturally only on Matinicus Rock and Machias Seal Island. In the late 1970s, puffins were successfully reintroduced on Eastern Egg Rock, a state-owned island in Muscongus Bay. Kathleen Blanchard photo.*

Matinicus Rock, Machias Seal Island, and Eastern Egg Rock in Muscongus Bay.

The tale of the return of puffins to Eastern Egg Rock is truly a success story.[6] Almost one hundred years after nesting puffins were eliminated from this island, taken by local fishermen for food, a National Audubon Society project directed by Stephen Kress began to reestablish the puffin colony. In 1973 chicks were transplanted from their native Newfoundland and placed in burrows on Egg Rock, where they were reared on a diet of smelt and vitamin supplements until fledgling age, about six weeks later. In the ensuing years, additional chicks were transplanted and raised. After years of anxious waiting, five pairs returned in 1981 to take up residence on the island and breed. By 1985, twenty pairs of puffins were returning to nest.

The puffin is the only alcid that mates on water and actively constructs a home—a burrow over a yard deep in which a single egg is laid. After forty-two days of incubation, the chick hatches. Both adults participate in feeding the young bird. It's a busy time; to accommodate a voracious chick, which can consume its entire weight in fish daily, one adult may load its capacious bill with as many as thirty small fish at a time. After about six weeks the adults abandon the chick, which spends another week in the burrow fasting and developing flight feathers. Then, under the protective cover of darkness, the chick flutters to the sea, where it must learn to fend for itself. After three years at sea the puffin normally returns to its native island to nest.

The most comon alcid on the Maine coast is the black guillemot, which is approximately the same size as the puffin but is distinguished by its black plumage, white wing patches, and bright red mouth and feet. Because of its stout body and rapid wingbeat, it flight is described as "bumblebeelike."

Few people ever see Leach's storm-petrel, an unusual member of an ancient group of sea birds—the tubenoses.[7] It is a small, dark bird with a white rump and forked tail, webbed feet, and a hooked bill. Most interesting are its tubular nostrils, through which it shoots out a salty fluid produced by glands beneath the eye sockets. The glands remove much of the salt the bird ingests while drinking sea water and eating, thus preventing dehydration.

Leach's storm-petrel is a bird of the open seas. Its name comes from its habit of appearing about ships in stormy weather. The term *petrel* is a diminutive referring to St. Peter, who, the scriptures say, walked on water;

A bird of the open seas, Leach's storm-petrel has declined in Maine since 1900.

Leach's storm-petrel, Oceanodroma leucorhoa, *chick. A nocturnal oceanic bird, Leach's storm-petrel nests in burrows on only a few of Maine's islands. Adult birds are rarely sighted. Joel Cowger photo.*

UNCOMMON WILDLIFE

when feeding, this sea bird hovers over the water, often patting it with its feet while catching fish, small shrimp, and crustaceans just under the surface. When it does come to land, it is only at night, to offshore islands where it breeds.

The nest is a deep burrow from which the petrel emerges only at night. The pair takes turns incubating a single white egg. While one parent is on the nest the other travels long distances out to sea in search of food. Truly remarkable is its homing ability; one test demonstrated that a petrel could fly directly home over a distance of at least three thousand miles. After leaving the nest, the young spend their first two summers at sea before returning to their breeding grounds. However, most do not begin breeding until their fifth summer.

Since 1900 Leach's storm-petrel, the only tubenose to nest in Maine, has declined in the state. A number of factors are blamed: a decrease in its food supply of copepod crustaceans; human introduction of predators, including cats, dogs, and rats; predation by herring gulls and great black-backed gulls, which wait for petrels to return to their nests at night and capture them as they land; and increased island development and habitation. The protection of this fascinating sea bird is of concern, and already several nesting islands, includ-ing Eastern Egg Rock, Matinicus Rock, Seal Island, Little Duck Island, and Great Duck Island, are designated as Critical Areas. Great Duck Island, owned by The Nature Conservancy and the State of Maine, contains the largest colony of Leach's storm-petrels in the United States.

Bonaparte's gull is the smallest of the American gulls. Its plump and petite form has also inspired the name sea pigeon. One of the hooded gulls, the Bonaparte's head plumage is black in summer, white (except for a black ear spot) in winter. In the summer its preferred habitat is muskeg in Alaska and Canada, where (surprisingly for a sea bird) it nests in trees of spruce-fir forests and feeds largely on insects. By chance—and an extraordinary extension of range—a small breeding colony summers on a remote island in northern Maine. In winter Bonaparte's gull is found along the Pacific and Gulf coasts and up the Atlantic coast as far as Nova Scotia. In Maine it rests in ocean bays, feeding on fish, crustaceans, and marine worms, and is known to migrate through Passamaquoddy Bay.

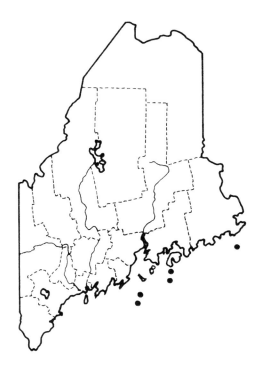

Major nesting sites of Leach's storm-petrel. Redrawn from Maine Critical Areas Program (1982).

Bonaparte's gull, Larus philadelphia, watch listed in Maine, has a small breeding colony on a remote island in the northern part of the state.

Barrow's goldeneye, Bucephala islandica, *is an uncommon diving duck that winters along the Maine coast.*

Male common eider, Somateria mollissima, *a seabird that was almost extinct in Maine at the turn of the century, now nests abundantly on about 250 Maine islands. The current population numbers about twenty-five thousand pairs. Courtesy of Maine Department of Inland Fisheries and Wildlife.*

Barrow's goldeneye is an uncommon diving duck, which in winter may be found in flocks on salt or brackish waters. As its name suggests, its eyes have rich yellow irises. Coloration is similar to the common goldeneye: males of both species have a large amount of white on their bodies, but the Barrow's is blacker above. The Barrows male also has a more crescent-shaped white spot on its face, and its dark head has a purple gloss rather than green. During its swift flight, its wings make a musical whistle. The Maine coast lies within the goldeneye's eastern wintering range, which extends primarily along the northeast coast to the Gulf of St. Lawrence. Breeding occurs mainly in western North America and in Iceland.

The common eider duck is not listed in any endangerment category, but its story is worth including here because it demonstrates the remarkable comeback of a sea bird once driven almost to extinction by egg collectors and market hunters.[8] In 1907 only one breeding colony was reported on the Maine coast, but over twenty thousand pairs are known to exist today. In fact, Maine, which is near the extreme southern edge of the duck's breeding range, is the only state that has a major breeding population.

The beautiful and strikingly patterned black-and-white male eider contrasts sharply with the camouflaged brown female. It is her responsibility to build the down-lined nest, usually on a relatively small uninhabited island. After she lays three to five eggs and begins incubation, the male leaves.

During the twenty-six-day hatching period, she "sits tight," rarely feeding and relying instead on accumulated fat reserves for energy. Within a day of hatching she leads the ducklings to the water, where they congregate in protective groups known as creches. These consist of several families and often number six to ten adults and twenty or more ducklings. The adults are ever alert for danger; when one quacks out a warning, all the ducklings rush together into a tight cluster and the adults surround them, quacking and thrashing their wings at the hovering gull or other predator.

Surprisingly, although the common eider is preyed upon by herring and great black-backed gulls, it often nests in close association with these predators. It appears that the gulls' loud alarm calls help to warn the eider of the presence of other dangers. As with other colonial nesting sea birds, eider ducks are disturbed by human activities, and a continuing effort is required to protect nesting islands and sites.

Wading Birds

The configuration of a wading bird reflects 100 million years of evolutionary development and is a well-tested example of form following function: sleek, flexible, long neck with deadly spearlike bill atop a tall, stilt-supported, mobile launcher. For fish, amphibians, reptiles, and insects living in shallows and wetlands, the shadow of one of these long-legged waders would likely warn of an imminent attack.[9]

Most of the nine species of waders living in Maine nest in colonies. This habit of congregating during breeding season almost spelled the demise of herons and egrets along the Atlantic and Gulf coasts of North America. Many of the colonial nesting birds are elegantly feathered, and the splendor of their mating plumage once attracted more than just females of their own species; Victorian ladies also found them appealing, and market hunters responded with such vigor that by the turn of the century the birds were nearly eradicated. Among those killed for their plumage were the great blue heron and black-crowned night heron, the only colonial nesting birds living in Maine at that time.

Protection was afforded with the passage of the Federal Migratory Bird Act of 1918, and the great blue heron reestablished itself. By 1983, twenty coastal island colonies existed, containing over twelve hundred nests. It's estimated that up to 25 percent of the Atlantic coast's population of blue herons now breed in Maine. As of 1986, there were also sixty-three known mainland colonies, with a total of 841 nests.[10] The number of black-crowned night heron nests, however, has remained low.

Now well-reestablished, great blue herons, Ardea herodias, *nest in almost every major coastal bay east of Portland. The larger heronries are commonly on islands near food supplies in shallow estuarine waters, but great blue herons are found in smaller inland colonies as well. Hank Tyler photo.*

Among Maine's wading birds, the relatively uncommon least bittern is the only species with indeterminate status. Although the least bittern breeds throughout the eastern half of the continental United States, only a relative few breeding sites are known to exist in Maine. The smallest member of the heron

The least bittern, Ixobrychus exilis, *is an uncommon wading bird of indeterminate status in Maine.*

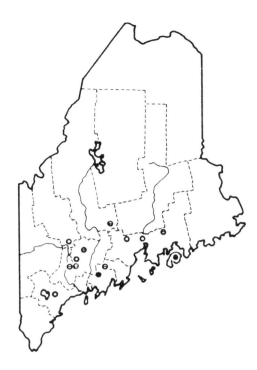

Distribution of least bittern in Maine. Redrawn from P.R. Adamus, comp. Atlas of Breeding Birds in Maine, 1978–1983 *(Augusta: Maine Department of Inland Fisheries and Wildlife, 1987).*

family, it stays well hidden, thanks to its protective coloration—dark cap and back and buff and chestnut wing patches—and its shy and secretive nature.

Unlike most other wading birds, the least bittern is a solitary nester. The male appears to choose the site, usually among dense cattails, and builds the nest with materials gathered by the female. Between May and July an average of four to five eggs are laid. Incubation lasts approximately seventeen days. When the young are only three to four days old, they assume the hiding posture characteristic of adults by pointing their bills straight up in the air and swaying as would cattails in the wind.

The black-crowned night heron, like the least bittern, is a wading bird of indeterminate status. This night-stalking wader has a shorter, thicker neck and shorter legs than the other herons. It is distinguished by its black crown, dark green back, pale gray wings, bright red eyes, and two long, narrow, white plumes on the back of its head.

The black-crowned night heron, Nycticorax nycticorax, *is a rare wading bird that once frequented all of Maine. It now nests on only a few southern and mid-coast islands. Fred Bavendam photo.*

Except perhaps for Australia and China, the black-crowned night heron has a worldwide distribution. It breeds throughout much of the continental United States, and on the east coast reaches the northern extent of its range in New Brunswick and Quebec. In 1977 Maine's Critical Areas Program estimated that about 120 pairs nested on eight islands along the Maine coast. These include islands in Kittery, Biddeford, Scarborough, Harpswell, Bristol, and an unorganized township in Hancock County.

Nests are built of twigs, usually about six to twenty feet above the ground. Being very social, black-crowned night herons will often nest together, with several pairs building nests in the same tree, or with other species of herons. Between May and July, one to six eggs are laid. Both sexes participate in the incubation. After the young leave the nest, they pursue the adults for food, which consists of whatever is available at the time and place: small fish, snakes, salamanders, frogs, crabs, clams, insects, and even the young of other nesting birds.

From the 1950s through the 1970s, five wading birds—the snowy egret, little blue heron, tricolored heron (also known as the Lousiana heron), cattle egret, and glossy ibis—began moving into Maine from states to the south where they are common. Today, they are seen with greater frequency and are expected to increase. It is still unknown whether this expansion of their ranges is due to population increases, disturbances within the centers of their populations, or some other cause.

These five species of wading birds nest in dense concentrations, often on offshore coastal islands. The control of excessive visitation and other disturbances during nesting is absolutely necessary to prevent abandonment of nesting areas and the death of young birds. So is protection of their food sources—the marshes and tidal flats of estuaries, which are vulnerable to pollution and other effects of human activity. For these reasons, populations of these species are on the state's watch list and will be monitored.

The snowy egret is perhaps the handsomest of all herons in Maine, especially in the breeding season when lacy nuptial plumes adorn its snow white plumage. Its black bill and bright yellow feet, contrasting sharply with its black legs, distinguish it from other white herons and egrets. When feeding

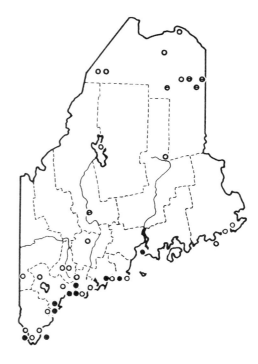

Distribution of black-crowned night heron in Maine. Redrawn from P.R. Adamus, comp. Atlas of Breeding Birds in Maine, 1978–1983 *(Augusta: Maine Department of Inland Fisheries and Wildlife, 1987).*

Snowy egrets, Egretta thula, *have nested in Maine only since the 1960s. They are found on several bird sanctuaries off the coast of York and Cumberland counties. Leonard Lee Rue III photo.*

Glossy ibis, Plegadis falcinellus, *nests throughout the world in tropical and mild latitudes, including a few islands off the southern Maine coast. Chris Ayres photo.*

in shallow water for small fish and other aquatic organisms, it uses one foot to stir the bottom, attracting prey by the movement of its bright yellow toes.

Since the 1950s, the snowy egret has been seen with increasing frequency in Maine. The first nests were discovered in the early 1960s. It can now be found in the marshes and estuaries of York, Cumberland, and Sagadahoc counties, and has been observed nesting on Islesboro and other coastal islands in Kittery, Biddeford, and Scarborough.

It wasn't until the late 1960s that another unfamiliar wader, the glossy ibis, appeared in Maine. Distributed throughout much of the world, this heronlike bird is rapidly extending its range along the Atlantic coast. The first nesting pair in the state was recorded on Stratton Island in Saco Bay in 1972. Since then, the population has increased from fewer than one hundred to several hundred nesting pairs per year. Generally they are found in rookeries with black-crowned night herons and snowy egrets on islands off York County. The glossy ibis is an unusual-looking bird, easily distinguished by its long, down-curved bill and glossy dark maroon, almost black, plumage. In flight it holds its neck outstretched and beats its wings rapidly.

The late 1960s also produced the first sighting in Maine of the little blue heron, but it wasn't until 1975 that it was confirmed as nesting in the state, on Wood Island, a Maine Audubon Society sanctuary in Biddeford. A little over half the size of the great blue heron, this small, dark heron is more shy and retiring. Unlike other herons, it is snow-white when immature. In this phase it can be distinguished from other white waders by its olive legs and pale, bluish-tipped bill. Like most other herons, it constructs a loose, flimsy clump of sticks

The little blue heron, Florida caerulea, *was first sighted in Maine in the late 1960s.*

in a tree for a nest. At night it roosts in trees in groups, but during the day may be seen hunting near shores for fish, frogs, crayfish, and insects and other invertebrates.

Often associated with the little blue heron is the tricolored heron. Only slightly smaller, it is easily distinguished from the little blue by its body color—slate blue, with white rump and chestnut throat. Along with the little blue heron, it escaped hunting pressure from the millinery trade because its plumes were not considered as attractive as some other species'.

Ordinarily the tricolored heron breeds near salt water, from northern South America to the southeastern United States, and wasn't discovered nesting in Maine until 1977. Today this active feeder can sometimes be seen just offshore in southern coastal Maine, running with its wings raised or sticking its foot in the shallows and moving it rapidly to flush its prey of fish, tadpoles, crayfish, leeches, insects, and other small animals.

Another white wader, seen first in the late 1970s in Maine, is the ubiquitous cattle egret. Formerly found exclusively in Portugal, Spain, and Africa, it has rapidly expanded its range to almost every continent. The first reported sighting in North America occurred in Florida in the early 1940s. The cattle egret is now found scattered over a wide area of the eastern half of the United States, where it is usually seen feeding in pastures and fields with cattle and horses. In fact, it will often perch on cattle, which, while grazing, frighten insects and other small animals from the grass and into the beaks of waiting egrets.

Upward of forty colonies of wading birds are estimated to exist along Maine's coast. To protect these important but vulnerable natural areas, more than twenty rookeries have been designated as Critical Areas, including sites in Kittery, Biddeford, Machiasport, and Islesboro.

Shorebirds

Most shorebirds live about half their lives along the edges of sandy shores and mudflats, particularly in the intertidal zone. The remainder of their time is spent on the wing or in marshy meadows or fields. They are generally long-legged, graceful, and skittish. As a group they include plovers, turnstones, and sandpipers—some two hundred species worldwide.

Among Maine's many shorebirds only the piping plover is listed as endangered by the state (any by the federal government as well).[11] This small,

The cattle egret, Bubulcus ibis, *was first seen in Maine in the late 1970s.*

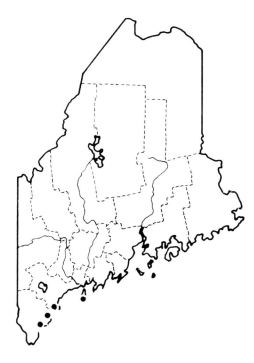

Distribution of piping plover in Maine. Redrawn from P.R. Adamus, comp. Atlas of Breeding Birds in Maine, 1978–1983 *(Augusta: Maine Department of Inland Fisheries and Wildlife, 1987).*

Piping plover, Charadrius melodus, *is a very rare sandpiper that nests on coastal sandy beaches and is found on only a few south coastal beaches in Maine. Patrick W. Grace photo.*

plump bird is protectively colored, matching the sandy beaches it inhabits. In summer it can be identified by its complete or incomplete dark neck ring, yellow legs, and yellow, black-tipped bill. Resembling a robin in feeding behavior, it picks up marine worms and other small animals on the beaches. Its nest is out in the open, simply a shallow depression in the upper beach. All told, about seventy-five days are required for incubation and care of the young before they leave their vulnerable nesting site.

Once plentiful, the piping plover was severely diminished by unlimited hunting during the last half of the 1800s. After federal law removed it from the gamebird roster it made somewhat of a comeback, but today it appears to be in a serious noncyclical population decline throughout its range. In Maine it finds few natural sand beaches, and it must compete with humans and natural predators for those it does find. People pose the greatest threat, and the plover must contend with beach walkers, vandals, and housing developments. It is now a rarity, with only a half dozen or so nesting sites in the state. In an effort to prevent the loss of this delightful and interesting beach bird, five piping plover breeding sites were designated as Critical Areas in 1977: one site in Scarborough, two in Phippsburg, and two in Wells. In the mid 1980s, observers reported only one Phippsburg site in use. Statewide in 1986, only five coastal sites with fifteen nesting pairs of piping plovers were reported.

The upland sandpiper, though not endangered, is a species of indeterminate status. Low numbers and possible alteration of habitat provide justification for concern about the future of the upland sandpiper in Maine until more information is obtained. In the United States, it suffered widespread destruction by market hunters in the late 1800s as a substitute for the disappearing passenger pigeons. As a consequence, it never regained its former population numbers. Today the upland sandpiper is rare in Maine; only a few nesting sites are known, the most productive of which are in eastern parts of the state.

Distribution of upland sandpiper in Maine. Redrawn from P.R. Adamus, comp.
Atlas of Breeding Birds in Maine, 1978–1983 *(Augusta: Maine Department of Inland Fisheries and Wildlife, 1987).*

The upland sandpiper, Bartramia longicauda, *is a species of indeterminate status in Maine.*

Like most sandpipers, the upland species is a small- to medium-size brownish shorebird with a bill that is more slender than those of the plovers. Unlike most other sandpipers, however, it is seldom seen near water in Maine, preferring to live in blueberry barrens or in hayfields and meadows. In these habitats, most of its diet consists of insects.

After arriving in the spring from its wintering site on the pampas of Argentina, the upland sandpiper constructs a grass-lined nest on the ground.

Four eggs are usually laid in May or June. About two months later the young are ready to fly.

Several species of shorebirds are on the state's watch list and recommended for monitoring primarily because significant numbers of them migrate through Maine and therefore depend on the availability of unpolluted and productive coastal mudflats, beaches, and marshes for feeding and resting spots. Three are in the plover family: the semipalmated plover, black-bellied

Black-bellied plover, Pluvialis squatarola. *From* Introduction to Our Bird Friends, *Maine Audubon Society, Orville O. Rice, artist. Reprinted with permission of Capper's Books.*

plover, and ruddy turnstone. As a group, plovers can be distinguished from sandpipers by their compact size, thicker necks, shorter, pigeonlike bills (slightly swollen at the tips), larger eyes, bolder colors and markings, and habit of running in short starts and stops. All three species nest on Arctic tundra in summer, and they winter from the coastal United States to the southern hemisphere.

Nine other species of shorebirds on the watch list belong to the sandpiper family: the short-billed dowitcher, whimbrel, greater and lesser yellowlegs, sanderling, dunlin, least sandpiper, semipalmated sandpiper, and white rumped sandpiper. Generally they are more slender than plovers, with more tapered bodies, longer and thinner bills, and longer legs. Their sizes range from the sparrow-sized least sandpiper (5 to 6.5 inches long) to the whimbrel (nineteen inches long).

The ruddy turnstone, Arenaria interpres, *and the black-bellied plover*, Pluvialis squatarola, *are two shorebirds in the plover family recommended for monitoring. From* Introduction to Our Bird Friends, *Maine Audubon Society, Orville O. Rice, artist. Reprinted with permission of Capper's Books.*

The sanderling, Crocethia alba, *is one of the nine species of shorebirds in the sandpiper family on Maine's watch list. From* Introduction to Our Bird Friends, *Maine Audubon Society, Orville O. Rice, artist. Reprinted with permission of Capper's Books.*

Northern, or red-necked, phalarope, Phalaropus lobatus, *a sandpiperlike bird on Maine's watch list, migrates through Passamaquoddy Bay during August and September.*

Another shorebird that bears watching is the northern, or red-necked, phalarope. A large portion of its population migrates through Passamaquoddy Bay during August and September. It looks much like a sandpiper and has lobed toes, which make it equally at home wading or swimming. In winter, when it is seen in Maine, it is gray with a dark patch through its eyes and streaked above. Its bill is black and needlelike. When feeding, it picks at the water for plankton, insects, and other tiny aquatic life, upending like a duck, and often spinning around and around. On shore, it runs around much like a sandpiper.

Inland Water Birds

Maine's profusion of freshwater lakes, ponds, and waterways provide havens for a variety of inland water birds. Not only do they have vital roles in these ecosystems, but they bring enjoyment to thousands of residents and summer visitors. Three are of special interest: the black tern, watch-listed because of its critical habitat requirements; the American black duck, which is seriously declining along its eastern flyway and is also on the state's watch list; and the common loon because of its popularity and the widespread public involvement in the monitoring of its numbers.

The black tern is a sleek, mostly black, water bird, easily distinguished from its generally white coastal relatives.[12] Unlike them, it nests on inland marshes and lakes. It arrives from its winter home in South America in late May and begins nesting in early June. Nests are built on abandoned muskrat houses or masses of floating dead vegetation just above the water. Normally three eggs are laid. After hatching some twenty days later, the young begin eating insects within two hours and start swimming a day later. In a month or less they are able to fly, and they begin to feed by skimming the water or vegetation for insects. Small fish near the water's surface may also be taken. By mid August they begin their fall migration.

The black tern breeds over a large part of the northern hemisphere, but Maine is on the eastern edge of its North American range so it has never been

Black tern, Chlidonias niger, *is very rare in Maine and nests in only a few freshwater marshes in central Maine. Fred L. Knapp photo.*

abundant in the state. The largest and only continuously used nesting site is in Belgrade, where up to six to eight pairs have been observed in an extensive marsh system. This area was designated as a Critical Area in 1977. (It is especially important to avoid nesting areas from the middle of May to the end of July to prevent parents from unnecessarily leaving the nest and exposing eggs and chicks to the sun, rain, or predators.)

Those who have heard the eerie laugh and haunting, echoing call of the common loon on a northern lake will never forget its startling and captivating sound. But its call is not its only attraction: the summer plumage of this red-eyed bird of inland waters is exquisitely patterned in black and white stripes and checks. In winter, however, it becomes nondescript, darkish above and whitish below. The loon is a large bird, up to three feet long with a wingspread of almost five feet.

The common loon nests in Iceland, Greenland, Canada, Alaska, and across the northern United States. It winters to the south along the Atlantic, Pacific, and Gulf coasts, as well as on the Great Lakes. Spring migration usually takes place in April and May, when it flies to northern lakes and ponds where food is plentiful. It feeds primarily on fish, which it captures by diving and chasing them underwater. Crayfish, frogs, salamanders, leeches, and aquatic insects also add to its diet. Loons are able to dive to depths of two hundred feet and may, when pursuing or pursued, stay under water for up to three minutes.

Common loon, Gavia immer. *Maine is fortunate to have a healthy loon population. Fred L. Knapp photo.*

Loon nests are close to the water and are constructed of grasses, rushes, and twigs. The same pair generally returns to the same nesting site year after year. Usually two eggs are laid between mid-May and the last half of June. Both parents incubate the eggs for about four weeks. After hatching, the young can swim within twenty-four hours but are sometimes seen riding on their parents' backs instead.

Although loons breed throughout the state and their numbers appear fairly stable, they are scarcer in southern sections. Shoreland development and the increased human presence probably are responsible for their decline in these areas. In the 1980s, monitoring was stepped up in Maine because of declining loon populations in New Hampshire and Massachusetts.

Female and male American black ducks,
Anas rubripes. *A seriously declining
population since the mid 1950s accounts
for this species being placed on Maine's
watch list. Leonard Lee Rue III photo.*

The American black duck is a wary, alert, and quick game bird, very dark in color with violet wing patches. When the bird is in flight, its wing linings display flashes of white. Found throughout northeastern North America, the black duck nests over much of Maine, usually on the ground near marshes or open water. Broods average nine or ten ducklings. Some, when they leave the nest, must waddle after the mother for a mile or more to reach water. There they quickly learn the dabbling technique of feeding on submerged plants and small aquatic animals.

Since the middle of this century, the black duck population has declined—as much as 76 percent for the wintering population since 1955. Causes of the decline are not completely known, and some explanations have generated controversy. Changing land uses of wintering areas, competition from other species, overharvesting, hybridization with mallards, poisoning by lead shot injested during feeding, acid rain, and commercial insecticides have all been suggested as contributing causes.

Songbirds

Some of the best known and most enjoyed birds are those that make music—the songbirds. During spring and summer, it is the male of most species that sings to advertise his territory and his availability as a mate. The mating songs are the primary songs, and consist of complex, elaborate patterns and phrases of notes. They are believed to be completely inherited behavior in some songbirds, a partly learned skill for others. The height of the musical season occurs during the spring and early summer breeding season, when some birds sing over two thousand songs in a single day.

Songbirds add immense pleasure to our lives. Not only do many have melodious voices, but they are colorful and interesting to observe. The value of any outdoor setting is enriched by their presence. Unfortunately, and mostly due to our ignorance of how human activities affect them, some songbirds have declined in recent years. One, the loggerhead shrike, is extirpated from the state.

The grasshopper sparrow is one of Maine's two endangered songbirds, a designation reflecting its dangerously low numbers and its reliance on a small patch of unique and threatened habitat.[13] Most would probably describe this small, secretive sparrow as unimpressive, especially in comparison with such attention-getting birds as the raptors. A sharp tail and flat head characterize its shape. Its colors, rather drab browns and yellows above and unstreaked buff below, serve it well for an unobtrusive life scurrying through the weeds and grasses in search of insects.

Each spring the grasshopper sparrows leave their wintering region, which extends from the southern states as far south as El Salvador, to nest over a wide

The grasshopper sparrow,
Ammodramus savannarum, *is one of
Maine's two endangered songbirds.*

UNCOMMON WILDLIFE

area of the United States. The principal attraction for those which arrive in Maine is a six-hundred-acre area of commercial blueberry barrens in York County—the Kennebunk Plains. Here, at the northeasternmost edge of the sparrow's range, a burning/harvesting cycle has produced a distinctive ecosystem of short, woody blueberry bushes, bunching grasses, and other herbaceous plants in which the species thrives.

A high, thin, dry, insectlike buzz, sung day and night by both male and female, announces the sparrows' arrival. At some time during the spring and summer four to five creamy white, speckled eggs are laid in a well-camou-flaged ground-nest constructed of grasses. After twelve days of incubation the young hatch, and in another nine days they are ready to leave the nest. It is not uncommon for a pair to have two broods during a season.

In the early 1980s, about thirty pairs of grasshopper sparrows were discovered nesting on the Kennebunk Plains—the second largest colony in New England. Since the early 1900s there had been no record of their breeding in Maine. The excitement of the discovery soon turned to concern, however, for in 1983 the herbicide hexazinone (known by the trade name Velpar) was introduced in Maine to increase blueberry production. It kills a wide variety of the plants that compete with blueberries. The effect was a drastic alteration of the ecosystem upon which the sparrows depended. By the latter half of the 1980s, only about a dozen pairs of grasshopper sparrows nested on the plains, apparently as a result of the Velpar treatment. Also threatened by the herbicide was the rare northern blazing star: 60 to 80 percent of the world's population of this beautiful purple wildflower grows on the plains. Fortunately, the Maine Chapter of The Nature Conservancy was able to raise funds to purchase over 100 acres of the Kennebunk Plains, and with the continued cooperation of public and private interests, the grasshopper sparrow and the wild plants in its habitat may still have a future in Maine.

Another songbird on the endangered list is the sedge wren. Catching a fleeting glimpse of this small and quick bird would be an unusual experience in Maine, and finding a nest would be a singular event indeed. Although in the past nests have been recorded, there are no current reports of any in the state.

The sedge wren is a very small bird, 4 to 4.5 inches long. Its short, slim bill once gave it the name short-billed marsh wren. It is brown like other wrens, but can be identified by its streaked crown and back and the buff-colored feathers under its short, cocked tail. Energetic and elusive, it flits among the grasses and sedges of freshwater meadows, capturing insects and spiders.

In the spring, the sedge wren migrates from its wintering range in South America and the southern United States to nest in local areas over a wide area of southern Canada and the eastern half of the United States. Arriving first, the male builds dummy nests, perhaps as a courtship gesture or a method of marking its territory. Interestingly, when the young of some species of wrens leave their nest, the male may lead them to one of these dummy nests for overnight sleeping. The sedge wren often has two broods of six or seven young per season. They are raised in a ball-shaped, well-hidden nest of woven grasses and sedges, one to two feet above the wet ground.

The water pipit is the only species of songbird in the special concern category. Although it is a widespread migrant and breeds over a large area of northern Canada and Newfoundland, only one nesting location is known in Maine. This is on Mt. Katahdin in Baxter State Park, and it breeds there only in small numbers. The water pipit is a sparrow-size ground bird, identified by its brownish color, streaked underparts, white outer tail feathers, thin bill, and long hind claws. It walks briskly, bobbing its tail constantly as it searches for

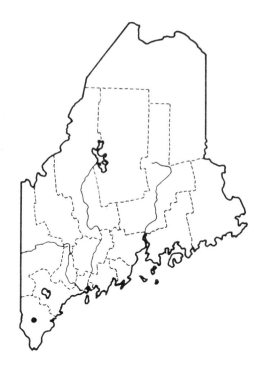

Distribution of grasshopper sparrow in Maine. Redrawn from P.R. Adamus, comp. Atlas of Breeding Birds in Maine, 1978–1983 *(Augusta: Maine Department of Inland Fisheries and Wildlife, 1987).*

The sedge wren, Cistothorus platensis, *is the second songbird on Maine's endangered species list.*

insects and seeds. In flight its song consists of thin, weak, paired notes. While migrating, it is sometimes seen on bare fields and along shores. Nests of dried grasses and twigs are built and occupied from June to July on tundra and alpine slopes. About a month is required to raise the four to five young it commonly has each year.

Left: *Distribution of water pipit in Maine. Redrawn from P.R. Adamus, comp.* Atlas of Breeding Birds in Maine, 1978–1983 *(Augusta: Maine Department of Inland Fisheries and Wildlife, 1987).*

Right: *Distribution of horned lark in Maine. Redrawn from P.R. Adamus, comp.* Atlas of Breeding Birds in Maine, 1978–1983 *(Augusta: Maine Department of Inland Fisheries and Wildlife, 1987).*

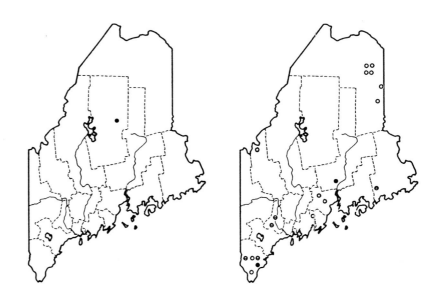

The horned lark, Eremophila alpestris, *is a small songbird about which more information is needed to determine its status in Maine. From* Introduction to Our Bird Friends, *Maine Audubon Society, Orville O. Rice, artist. Reprinted with permission of Capper's Books.*

The horned lark is a songbird of indeterminate status in Maine. Small, but larger than a sparrow, it has distinctive black sideburns and breast splotch, and small, black, horn-shaped feathers on its head. When flying overhead it displays a black tail and folds its wings after each beat. The claws on its hind toes, known as larkspurs, are very long.

A bird of prairies, open fields, airports, golf courses, and (in migration) beaches, the horned lark breeds over a wide area of the northern hemisphere. Courtship involves a spectacular aerial display in which it climbs to more than eight hundred feet. There it circles, emitting a high-pitched flight song. Then it plummets headlong to earth, keeping its wings closed almost to the very end. Nesting consists of simply selecting a slight hollow in the open on bare ground in which four eggs are laid.

The orchard oriole, another songbird of indeterminate status, lives in Maine in low numbers. Unlike its more common and colorful relative, the Baltimore oriole, the male is all black except for deep chestnut underparts and rump and two white wingbars. The female is olive green and yellowish in color. It is a slimmer bird than the robin and measures six or seven inches long, compared to the robin's nine to eleven inches.

The orchard oriole flies in the spring from South America to its summer breeding range, which extends from central Mexico through the eastern and central United States to southeastern Canada. Here it searches the fringes of woods, orchards, and shade trees for insects, which make up 90 percent of its diet. Its cup-shaped nest of beautifully woven grasses hangs suspended from a tree or bush six to twenty feet high. An average of four to five young are hatched each year.

Three songbirds are being watched in Maine for possible population problems: the eastern bluebird, vesper sparrow, and sharp-tailed sparrow. The bluebird now appears to be recovering from a severe population decline. Competition from starlings and house sparrows is considered a major cause, along with the loss of old orchards through changing land use. It is also possibly the hole-nesting songbird most victimized by cowbirds, which lay their eggs in the nests of other birds, leaving the unwitting "host" birds to hatch and raise the cowbirds' young rather than their own.

Although secure in Maine at the present time, the vesper sparrow is declining in numbers, probably due to its dependence on the limited (and shrinking) availability of the short-cropped dry upland fields, pastures, and meadows in which it nests and feeds on insects and seeds. It is another species known to live on the Kennebunk Plains. The sparrow's breeding range extends into Canada and the central United States. Identifying marks include white outer tail feathers and white eye ring.

The sharp-tailed sparrow is another bird with critical habitat requirements—it breeds only in coastal salt marshes. Its more distinguishing characteristics are a yellow face surrounding gray ear patches and an unstreaked, blackish cap. Secretive in its habits, it runs through the grass hunting for insects and spiders and looking for seeds. It summers along the northeastern Atlantic coast and the Canadian prairies and winters along the southern Atlantic and Gulf coasts.

The variety of birdlife in Maine can be directly attributed to the diversity of habitats present in the state. Protecting those areas where birds live is the key to their survival. To this end, it is important that each of us exercises a watchful and protective eye. Sightings and concerns may be reported to any one of a number of agencies and organizations, such as those listed in Appendix B.

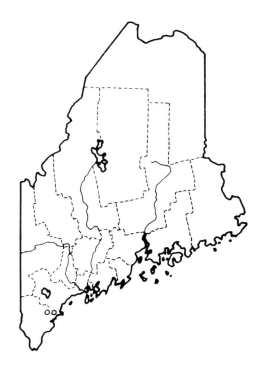

Distribution of the orchard oriole in Maine. Redrawn from P.R. Adamus, comp. Atlas of Breeding Birds in Maine, 1978–1983 *(Augusta: Maine Department of Inland Fisheries and Wildlife, 1987).*

The eastern bluebird, Sialia sialis, *is one of three songbirds whose populations are being watched in Maine. From* Introduction to Our Bird Friends, *Maine Audubon Society, Orville O. Rice, artist. Reprinted with permission of Capper's Books.*

Mammals

Mammals descended from flesh-eating reptiles 190 million years ago, before the birds. Even these earliest species were insulated by fur, had glands to provide milk for their young, and, most important, showed the first indications of a complex brain. For the next 120 million years their development was slow, but they proliferated during the past 70 million years; today, an estimated four thousand species roam the earth. Of the more than three-hundred and fifty terrestrial species that live in North America, about sixty are found in Maine. Another twenty-six species of marine mammals have been reported at one time or another in the Gulf of Maine.

We human beings belong to this class of vertebrates, and historically we have always looked to other mammal species for pleasure, comfort, and survival. For most of us, an encounter with a wild mammal creates interest, if not curiosity and excitement. We often come upon them with unpredictable suddenness, and many a tale has been told and retold about these face-to-face meetings—a wandering moose peering through a window, a deer on the edge of the road, or a fox in the field. Other encounters are more of a nuisance: the woodchuck in the garden, a mouse in the house, the porcupine that leaves the dog's nose studded with quills. But despite the problems some may present, mammals on the whole are beneficial to us.

They provide untold hours of pleasure to painters, photographers, writers, and other observers. Mammals provide sport for hunters and are sought by trappers, furriers, and others with commercial interests. But their greatest value, we are beginning to surmise, is their role in maintaining a healthful environment. Much is still unknown about mammals and their roles in the ecosystem, and for this reason they are of great scientific interest.

The long association of people and wild mammals in Maine is not unlike that in other places. For the early natives and European settlers, deer, moose, bear, and others were a source of food. Lynx and beaver pelts were used for clothing and blankets. However, over the years the kind and number of mammal species varied due to both natural causes and human activities. Some were forced out of the state, or extirpated: the wolf in the mid 1800s, the eastern mountain lion at the turn of the twentieth century, and the woodland caribou by the early 1900s. The giant sea mink was less fortunate—it was actually driven into extinction. Other species, such as the moose and the fisher, overcame severe declines in their populations and made dramatic comebacks during the twentieth century. Once protected by law, both can now be taken in limited numbers. Although land use changes have taken their toll on mammal populations, Maine still provides a diversity of habitats unparalleled in the eastern United States.

Protection of habitat remains the key to the survival of mammals. Because we do not yet fully understand the natural regulation and interrelationships of wild animals, it is imperative for their future that we think carefully before altering the landscape. We still have little detailed knowledge of the natural history of many mammals, but we do recognize the importance of preserving habitats such as bat caves, deer wintering yards, and seal haulout ledges. In addition, we have been able to identify some species that are threatened by low or declining numbers or problems of habitat and need our attention now.[1]

Marine Mammals

Few mammals fascinate us as much as do whales and porpoises (cetaceans) and seals (pinnipeds).[2] For example, the songs of humpback whales—combined with other evidence of cetaceans' high intelligence—have captured the interest of the public, creating a desire to learn more about the remarkable habits and abilities of these sea creatures.

Humpback whale, Megaptera novaeangliae, *a federally endangered species, summers in the Gulf of Maine. Steve Savage photo, courtesy of Allied Whale.*

Twenty-one species of whales and porpoises (a term used broadly to include dolphins) and five species of seals have been reported in the Gulf of Maine. Those seen most often are the finback, minke, and humpback whales, the harbor porpoise, and the harbor seal. These are usually sighted along the coast and in the offshore waters of eastern Maine. At one time the walrus was also an occasional visitor and may have been hunted by early native peoples.

Maine's coastal waters from the Bay of Fundy to New Hampshire are important habitat for a number of populations of sea mammals. The area is a feeding and breeding range for the harbor porpoise and the harbor seal and part of the native range of the gray seal. Whales migrate along the coast in spring and summer, following the movement of zooplankton, squid, and schools of herring and other fish. During the summer, humpback and finback whales appear to feed east of Penobscot Bay in the region of Mt. Desert Rock and the approaches to the Bay of Fundy. The humpback, right, and other large whales are most often found in waters between 120 and 300 feet deep. At the end of October or during November, the humpback, minke, and right whales begin their migration south to breed, while the pilots and finbacks move offshore to winter in warmer waters.

Humankind has a long history of hunting marine mammals. Records show that whaling occurred as early as 890 A.D. off the coast of Norway. Native Indians are thought to have hunted whales from canoes using stone-headed arrows and spears. Whaling took on greater significance with settlement of the New England colonies; both whale and seal harvesting became commercially important, and the industry became a way of life for many coastal residents. Demand was high for whalebone—used in ladies' corsets—and whale oil for lamps. Whalers spent quiet hours on the long, monotonous voyages carving scrimshaw designs on whale "ivory"—usually the teeth. Ambergris, an infected mass sometimes found in the whale's intestines, brought a high price from the perfume industry. The period from 1825 to 1860 became known as the "golden age of whaling." Since then whaling has declined, due as much to diminishing demand and readily available substitutes for whale products as to the decreasing numbers of animals. With passage of the Marine Mammals Protection Act in 1972, whaling activities ceased in the United States and Canada. As of 1986, however, Japan, Russia, and one or two European countries still continued to hunt whales.

During the nineteenth century, a regular fishery for harbor porpoises existed in the Bay of Fundy and at Grand Manan Island, where several thousand were taken yearly. Elsewhere along the New England coast, porpoises were taken less regularly. They were primarily hunted for their oil, which was marketed for lamps and lubrication.

Gray and harbor seals were also hunted by the Indians of New England. European settlers continued to take them, sometimes for the meat and hides, but more often to reduce competition for fish. In fact, seals came to be considered such a threat to fisheries that Maine and Massachusetts initiated bounties in the late 1800s that lasted well into the middle of the twentieth century.

Today, gray and harbor seals still inhabit the Maine coast. Forty-four significant haulouts have been identified, over three-quarters of them located from Penobscot Bay east. Haulouts are gently sloping rocky areas—usually small, unvegetated islands or half-tide ledges—used by seals for resting, breeding, pupping, and feeding.

Marine mammals are subjects of increasing scientific and educational study. They are also objects of a growing public interest, as evidenced by the increasing number of commercial sightseeing excursions. However, during this time when we are becoming increasingly aware of their unique and valuable qualities, the survival of many species is being threatened. In addition to continued hunting by a few countries that choose to ignore protective international laws and regulations, a number of other human activities appear to be important issues: accidental entrapment in commercial fishing nets, oil and gas development on the outer continental shelf, and alteration and contamination of coastal habitat.

Two factors make marine mammals particularly susceptible to the effects of contaminants: their relatively high position in the aquatic food chain, which concentrates pollutants in the organisms they eat in their tissues; and their long life spans, which allow debilitating and deadly quantities of toxins to accumulate. Pesticide compounds, including DDT and dieldrin, polychlorinated biphenyls (PCBs), and heavy metals, particularly mercury, could be especially harmful. However, more data on the effects of contaminants are needed before we can fully assess the threat they present.

Five species of whale found off the Maine coast are now federally listed as endangered: the right, humpback, finback, sperm, and sei whales. The right whale is found primarily in northern oceans. It was named by whalers, who considered it the "right" one because it swims slowly (and so was easier to catch), has thick blubber, which could be melted for the valuable oil, and floats when dead, making it possible to flense the whale as it lay alongside the ship rather than having to winch it aboard. It also has long baleen, the rows of "whalebone" (actually plates of keratin) hanging from the upper jaw that act as a giant sieve to filter great quantities of planktonic copepods and krill shrimps from sea water. It is a large whale; averaging about forty-four feet long, although it may reach as much as fifty to sixty feet. Unlike other large whales, it lacks a dorsal fin.

The right whale skims the water when feeding, either at or below the surface. It may be found feeding both in coastal waters and well out at sea. Mating occurs between May and July and is followed by a ten- to twelve-month gestation period. There is some evidence that a population, or pod, of right whales breeds near the entrance to the Bay of Fundy.

Because it was easier to kill, the right whale was one of the first pursued

The right whale, Eubalaena glacialis, *is an endangered species sometimes found off the Maine coast.*

by early whale hunters. And a prize it was, for a single whale might yield up to thirty tons of oils. Severely depleted by hunting, which continued until the early 1900s, the right whale population still shows little sign of recovery. Total world population is estimated at between three and four thousand, with only a few hundred of these in the North Atlantic.[3]

In spite of being protected by law, the right whale still faces a number of problems. There are documented instances of whales becoming entangled in fishing gear and drowning; also, due to its method of near-surface feeding, it may be affected by oil spills. It is also speculated that the sei whale may outcompete the right whale for food, displacing it from its northern feeding grounds.

The humpback whale is another of the nine species of giant baleen whales. It is forty to fifty feet long, relatively short when compared with the others. Identifying characteristics include rough skin, long, white, irregular flippers,

Feeding humpback whales filter mouthfuls of seawater through the baleen plates that fringe their upper jaws, trapping herring and other small fish. Scott Mercer photo, courtesy of Allied Whale.

individual fluke patterns, paired blowholes, and an acrobatic habit of jumping from the water. Humpbacks live in schools for companionship as well as protection, for they are sportive and sociable. However, it is only the adult males that compose and perform the songs for which the humpback is noted.

World population is estimated at around ten thousand animals— alarmingly few considering that the humpback's numbers may have at one time exceeded a hundred and twenty thousand. By current estimates, the western North Atlantic population is less than six thousand.[4]

During the summer, humpbacks are found in the western North Atlantic from Long Island to Greenland. They are popular with whale watchers and are often spotted in waters off the coast of Maine. In fact, they appear to be increasing in the herring-rich approaches to Cobscook Bay and Passamaquoddy Bay. They also feed regularly in the Mt. Desert Rock area. In winter, humpback whales migrate to warm waters, such as Silver Bank in the Caribbean. Mating occurs between January and March, and calves are born in the same waters eleven to twelve months later. It is only at their wintering grounds that humpbacks compose their famous songs; feeding, not singing, is their primary activity during the summer months in the Gulf of Maine and other northern waters.

Each year, an undetermined number of humpbacks become entangled and killed in fishing gear—weirs, nets, lines, seines, and traps. PCBs and pesticides have also been found in their tissues, although information on their long-term effects is lacking. More research is urgently needed so that we may properly manage and protect these rare mammals.

The finback whale is the most common of the large whales in the Gulf of Maine. It averages sixty feet long, and is flat-headed with a gray upper body. Its belly, the inner sides of its flippers, and the undersides of its flukes are white.

A finback whale, Balaenoptera physalus, *at Mt. Desert Rock. Bob Bowman photo, courtesy of Allied Whale.*

A white stripe also crosses the right side of its jaw. Another distinguishing characteristic is the spout, which can reach fifteen to twenty feet high and is accompanied by a loud whistling sound.

Finback whales were in 1977 estimated to number 7200 off the coasts of Newfoundland and Nova Scotia. They are found all along the American and Canadian Atlantic coast, and groups of thirty to fifty are often seen inshore during late spring and summer, engaged in feeding frenzies—rushing, lunging, and circling as they capture krill, herring, and squid. From June to September, finbacks feed regularly in the Mt. Desert Rock region. In winter they move offshore to warmer waters. Mating occurs between November and March. After an eleven- to twelve-month gestation, a calf is born, usually exceeding a length of twenty feet.

The finback whale is the most common of the large endangered whales in the Gulf of Maine.

The endangered sperm whale, Physter catodon, *rarely strays into Maine waters.*

Sperm whales are generally found in the Atlantic Ocean from the West Indies to Labrador. They tend to stay in offshore waters well out to sea, very rarely straying into the Gulf of Maine. About twenty thousand are estimated to live in the North Atlantic. Males can reach sixty feet in length and weigh up to fifty-three tons. Females are about half that size. Identifying characteristics include a square snout on a large head (which accounts for about one-third the length of the animal), absence of a dorsal fin, and blue-gray coloration, darker on the back and sides. The lower jaw has many teeth, some up to eight inches long. Food consists primarily of squid.

The sperm whale appears to have a complex communication system of sounds and, at various times of the year, a social structure based on sex and age. In summer, mature males migrate further north than females and juveniles, which tend to remain in warmer waters.

The sei whale is a member of the finback family. In appearance it is similar to the finback but darker and smaller, reaching fifty feet, or perhaps more, in

The sei whale, Balaenoptera borealis, *is an endangered mammal that usually stays well away from the coast.*

length. Its dorsal fin is relatively large. Food consists of plankton and small fish. Like the sperm whale, it usually stays well out to sea. Distribution in the North Atlantic includes a wide area from the Gulf of Mexico and the Caribbean to Nova Scotia and Newfoundland. Three stocks are thought to exist; the whales off the coast of Maine belong to the Nova Scotia stock, while the other two groups are to the north and south. Estimates for the Nova Scotia stock range from less than one thousand to over two thousand individuals.

Seals are another group of marine mammals inhabiting the North Atlantic. Two, though presently secure, are of special interest: the gray seal because it is rare in the United States, and the harbor seal due to its having made an unusual comeback after its numbers were severely reduced around the turn of the twentieth century.

The gray seal, Halichoerus grypus, *which stays well out to sea, is seen less frequently than the harbor seal in Maine.*

The gray seal is also called the horsehead seal because in profile its raised Roman nose and large muzzle resemble those of a horse. It is a large seal, averaging seven to nine feet in length. Major populations exist in eastern Canada, Iceland, and northwestern Europe. The number in the North Atlantic is estimated at over one hundred thousand, but only a hundred or fewer individuals are thought to summer in Maine. The gray seal stays out to sea, where the fish that make up the bulk of its diet are more readily available, and so it is seen less frequently than is the harbor seal. Sightings are occasionally made around Mt. Desert Island, Swans Island, and the lower Penobscot Bay area.

The nearest known breeding ground is at Sable Island in Nova Scotia. Minor breeding populations are found around Grand Manan, New Brunswick, and Muskeget Island off Massachusetts. Unlike other marine mammals, which mate only in water, the gray seal mates either on land or in water. Mating occurs in March, and pups are born in January or February of the next year.

The harbor seal is small, about five to six feet long. Its coarse hair varies from yellow-gray to gray. It hunts alone for herring, squid, flounder, alewife, and other fish, but on land it congregates in herds. Mating occurs from early May to August. Pups are born the following year from late April to mid-June.

A young harbor seal, Phoca vitulina, *the commonest marine mammal along the Maine coast. Harbor seal populations have rebounded since the seals were afforded protection through the Federal Marine Mammals Protection Act. Harriet Corbett photo, courtesy of Allied Whale.*

Although it was nearly exterminated in the state around 1900, today an estimated fourteen thousand harbor seals are permanent residents of coastal Maine. Sightings occur throughout the year, most often in lower Penobscot

Bay near Mt. Desert Island and in Machias Bay, where the animal is seen on half-tide ledges, small harbor islands, or swimming. It is also known to enter estuaries and rivers.

Land Mammals

We might expect that Maine's rare land mammals would be more familiar to us than their marine relatives, but that doesn't appear to be completely true. In fact, some rare terrestrial mammals actually seem to be even more elusive and difficult to study than those of the sea. Fifteen species have been listed by Maine's Endangered and Nongame Wildlife Project, many because we simply do not know that much about them.

The northern bog lemming is an elusive, volelike mammal that is threatened in Maine. Although this rodent's range extends over a wide area of Canada to southern Alaska, only five have been recorded in Maine—all in the Katahdin area of Baxter State Park, where two populations are known to exist. The first two specimens were captured in 1902, but it wasn't until eighty-three years later, in 1985, that three others were trapped.[5]

Much like a meadow vole in appearance—about four inches long, brown, with hidden ears and small eyes—the northern bog lemming can be distinguished by its shorter tail (about one inch compared to the vole's two-inch tail). Any doubts about a specimen's identity, however, can be resolved by observing its upper incisors: the bog lemming's are grooved.

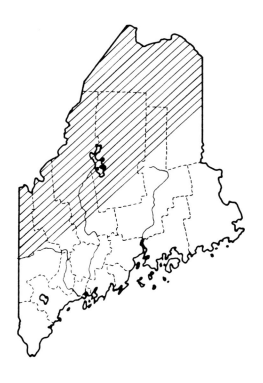

Distribution of the northern bog lemming in Maine. Redrawn, with permission, from A. J. Godin, Wild Mammals of New England *(Baltimore: Johns Hopkins Univ. Press, 1977).*

The northern bog lemming, Synaptomys borealis, *is a threatened species in Maine.*

For those who go looking for this rare mammal of bogs, alpine meadows, tundra, and spruce woods, a sharp eye is required to discern the subtle signs of its presence. These include piles of green fecal pellets along runways, grass cuttings, and round, grassy nests about eight inches in diameter.

The New England cottontail rabbit, often called "cooney" by hunters, is another mammal that rarely ventures from its habitat.[6] It is smaller than its Maine relative, the snowshoe hare, weighing 1.5 to 2.5 pounds. It also has shorter ears and a short tail, cottony white below. The most conspicuous difference shows up in winter, when the hare turns white but the cottontail retains its brownish color and identifying black patch between its ears. Like all hares and rabbits, the cottontail has long, sensitive ears, long hind legs, keen nose, and bulging, wide-visioned eyes as its built-in defense system to detect and escape its enemies.

The cooney inhabits woodlands and brushlands from New England southwest through the Allegheny Mountains. It prefers areas with numerous brushpiles and low, dense vegetation for cover and with abundant sprout growth, grasses, and other herbaceous plants for food. Such a habitat also provides protection from foxes, hawks, and other predators. In addition, the cottontail has a number of protective habits, including nocturnal feeding, thumping the ground with a hind leg when alarmed (which also warns other rabbits of danger), and freezing in place when threatened.

The cooney also has an amazing reproductive rate, averaging three to four litters each year and five young per litter. Mating, which occurs from March to August, is followed by a one-month gestation period. The young, which weigh less than an ounce at birth, are born naked and blind in a concealed nest lined with the mother's downy fur. Within hours of giving birth, the female mates again.

Despite its fecundity, the New England cottontail is declining over all its range, including Maine, probably as a result of vanishing habitat (and possibly hybridization). Loss of its brushland habitat to development, natural succession in abandoned farmlands, and maturing of burned and cut-over forested areas have all taken their toll, and the cooney is now limited to scattered populations in coastal towns in southern Maine. Following the large forest fires of 1947, there was an especially notable build-up of the cottontail population in York and southern Oxford counties, but these forests are now well beyond their young, brushy growth stages. For these reasons, the New England cottontail is placed in the special concern category.

Several mammals in Maine currently have indeterminate status, principally because information about numbers, population trends, distribution, and real and potential threats is difficult to obtain. One is the Canada lynx.[7] Because of its shy habits, scarcity, and limited range, this cat of the deep north woods is one of Maine's least known mammals. Only a practiced eye can detect the subtle signs of its presence: indistinct trails, occasional scat, and inconspicuous scratching posts.

Similar in size to its relative the bobcat, the lynx measures up to three feet

A litter of cottontail rabbits. The New England cottontail, Sylvilagus transitionalis, *is declining over all its range, including Maine, where scattered populations exist in southern sections. Leonard Lee Rue III photo.*

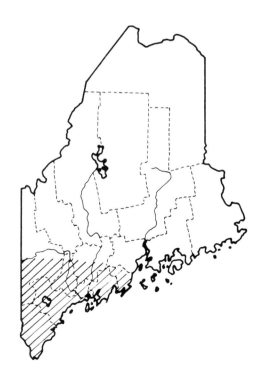

Distribution of the New England cottontail in Maine. Redrawn, with permission, from A. J. Godin, Wild Mammals of New England *(Baltimore: Johns Hopkins Univ. Press, 1977).*

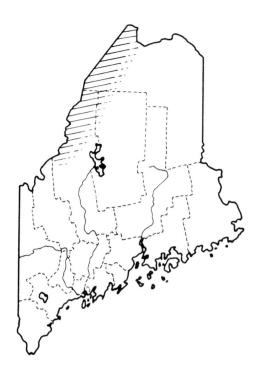

Approximate distribution of the Canada lynx in Maine. Redrawn from John H. Hunt, Maine Dept. of Inland Fisheries and Wildlife.

long and eighteen inches high and weighs up to forty pounds. Its relatively long tawny fur is mixed with blackish guard hairs and its short tail is also tipped with black. Long, prominent black ear tufts provide sensitive antennae to enhance its hearing. Its long legs and well-furred feet move it quickly and powerfully over snow in pursuit of its principal prey, the snowshoe hare. So tightly linked is this predator-prey relationship that the lynx's numbers in a given area appear to coincide with the nine- to ten-year population cycles of the hare. In its catch-as-catch-can world, however, the lynx will not pass up opportunities to take birds, voles, and even small winter-weakened deer. Once a kill is made, the lynx will sometimes cache it for a later meal.

In the spring, three or four kittens are born in a nest, which is often located in a ledge or fallen tree. (Unlike many cats, the young lynx have their eyes open at birth.) The parents step up their hunting during the summer, when the young must be fed, but by fall the kits have learned to hunt for themselves. However, they stay with their mother until mating occurs in late winter. At that time, the adults may break their habit of silence by uttering shrieks or screams ending in long wails.

The Canada lynx is found over much of Canada and Alaska and across the far northern areas of the United States—Washington, Oregon, Idaho, Montana, Wyoming, Michigan, Wisconsin, New York, and New England. In

The Canada lynx, Lynx canadensis, *is rarely found south of Moosehead Lake or east of the St. John and Allagash rivers. Leonard Lee Rue III photo.*

Maine it is rarely found south of Moosehead Lake or east of the headwaters of the West Branch of the Penobscot, St. John, and Allagash rivers, although one was found dead in York County in 1973.

The lynx, like the bobcat, once could be hunted year round, and fifteen dollars was paid by the state for every kill. Then, in 1967, the State Legislature removed the bounty and protected the lynx. However, its life in the state since then has not been without difficulty. Accidental trapping of the lynx in bobcat traps has been a problem. Also, increased cutting of northern forests, plus spruce budworm damage, has drastically changed large areas of its habitat. Finally, the widespread construction of new roads has increased human access and thus the temptation to poach the lynx for its valued pelt. For these reasons, Maine's Canada lynx populaiton warrants further study.

The southern flying squirrel is another species about which we lack specific knowledge. This is an appealing little mammal with a thick, glossy coat of fur, grayish-brown above and white below.

Flying squirrels are among the most fascinating of our small mammals. These four-footed land creatures perform the amazing feat of gliding between trees on a flight path of eighty yards or more. The flying squirrel leaps spread-eagle into the air from the top of a tree, the folds of skin between its hind legs and forelegs forming a combination sail and parachute that enables it to maneuver in flight and brake to a light four-footed landing on the trunk of another tree. Unfortunately, its nocturnal habits deprive most of us of the opportunity to marvel at this special adaptation.

The southern flying squirrel is widely distributed throughout the eastern half of the United States. Its range extends into the deciduous forests of southern Maine, where this small tree squirrel finds the acorns, seeds, and berries that make up the bulk of its diet. Abandoned woodpecker holes are a favored nesting site. In winter, several may nest together in one hole. Mating occurs in late winter to early spring. Forty days later, a litter of two to six young are born, and there may be a second litter in late summer.

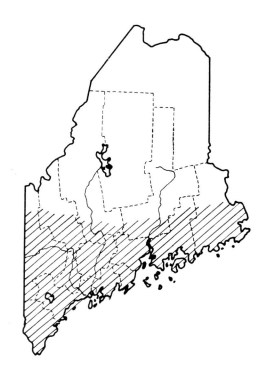

Distribution of the southern flying squirrel in Maine. Redrawn, with permission, from A. J. Godin, Wild Mammals of New England *(Baltimore: Johns Hopkins Univ. Press, 1977).*

The southern flying squirrel, Glaucomys volans, *although widely distributed throughout the eastern United States, is of indeterminate status in Maine.*

The yellow-nosed vole, also called the rock vole, is a mouselike rodent related to lemmings and muskrats.[8] It is five to seven inches long, with a tail relatively long in proportion to its body. Brownish above and gray below, the vole sports a yellow-orange nose as its most distinguishing characteristic.

This small mammal inhabits moist, rocky areas and woodland slopes of mountains from North Carolina to Labrador, preferring cool crevices in moss-covered rocks with abundant moisture and water near by. Its dietary requirements are satisfied by bunchberries, blackberries, blueberries, grasses, and thread moss. Moss also is used for its nest, in which it raises two to three litters each summer. Four is the average number of young per litter.

The yellow-nosed vole was first discovered on Mt. Washington in New

The yellow-nosed vole, Microtus chrotorrhinus, *was first discovered in Maine in 1923.*

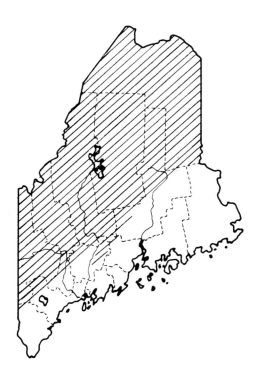

Distribution of the yellow-nosed vole in Maine. Redrawn, with permission, from A. J. Godin, Wild Mammals of New England (*Baltimore: Johns Hopkins Univ. Press, 1977).*

The eastern pipistrelle, Pipistrellus subflavus, *is the smallest bat in the eastern United States.*

Hampshire in 1893. In 1923 it was discovered in Maine, on Mt. Coburn in Somerset County. Since then it has been collected from only a few sites, including Sugarloaf Mountain and Mt. Katahdin. Although this vole was previously found only above three thousand feet in Maine, a specimen was trapped at thirteen hundred feet on the western border of Baxter State Park in the summer of 1985. Until more information is available, the yellow-nosed vole is classified as having indeterminate status.

Eight bat species also have indeterminate status on Maine's list of endangered and threatened species: the silver-haired bat, red bat, hoary bat, big brown bat, Keen's myotis, little brown myotis, small-footed myotis, and eastern pipistrelle.[9] Additional information is required about their wintering and breeding sites, distributions, population sizes and trends, and potential threats before a more precise classification of each can be made.

Bats are amazing mammals in many ways. They hold the distinction of being the only mammals capable of true flight, and, despite poor vision and nocturnal flight habits, they fly with uncanny maneuverability, guided by their internal sonar. Echoes of self-emitted supersonic waves bounce back from objects in their paths to be picked up by the bat's dished, antennalike ears. Bats are able to determine the size, location, and movement of obstacles and prey with astounding accuracy.

All bats in North America are insectivorous, and they catch astonishing quantities of flying insects on the wing, either directly in their mouths or in a scooplike membrane between their hind legs and tail. Only slow-motion films reveal to our slower human senses the truly amazing precision and grace of

bats' flight. During the summer months, when insects are plentiful, bats are among the most numerous of our wild species of mammals.

The wings of bats are a marvel of adaptation. Arm bones and muscles have become enlarged to support their "flying hands"—greatly elongated fingers connected by naked, translucent membranes. Thumbs have evolved into claws, by which bats can hang. When their wings are folded, they can also walk and climb.

Like all small mammals, bats have their enemies. Probably owls are the major predators, although hawks may catch them as well. Blue jays are also known to prey on red bats. On a much smaller scale, bats are affected by fleas, ticks, and mites. Some cases of rabies have also been reported among bats, but incidences of rabid bats attacking humans or other animals are extremely rare.

Three bats (the silver-haired, red, and hoary) migrate in winter to southern parts of their range, where food is plentiful, though they are also known to hibernate. All are heavily furred on the upper portion of their tails. Because they hide in hardwood foliage and fissures in the bark of trees in the summer, their numbers are affected by the abundance of hardwood trees in a given area.

The silver-haired bat, approximately 3.5 to 4.5 inches long, is a beautiful mammal, nearly black, with silvery-tipped hairs on its back, giving it a frosted appearance. Its range covers most of the United States and southern Canada.

The silver-haired bat, Lasionycteris moctivagans, *has indeterminate status on Maine's list of endangered and threatened species.*

A red bat, Lasiurus borealis, *carrying her young. This is one of eight bat species needing further study to determine their status on Maine's list of endangered and threatened species. Leonard Lee Rue III photo.*

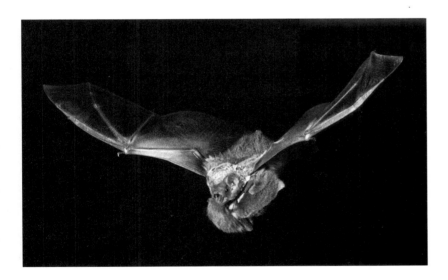

The red bat, which is similar to the silver-haired in size, is one of the few mammal species whose coloration differs between the male and female. The male is brick red or orange-red, whereas the female is distinctly darker. Both are frosted white on their backs and breasts. The range of the red bat, like that of the silver-haired, extends over much of the United States and Canada. Unlike most other bats, which usually have one or two young, this bat has four or five offspring and is the only bat with four nipples rather than two.

The hoary bat, which can be up to six inches long, is the largest bat in the East. Its fur is light brown on the back, heavily frosted with white. Although widely distributed throughout southern Canada and the continental United States (except for the Florida peninsula), it is rarely seen because there are so few in any one location. It is also the only known bat in the Hawaiian Islands.

Rather than migrate, some bats go into a deep sleep or hibernate through the winter period of food deprivation. These are the cave bats. They must find

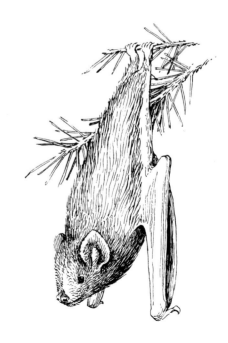

The hoary bat, Lasiurus cinereus, *is the largest New England bat.*

Keen's myotis, Myotis keenii, *is a long-eared bat that hibernates in caves or mines.*

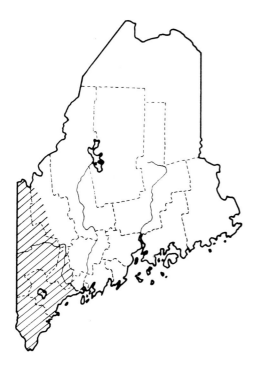

Distribution of the eastern pipistrelle in Maine. Redrawn, with permission, from A. J. Godin, Wild Mammals of New England (*Baltimore: Johns Hopkins Univ. Press, 1977*).

The big brown bat, Eptesicus fuscus, *commonly frequents buildings and other structures.*

The little brown myotis, Myotis licifugus, *one of the most common bats in the United States, needs further study before its status in Maine can be asessed.*

places for hibernation that are suitably quiet, dark, and—of critical importance—the right temperature. A few such caves have been discovered in Maine. Since most bats mate in the fall, females of many hibernating species have the ability to store sperm, delaying fertilization until spring and thus preventing the young from being born during the winter.

Keen's myotis is a long-eared brown bat, 3 to 3.5 inches long. It feeds on small insects, especially flies. Its range includes the northern Pacific coastal region and a large area from Saskatchewan to Newfoundland and south to Georgia. Hibernation occurs in caves or mines, either singly or in groups of four to six.

The reddish to light brown eastern pipistrelle is the smallest bat in the eastern United States, weighing only an eighth to a quarter of an ounce. During the daytime it usually hangs in vegetation, emerging in early evening to feed on small insects, including beetles, flies, and leafhoppers. Hibernation occurs in caves, mines, and crevices. Its range covers the eastern United States, west to Texas and southeastern Minnesota.

The big brown bat, twice the weight of the eastern pipistrelle and up to five inches in length, is found over much of the United States and southern Canada. It is reported to be able to fly at forty miles per hour, the fastest speed of any bat.

The little brown myotis is one of the most common bats in the United States. It can reach 3.75 inches in length and weigh up to half an ounce. In spring it forms nursing colonies. If disturbed, the mother may flee carrying the young. In the fall, the bat may fly several hundred miles to find a suitable cave or mine for hibernation. Its range covers much of North America in a wide belt from central Alaska and Hudson Bay southward through most of the United States except Florida, Texas, and southern California.

The small-footed myotis is light tan to golden brown above and buff or nearly white below, with a black mask and ears. It is small, measuring up to 3.75 inches long and weighing about one-quarter ounce. Populations are concentrated over much of the western United States and, in the East, from Maine south through the Appalachians.

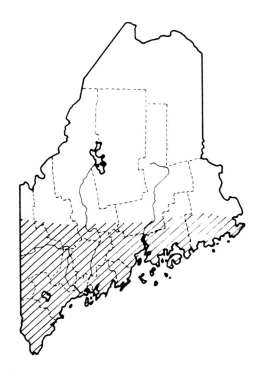

The small-footed myotis, Myotis leibii, *is a small bat of indeterminate status in Maine.*

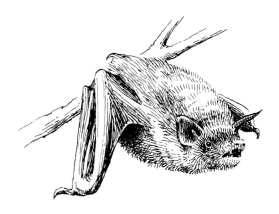

Two species of mammals are on the state's watch list: the southern bog lemming and the long-tailed shrew. The southern bog lemming looks similar to the northern bog lemming except that it lacks the northern lemming's rust-colored hairs at the base of the ears. It is brown above and silvery below, with a very short tail and inconspicuous ears and eyes. Contrary to its name, the southern bog lemming seldom lives in bogs, preferring instead grassy meadows, where grass and clover form the bulk of its diet. In turn, the lemming provides food for many other mammals, birds, and snakes. Its range includes a large portion of the central and eastern United States, running north to Manitoba and Newfoundland.

The long-tailed shrew is dark gray with a long, slender body and a tail that

Distribution of the small-footed myotis in Maine. Redrawn, with permission, from A. J. Godin, Wild Mammals of New England *(Baltimore: Johns Hopkins Univ. Press, 1977).*

The long-tailed shrew, Sorex dispar, *is a seldom observed mammal on Maine's watch list.*

accounts for almost half its four- to five-inch length. It is found in mountainous areas from Maine south to North Carolina and Tennessee. It is also known as the rock shrew because it prefers cool, moist environments in deep recesses among boulders, where it hunts spiders, beetles, and other small invertebrates. Only a few living specimens have been observed.

Mammals are among the most fascinating of animals. Because most of them are quiet, nocturnal, and secretive, a sighting of one usually attracts much interest, though these very qualities tend to limit our knowledge of them. Nonetheless it is very important that we learn more about these uncommon species in order to better evaluate their status on the endangerment list, and the task of expanding our knowledge about them is one to which everyone can contribute by reporting sightings to appropriate agencies and organizations, such as those listed in Appendix B.

Natural Regions of Maine

Perspective

Nature, of course, is not uniform but varies as a function of historical geology, climate, physiography, soils, plants, animals and—consequently—intrinsic resources and land uses. Lakes, rivers, oceans and mountains are not where the economist might want them to be, but are where they are for clear and comprehensible reasons. Nature is intrinsically variable.

Ian L. McHarg[1]

A traveler anywhere in Maine cannot help but be struck by the changing landscape: narrow and V-shaped valleys wind among rolling hills and mountains, becoming gentler and broader as they approach the sea; rivers and streams drain bogs and marshes, occasionally widening into lakes and ponds as they, too, make their way to the ocean; and everywhere the forest, with its infinite wardrobe of colors and textures, cloaks the countryside. As unplanned and random as it may seem, this varied landscape shows detectable rhythms and patterns, which in turn reflect underlying natural laws. No single feature—plant, animal, or rock—stands alone; each is connected to all the others in a web of complex interrelationships, the results emerging on the landscape as distinguishable geographic regions.

Why is it important to know about geographic regions? Everything in nature has its place, either as the result of geologic events, as in the case of waterfalls and gorges, or as a matter of ecological relationships, as demonstrated by plants and animals. Understanding how elements of land, climate, and life intermesh and how they vary from place to place makes us better able to manage and protect natural features, because we can fully appreciate the delicate relationships that have developed in each setting. Nowhere is this more crucial than in our treatment of endangered and threatened species, for the consequences of our failure to intervene on their behalf may be that we are left with only an image on paper or a specimen under glass to remind us of our failure.

Virginia Lake, Oxford County,
is part of the White Mountain National
Forest. E.T. Richardson, Jr., photo.

14

A Richly Varied Landscape

The fact that several distinct natural regions can be identified in Maine is confirmation natural elements do not exist in isolation, but are grouped by forces and affinities they have in common. How one divides an area (any area—one's backyard, or a city) is determined by what one views as important. So it is with the natural environment of Maine; over the years scientists have divided and classified the land in literally hundreds of ways. Divisions have been based on soils, bedrock geology, surficial geology, elevation and relief, slope of the land, watersheds, wetlands, forest types, climate, and wildlife habitats—to name but a few. Four factors, however, have special influence in determining Maine's natural regions: land, water, biota, and climate.

Landform, in particular, influences the regional variations, affecting both climate and vegetation. Cooler, higher elevations favor the alpine plant communities usually associated with colder regions. North-facing slopes receive less sunlight and are subject to colder winds, and these conditions also tend to support plants related to northern areas. Logically enough, plant communities that prefer more southerly latitudes and drier soils tend to grow on sunwarmed, south-facing slopes.

Landform also influences the location and character of lakes and ponds, rivers and streams, and wetlands, which in turn profoundly affect the terrain. The presence of water also alters the characteristics of soil, local conditions of climate and weather, and the distribution of vegetation and wildlife.

The composition of the bedrock and the layer of weathered materials near the surface directly influence both the landform and soils in a region and, ultimately, its plant communities. An unusual number of soil types are found in Maine, ranging from the rich alluvial and calcareous loams of Aroostook County to the sandy soils of river valleys, and from the sandy and gravelly southern outwash plains to the thin, rocky, acid soils of mountaintops and the eastern coastline.

The biota is another important factor in demarcating Maine's natural regions. Vegetation affects the character of soil by contributing organic matter, the shape of the land by limiting runoff and controlling erosion, and local climate by influencing the amount of sunlight reflected and the amount of moisture retained near the surface or transpired into the atmosphere.

Vegetation also exerts a strong influence on which species of wildlife will be present in an area. This is understandable, since most animals ultimately depend on plants for food and shelter. Animal life, in turn, affects vegetation— for example, through pollination and grazing —and soil, through such activities as burrowing and adding organic matter.

In the short term, climate influences the distribution of vegetation and wildlife; in the long term, it affects the weathering of landforms and development of soils. Elevation and landform exert an influence on climate by modifying temperature, precipitation, and wind. So too does the ocean, which has a marked effect on climate in the coastal region.

Based on these considerations, seven natural regions have been identified in Maine for the purposes of this book: (1) coastal, (2) southern oak-forest, (3) upland-hilly, (4) mountain, (5) northern forest, (6) Aroostook limestone, and (7) eastern peatlands. Although the boundaries are in reality less distinct than those shown on the accompanying map, the regions nevertheless represent distinguishable areas having common features. (The definitions and descriptions of these regions draw heavily on *The Natural Regions of Maine*, a report prepared for Maine's Critical Areas Program by Paul Adamus.)[1]

Coastal Region

One of the most distinctive regions is the coast, notable for its low elevation and relief and convoluted profile, with numerous peninsulas, harbors, and islands. The boundary between this region and the adjacent hilly sector is principally a difference in relief and climate, and thus not sharply defined.

Elevations in the coastal region are generally less than two hundred feet, and in some areas, under one hundred feet. As anyone who has traveled up and

Great Wass Island, in Washington County, is a Nature Conservancy preserve supporting a great diversity of rare plant species and plant communities. (Coastal region.) Hank Tyler photo.

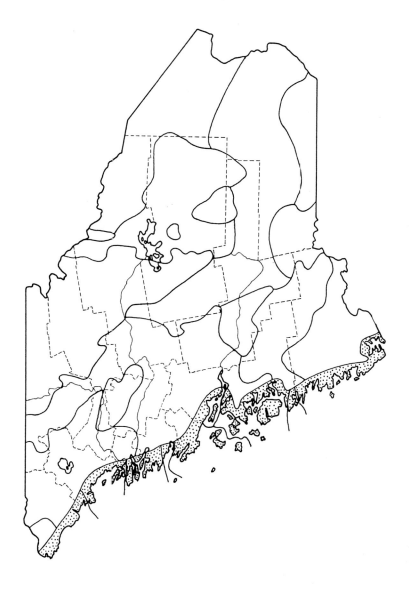

Coastal region

down its many peninsulas knows, Maine's coastline is extremely irregular. In fact, if it were stretched out, the "as the crow flies" measurement of 230 miles from Kittery to Quoddy Head would become nearer 3500 miles. Adding further to the coast's complexity — and to its attraction—are hundreds of islands.

Much of the basic shape of the land in the coastal region is due to the orientation and weathering of the ancient bedrock. Here the well-exposed rock reveals layers of sediments and lava, variously metamorphosed and intruded. Many strata are compressed into a series of parallel folds, running from northeast to southwest. Differences in the rock's susceptibility to erosion further contribute to the coastal landform.

More recently, glacial erosion and deposition changed the shape of the Maine coast. Only twelve thousand years ago, as the last glacier receded, the coastal plain was under sea water. Since then, gradual adjustments of the land mass and fluctuations in sea level have given the coast a relatively new rocky edge. Wave action continues to refine the irregularities: eroding headlands to form cliffs, filling depressions, developing and altering marshes and beaches. Sea cliffs and other erosional features are relatively numerous along some sections of the coast.

The last glacier also left an abundance of glacial debris and marine silts and clays. These materials, along with sorted sands and gravels, lie in scattered river deltas, eskers, and an assortment of mounds and plains. The soils are largely determined by the nature of these deposits and are generally shallower and more sterile than those inland.

Also included in the coastal region are the numerous estuaries where Maine's rivers meet the sea, with their associated salt marshes and mud flats. Ponds and lakes, however, are more scarce in the coastal region than in any other.

The Atlantic Ocean is the most important single factor affecting the region's climate. Due to its sheer mass, the sea responds more slowly to the changing temperatures of the seasons than does the land, and this effect is transferred to the surrounding atmosphere. This results in less severe winter temperatures and consequently a growing season longer than that of other regions—but, paradoxically, less productive, owing to cooler summer temperatures and (particularly in eastern Maine) frequent fogs that blot out sunlight.

Fog is caused by prevailing wind patterns that bring southern warm air in over the cold coastal waters. In July and August, fog banks hover offshore almost constantly, although they are usually less prevalent toward the heads of bays and along the warmer western parts of the coast. Of the total amount of sunshine possible in a year, the portion reaching the coastal region varies between 50 percent at Eastport and 60 percent at Portland.

Precipitation is greater along the coast than inland, averaging about six inches more a year. However, snowfall averages thirty to forty inches less than in northern regions. Fewer thunderstorms occur along the coast, for the storm cells usually weaken and dissipate as they reach the cool ocean air.

The climate is most responsible for the character of vegetation in the region. East of Casco Bay, where the climate is cooler, the spruce-fir forest prevails, undoubtedly the most noteworthy feature of the coastal region's vegetation. South of Casco Bay, the warmer climate and better-drained soils favor mixed northern hardwoods and hemlock. White pine is found on drier, sandier sites. Pitch pine is favored where areas have been burned, as is jack pine, which also occurs sporadically on shallow soils.

Especially noteworthy are the region's birdlife, marine mammals, fish, and invertebrates. Characteristic bird species nesting along the coast include bald eagle, osprey, alcids, terns, and a variety of waders. A great many birds stop for food and rest on their migrations, and others winter over in the sheltered, brackish waters of ice-free bays and estuaries.

Several species of whales (such as the humpback, finback, and minke) as well as dolphins are seen frequently offshore, and throughout the length of the coast, seals swim and bask on ledges. Beneath the waters live the Atlantic sturgeon, Atlantic salmon, shad, and numerous other species. At the sea's edge, the tidal zone is the home for an amazing diversity of invertebrates.

The coastal region is probably the most varied of all regions in Maine. Because of this, four coastal subregions can be distinguished: sandy beach, transition, Penobscot Bay, and eastern.

Sandy Beach Coastal Subregion

The sandy beach coastal subregion extends from Scarborough south to Kittery. It has a relatively straight coastline, a gentle slope to the sea, many sandy beaches, and the greatest acreage of salt marsh in the state. Overall, its

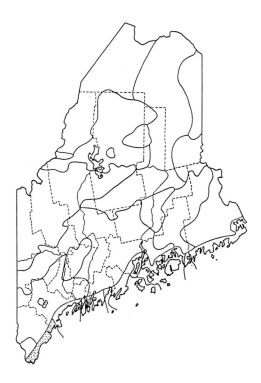

Sandy beach coastal subregion

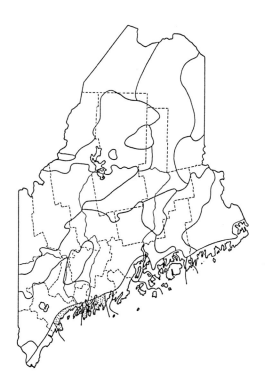

Transition coastal subregion

character is more similar to the coasts of New Hampshire and northern Massachusetts than to the rest of Maine.

Glacial outwash deposits of granitic sands and gravels cover most of the region and are particularly noticeable between Kennebunk and Moody. North of Kennebunk, marine clays give more evidence of glacial influence. Most notable are the many sand beaches, a distinct contrast to the other coastal subregions.

Beneath the cloak of sand and clay, belts of folded bedrock run parallel to the shoreline. These are responsible not only for the straightness of the coast but also for the position and direction of the few islands found here. Outstanding outcrops, such as the dike swarms in the Ogunquit area, graphically illustrate some of the area's geologic history. Extensive erosion of the abundant sedimentary and metamorphic crystalline rocks has worn and softened most marine features.

Meandering across the generally low, slightly rolling surface, cutting through the soft sands and clays, are many rivers and streams. The larger rivers—the York, Mousam, Kennebunk, Saco, and Nonesuch—supply the most productive salt marsh estuaries in Maine. Scarborough Marsh is the largest in the state. Others worthy of mention are at Kennebunkport and Wells.

Migrating birds following the Maine coast stop over at the productive marshes, mud flats, and estuaries in this section. Biddeford Pool is especially significant for its migratory bird concentrations—as is Scarborough Marsh, although the latter also supports many breeding species. Some of these, like the marsh's nesting willets, are rare in Maine due to the fact that they are at the northern edge of their range. So too are the little blue herons, glossy ibis, and snowy egrets, which nest in colonies on islands in Biddeford and the Isles of Shoals. In summer, a few colonies of least terns and piping plovers may be found nesting on the sandy beaches, and areas of brackish open water in coastal marshes and estuaries provide winter habitat for black ducks and other waterfowl.

Transition Coastal Subregion

Extending eastward from the sandy beach subregion to Penobscot Bay is the transition coastal subregion, so named because here the dominant forest type shifts from the white pine and hardwoods typical of the southern Maine coast to red and white spruce and balsam fir. From Scarborough to Rockland the coastline is unusually irregular, deeply indented, and rocky. Numerous islands clearly show the characteristic northeast-southwest folding of the bedrock formations of the Casco Bay Group. Superb coastal exposures of these rocks extend from Scarborough to the Kennebec River, providing valuable information about the complex geologic history of southwestern Maine.

Between the ridges and overlaying the old bedrock are deep marine deposits of sand, silt, and clay—evidence of glacial outwash. Noteworthy glacial features include the outwash plain of the Bristol-Pemaquid peninsula, the sand plains of Brunswick, kame fields east of Freeport and on the Boothbay peninsula, and a small esker north of Boothbay.

Flowing into the bays and inlets between the fingers of land are dozens of rivers. These include the Presumpscot, Royal, Sheepscot, and Damariscotta, but the largest is the Kennebec, which meets the ocean at historic Popham. Two of Maine's most outstanding sand beach systems are those at Popham Beach State Park and Reid State Park. Small ponds and kettlehole wetlands dot the peninsulas, although they are more scarce southwest of Brunswick.

Along the water's edge varied temperatures, wide-ranging salinities, and complex currents combine with an exceptional diversity of habitats—sandy beaches, rocky shores, mud flats, and bays and inlets—to support perhaps the greatest assortment of marine life in Maine. Here quahogs, oysters, and several other marine invertebrates reach their northern limits. In the lower reaches of the Kennebec and Sheepscot rivers live Atlantic and shortnose sturgeon. Just north of Bath, at the confluence of the Kennebec, the Androscoggin, and four other rivers, lies Merrymeeting Bay. This bay, along with the many other estuaries and back coves in the subregion, shelters thousands of migrating, wintering, and breeding birds.

Penobscot Bay Coastal Subregion

The beautiful Penobscot Bay coastal subregion—with its cool waters, rocky coastline, and forests of red spruce and balsam fir—typifies Maine. Extending from Muscongus Bay to Frenchman's Bay, this area is notable for Penobscot Bay, with its many domed granitic islands, and for the state's largest and most famous island, Mt. Desert, where Cadillac Mountain rises 1580 feet above the sea. To the southwest, Mount Megunticook, at 1380 feet, is the second highest coastal mountain.

Here, as on the rest of the Maine coast, the land's exposed, wave-washed, rocky edge displays the effects of powerful geologic forces. Large areas of granite, the darker and coarser gabbro, and other igneous rocks may be found. The glint of sparkling flecks of mica in the widespread grainy schists, particularly in the area southwest of Belfast, reveals the effects of tremendous heat and pressure on the bedrock. Only in a relatively few places did the rock escape these changes, and where it did, mainly in the strata of islands in Penobscot Bay, fossils are evident. Near Castine and on Mt. Desert Island, volcanic rocks are widespread. On one island, pillow lavas—where blobs of molten basalt cooled underwater in plump mounds—give further evidence of volcanism. Deposits of metal ores are also present in this coastal volcanic belt, in the Blue Hill area. On the Rockland-Thomaston-Union axis, extensive limestone bedrock occurs.

Sandy beaches are few and glacial outwash plains are not as extensive in this subregion as in the southwestern portion of Maine's coast. Nevertheless, ample evidence of past glacial activity can be found: eskers near Blue Hill and Lamoine, extensive boulder fields on the Blue Hill peninsula, and kame terraces near Brooksville. Mt. Desert Island abounds with exposed glacial features, including kettlehole ponds, striations, troughs, formed mountains, erratics, the fjord of Somes Sound, and "chattermarks" showing glacial flow at Seawall.

Cool marine waters surround the peninsulas and islands in this subregion, and heavy fog frequently hangs low in the atmosphere. Ponds and freshwater wetlands are more prevalent here than in the coastal areas to the southwest. Big Heath, on Mt. Desert Island, is a significant example of a coastal raised peatland. Among the many rivers and streams are the Medomak, St. George, Ducktrap, and Union, while the historic Penobscot, with its outstanding and picturesque estuary, is particularly noteworthy.

Vegetation is a mixture of spruce-fir forest, particularly on the islands, and transition hardwoods interspersed with hemlock and white pine. Along the sea's edge are the highest populations of nesting seabirds in the eastern United States. The rocky islands and ledges also provide haulout sites for hundreds of harbor seals and a few gray seals.

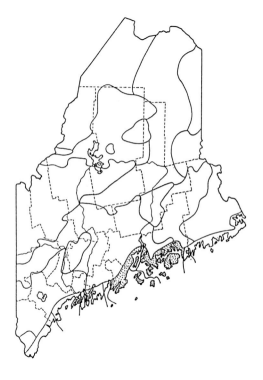

Penobscot Bay coastal subregion

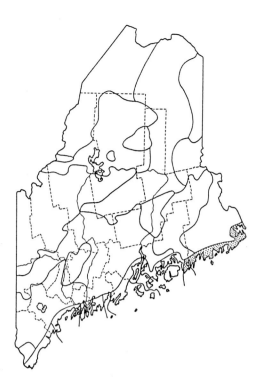

Eastern coastal subregion

Eastern Coastal Subregion

In the eastern coastal subregion, from Schoodic Point to Passamaquoddy Bay, one can view some of Maine's most beautiful and undeveloped coastline. The land is low, with scattered small hills, and in the indentations of the ragged coastline are several large bays: Narraguagus, Englishman, Machias, Cobscook, and Passamaquoddy. From Machias to Lubec, however, the coastline is unusually straight, indicating a fault line where two bedrock masses shifted. At Cobscook Bay the sea flooded a valley that cut across several other valleys parallel to each other, resulting in an unusually irregular and indented shoreline with many peninsulas, islands, and bays.

In much of the region, igneous rocks are evidence of past volcanic activity. The area around Eastport is of special geologic interest, for mixed in with layers of volcanic rocks are relatively unaltered sedimentary rocks containing fossils more closely related to those of Europe than to others in North America.

Most of the bedrock story lies buried beneath tons of marine sediments and glacial outwash. Exceptional glacial features include several sizable moraines near Jonesboro and Cutler, a kame field at Petit Manan, and a glaciomarine delta in coastal Washington County. Sand beaches exist at Jonesport. Extensive cobble and boulder beaches, including the unusual Jasper Beach at Machiasport, are also found in this subregion. Outstanding coastal cliffs add further geologic interest.

The greatest acreage of mud flats of any coastal subregion is here. Bogs also are more prevalent than in other coastal areas, although ponds are few. Especially noteworthy are the coastal raised peatlands. Feeding the many beautiful estuaries are a number of major rivers, including the Dennys, St. Croix, Narraguagus, Pleasant, Chandler, and Machias. And here, in the easternmost area of the coast, the cool marine waters rise and fall an average of eighteen feet—the highest tides anywhere in the United States except Alaska.

The cool, foggy, and wet climate of the eastern coastal subregion has a marked effect on the vegetation, providing ideal sites for several unusual subarctic plants, such as roseroot stonecrop, bird's-eye primrose, and blinks. The unusual conditions and relatively undisturbed sheltered coves, pockets, and nooks provide excellent habitat for wildlife. Several of the islands, including Petit Manan and Old Man, contain some of the state's most important seabird nesting colonies. Between Eastport and Deer Isle, Bonaparte's gulls, herring gulls, northern phalaropes, and black-legged kittiwakes gather in large concentrations each August to feed on the abundant marine life. The mud flats at South Lubec are habitat for shorebirds and in the spring attract large numbers of migrating brant. The majority of Maine's bald eagle population also reside in this subregion.

Southern Oak-Forest Region

This region, which includes the towns of Eliot and the Berwicks, is distinguished by tree species found almost nowhere else in the state. Covering approximately two hundred square miles, less than one percent of Maine's forest, this region's vegetation is more typical of areas to the south. Maine's most extensive stands of white and red oaks exist here, though much of the forest is white pine. Other species include black oak and shagbark hickory. Scrub oak is also found in association with pitch pine in the barrens communities. Flowering dogwood, chestnut oak, mountain laurel, rhododendron, and other species are near their northern limit here.

The topography is low and relatively flat. Mt. Agamenticus, with an elevation of 692 feet, is the highest point. It is the dominant bedrock feature, an intrusive granite formation. Glacial deposits of till, marine sediments, and sands and gravels are typical, as are numerous end moraines. One large moraine, Merriland Ridge, begins west of Wells and runs northeasterly for a few miles. Kettleholes are also present in the area. Soils of the region are primarily sandy loams, becoming more silty in river drainage areas.

Partly bounded by the Great Bay estuary, most of the region is within the drainage of the Piscataqua River, although some land is also drained by the York. These and other rivers of the region typically are slow-moving and meandering. There are relatively few lakes and freshwater marshes, and only a few peatlands.

Winter temperatures here are warmer than in the rest of Maine: daily maximum temperatures in January average thirty-four degrees Fahrenheit. Consequently, although slightly wetter than nearby southwest coastal areas,

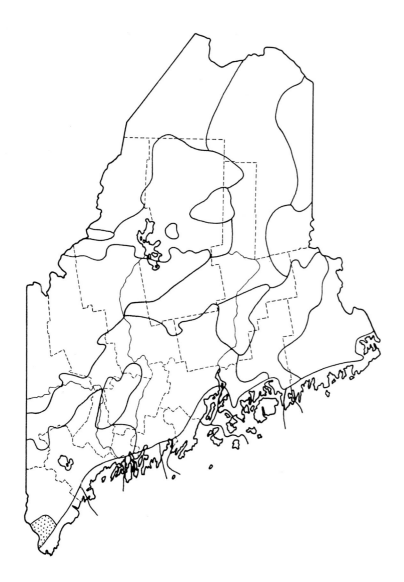

Southern oak-forest region

In extreme southern Maine are forests dominated by oaks. Patrick W. Grace photo.

the southern oak-forest region has the lowest snowfall of any in southern Maine.

The combination of large hardwood stands (especially the oaks) and open land provides good habitat for white-tailed deer, turkeys, flying squirrels, and an abundance of gray squirrels.

Upland-Hilly Region

As one moves inland from coastal Maine, the land begins to rise, forming a hilly belt of uplands that runs roughly parallel to the coast. From southwestern to central Maine, as one nears the 1,100-foot contour bounding the region to the north, low hills give way to the higher foothills of the western mountains. East of New Vineyard the border is much less defined, roughly following the northeastern limit of the transition forest. The region narrows northeastward of Bangor, cutting across lower elevations dotted with peatlands. Here, among the Norumbega Hills, the relief is significant, with elevations averaging five hundred to one thousand feet.

Within the upland-hilly region a number of subregions may be identified: pine forest, Belgrade-Cobbossee Lakes, upland-foothills, and Norumbega Hills.

Overlooking Mt. Christopher in Bryant Pond, in the Upland-Hilly Region. Dean Bennett photo.

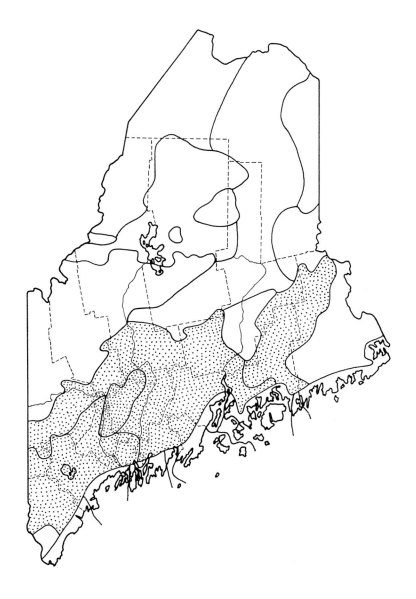

Upland-hilly region

Pine Forest Subregion

Characterized by a mixture of white pine and hardwoods, with a few red pines, this subregion extends northeast from Fryeburg to Livermore Falls and south to Lewiston and Richmond. The bedrock is heavily metamorphosed, containing extensive intrusions of igneous rocks. A distinctive zone of pegmatite, located in eastern and northern sections, has yielded many rare minerals, including tourmaline, quartz, and beryl. Bedrock outcrops are numerous, revealing major folds aligned along a northeast-southwest axis.

The influence of glaciation is readily apparent in this area. Till predominates, and much of the subregion is buried deeply in glacial drift. Extensive outwash plains cover large areas near Fryeburg, along the southern border, and in the lower Androscoggin and Kennebec river valleys near the eastern boundary. Eskers occur near Poland and Brownfield and along the west bank of the Kennebec River. A large moraine runs along the southern shore of Sebago Lake. Kame terraces and old river deltas are common, and large kame fields occur near Westbrook and Hollis. Near the coast, marine sediments influence the soils.

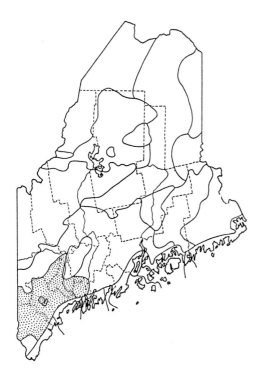

Pine forest subregion

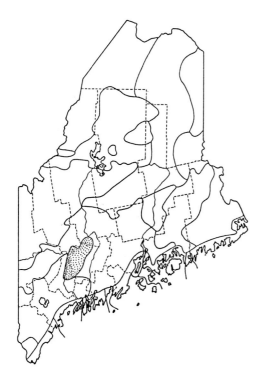

Belgrade-Cobbossee lakes subregion

Climatically, the warmest summer temperatures in Maine are found in the pine forest subregion. Average daily July temperature is around sixty-nine degrees Fahrenheit and precipitation is about average for the state.

This subregion encompasses much of the watersheds of the Saco and Androscoggin rivers. Other important rivers are the Piscataquis, Mousam, Royal, Kennebunk, Ossipee, and Crooked. Almost three hundred lakes lie within this area, the largest of which is Sebago. Peatlands are rather uncommon.

The Ossipee River provides some of Maine's finest fishing for smallmouth bass, while Sebago Lake is known for its landlocked salmon and lake trout. Along the Saco River, yellow-throated vireos and prairie warblers nest near the northern edge of their range. Opossum and gray fox also approach the northern edge of their range here.

Belgrade-Cobbossee Lakes Subregion

Near the middle of the western and central portion of the upland-hilly region lies the Belgrade-Cobbossee lakes subregion, which includes the towns of Monmouth, Winthrop, Wayne, Readfield, Mt. Vernon, and Belgrade. Lakes and wetlands are the most outstanding features; few other areas of corresponding size in Maine have as much of their surface covered by water. The numerous lakes and ponds among the pronounced but low hills (averaging under five hundred feet elevation) were formed in glacial kettleholes and in dammed and scoured valleys. Kames, eskers, and outwash areas are also present. Extensive shallow freshwater marshes also occur here, especially along portions of East Pond, Cobbossee Lake, and Messalonskee Lake. (The last named provides habitat for the uncommon black tern.) Annabessacook Lake is a classic example of a eutrophic lake.

Upland-Foothills Subregion

From Fryeburg to Madison, between the pine-forest and Belgrade-Cobbossee Lakes subregions and the mountain region, lies a belt of foothills. This subregion also includes an area of lower relief, extending south to Gardiner and east to the Pittsfield-Bangor area. Near the White Mountains, in the northwest section, are sizable areas of granite and other related igneous rocks, with smaller areas near Canaan, Bucksport, and the Blue Hill Peninsula. However, most of the region's rocks are metamorphosed and sedimentary.

Glacial outwash plains are less extreme in this subregion than in other parts of southern Maine. In western sections, kame terraces are common along river valleys, but east of the Kennebec River eskers are more prevalent. At Moscow, marine sediments found at 305 feet—the highest in the state—indicate the extent of seawater incursion.

Wetlands, though locally common, are not present in great concentrations. Groups of lakes occur near Lovell, China, and Jefferson. A large segment of the Kennebec River crosses this subregion, as do the Sheepscot, St. George, and Medomak rivers in Lincoln County.

Forest types are notably diverse. In the western foothills near the mountain region, maple-beech-birch predominate, interspersed with white pine on sandy upland sites. To the east, transition hardwoods and hemlock become prevalent, grading once again into maple-beech-birch in the upper Kennebec area. The most extensive and southerly inland stands of spruce-fir forest lie in a belt running northeast from Lincoln County to the Dixmont area.

Norumbega Hills Subregion

Extending northeastward from Bangor to the New Brunswick border at the northern tip of Washington County is the Norumbega Hills subregion. These hills are almost entirely underlain by igneous bedrock, particularly the granites, and most of them are rounded monadnocks. A major fault exists near Sabao Mountain in the unorganized township of T 41 MD.

A few of the mountains—Chick Hill in Amherst, for example—have sharp cliffs showing evidence of glacial plucking. (This phenomenon occurs on the lee sides of mountains where glacial ice "plucks," or breaks off and carries away, blocks of the bedrock.) Thin layers of till and extensive boulder fields with large erratics cover much of the area. Eskers cut across the northeast orientation of the ridges. Outwash sediments in lower elevations help smooth the relief.

In the lowlands are many lakes, the largest being Grand Lake and Graham Lake. Many of Washington County's rivers rise in this subregion. Northern hardwoods, especially white birch, occur on high ridges, while spruce and fir are more common on the lower slopes and poorly drained bottomlands.

Mountain Region

The mountain region is one of Maine's most picturesque landscapes, containing many of the state's unusual and rare natural features. This region's southern boundary follows the eleven-hundred-foot contour and is roughly separated from the Upland-Hilly Region by a long escarpment—a rather abrupt rise in the land. Its northern boundary generally follows the fifteen-hundred-foot contour. The average elevation is fifteen hundred to two thousand feet.

Within the region's boundaries lie several mountain groups: the Katahdin group, the Boundary Mountains, the White Mountains, and the Longfellow Mountains. Eleven peaks are over four thousand feet, and more than fifty are over thirty-five hundred feet. Katahdin looms above all, and is considered by some to provide the most impressive views east of the Rocky Mountains.

The bedrock for most of these mountains was created over 350 million years ago by granitic intrusions. Tremendous heat and pressure also metamorphosed the bedrock extensively during this time. This was followed by millions of years of erosion that removed the softer overlying rock to leave the granite mountains we see today. In the Rangeley Lakes area the bedrock is extremely varied, more so than in any other region of the state; slate, metamorphosed siltstone, many varieties of igneous rocks, and numerous faults exist there.

Rocks and boulders of glacial till are deposited across the mountains, river valleys, and lake shores, but glacial features are generally less apparent here than in other regions. Mountain soils are thin, acid, and infertile.

Climate is relatively severe. Altitudes over twenty-five hundred feet often experience a subarctic climate; average annual temperatures in some areas hover near freezing. Fog and low clouds increase the humidity, and the annual precipitation on mountaintops is greater than that at lower elevations. Strong winds are common, with wind velocities exceeding one hundred miles per hour recorded on the summits of many mountains. The climate becomes wetter and cooler as one moves north and west through the mountain region, but in the valleys, particularly in the Rangeley Lakes area, conditions are usually drier.

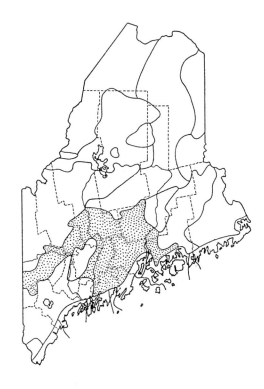

Upland-foothills subregion

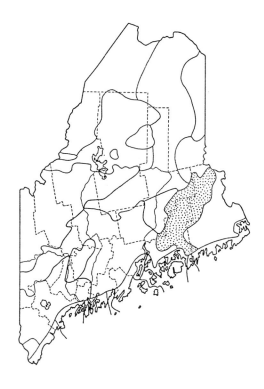

Norumbega Hills subregion

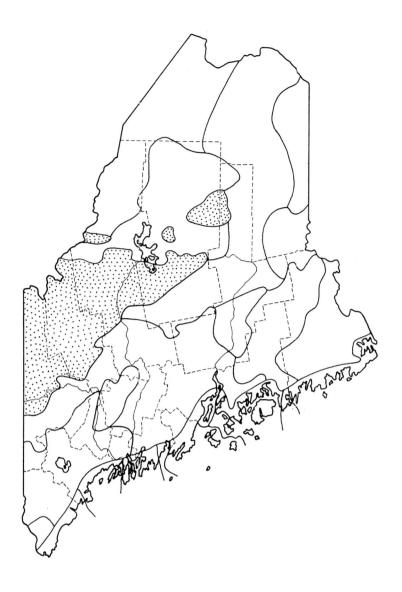

Mountain region

The low-lying, somewhat level area in the Rangeleys and to the northeast contains most of the lakes in this region, including Rangeley, Mooselookmeguntic, Umbagog, Aziscohos, and Cupsuptic. Cirque lakes, or tarns, exist in the higher mountains shaped by glaciers. Peatlands are numerous, and alpine bogs can be found on a few mountains.

Among the many small mountain ponds and streams rise the headwaters of nearly all of Maine's major rivers: the Saco, Kennebec, Androscoggin, and Penobscot. Within these river systems are many of the state's most outstanding gorges, waterfalls, and stretches of white water.

Running the length of the mountain region and providing access to many of its treasures is the Appalachian Trail. Spectacular vistas, cascading mountain streams, surprising encounters with wildlife, remnants of virgin forests, and unusual and interesting plant life await the hiker along this famous route. As one moves up the mountains, the spruce-fir forest becomes predominant, but in stunted form. This type of growth is known as krummholz. Above the timberline, the treeless summits of several mountains support rare, low-growing arctic alpine plants.

One of the most spectacular natural areas in the mountain region is Baxter State Park. The park boasts a variety of outstanding natural features, including

Mooselookmeguntic Lake is typical of the large lake systems in mountainous settings in western Maine. Scott Perry photo.

waterfalls such as Grand Falls and Green Falls, glacial cirques, mountain lakes and ponds, old-growth forests, and at least thirty-eight rare plant species.

As one would expect, the increasingly harsh conditions found higher up on the mountain slopes mean a decrease in animal life. Cold-blooded reptiles and amphibians are affected most. One of the few birds found above timberline in Maine is the water pipit, although hawks and ravens are often seen riding thermal updrafts. Gray-cheeked thrushes nest in the krummholz immediately below timberline, and spruce grouse, Canada jays, and boreal chickadees range over the upper parts of the forested slopes. In the krummholz and grassy alpine areas, red-backed voles, meadow voles, and long-tail shrews live. During the blueberry season, bears often browse above treeline.

Northern Forest Region

To the north and east of the mountain region lies the northern forest region, a large expanse of low and rolling hilly terrain forested with conifers and

Grand Lake. Northern Maine is characterized by flat or gently rolling topography and many large lakes. Fox Hollow photo.

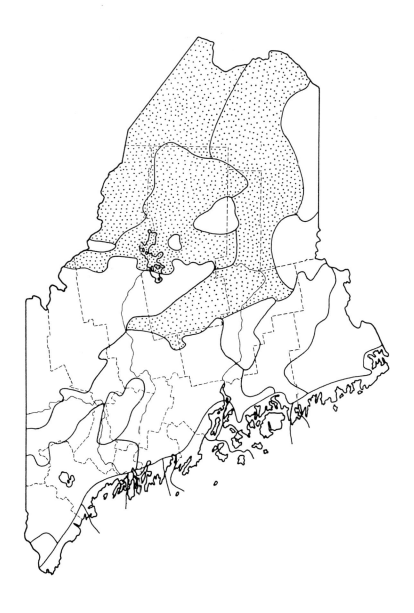

Northern forest region

northern hardwoods. It is an area with numerous wetlands and exceptionally beautiful lakes and streams, but it's also known for its severely cold, snowy winters.

Within this region, three subregions exhibit very distinct characteristics. They are the northern lakes, Allagash–St. John River, and forest lowlands subregions.

Northern Lakes Subregion

This subregion includes the headwaters of the Kennebec, Penobscot, and Allagash rivers. Although Moosehead Lake is by far the dominant feature, there are several other large lakes, including Chamberlain, Chesuncook, Eagle, Churchill, and Pemadumcook. Wetlands are also abundant, as are brooks and streams. Animal life, including lake trout, loons, goldeneyes, redbreasted mergansers, otter, beaver, and moose, reflects this diversity and abundance of aquatic habitat.

For those who enjoy boating and canoeing, Maine's northern lakes provide a very special experience. Always aware of the commanding presence of Mt. Katahdin, one is surrounded by miles of beautiful, undisturbed forested shoreline, from which at any time may emerge deer, moose, and bear. Along the lakeshores is the gray-white, bleached dri-ki (dried out, weathered skeletons of the trees that succumbed long ago to water levels raised by dams).

The relatively unmetamorphosed bedrock beneath the land's surface is composed mostly of gray slate and sandstone. Some of Maine's oldest bedrock strata, dating from 600 million years ago, occur west of Jackman. Northeast of Katahdin, fossils over 300 million years old are abundant in the Mississippian period strata of the Trout Brook area.

Allagash/St. John River Subregion

To the west and north of the northern lakes subregion, setting it apart from the others, lie the drainage basins of Maine's two most famous wild rivers. Here among the hills, the rivers flow over dark gray, 400-million-year-old Seboomook slate. Seen from the air, the rivers' many tributaries flow at right angles to the main branches, sectioning the land in trellislike patterns.

Because this is one of Maine's driest regions (annual precipitation is usually less than thirty-six inches), the free-flowing St. John shrinks as the summer progresses. When July and August have little rain, it can become nearly dry. June, therefore, is one of the most popular canoeing months. Ledges and limy soils along the river's banks combine with the cool climate to provide prime habitat for a host of rare plant species, including the nationally significant and endangered Furbish's lousewort.

Spruce-fir is the typical forest of the area west of the junction of Aroostook, Piscataquis, and Somerset counties, although stands of aspen and birch often grow where the forest has been cut or burned. South of the confluence of the Allagash and St. John rivers, the maple-beech-birch forest is most extensive. Peatlands and the rare ribbed fens occur in the low depressions.

As many a canoeist can attest, the Allagash-St. John subregion is also known for its opportunities to sight moose, deer, and, occasionally, black bear. In the valleys back from the rivers are important deer wintering areas. From time to time, bald eagles can be seen gracefully soaring overhead.

Forest Lowlands Subregion

Boot-shaped in outline, the forest lowlands subregion extends northeastward from Moscow to Lincoln and northward to Madawaska at the Canadian border. It is distinguished by its generally low elevation and relief, spruce-fir forest, and moderate number of lakes, ponds, and wetlands. Several isolated mountains approach seventeen hundred feet in elevation: Kelley, Green, Saddleback, Number Nine, and Mars Hill.

The bedrock geology throughout is predominantly metamorphosed sedimentary rock, including slate, shale, sandstone, and conglomerate. Extensive faults exist east of Mt. Katahdin. Unlike the rest of the state, the northern part of this subregion (and for that matter, northern Maine in general) shows little evidence of glacial deposition. Grooves in the rock indicating glacial movement are the major signs of past glaciation, and their irregular patterns reveal an unclear, complicated picture of glacial movement. For this reason, northern Maine is termed the "zone of confusion" with respect to the direction of movement of the last glacier.

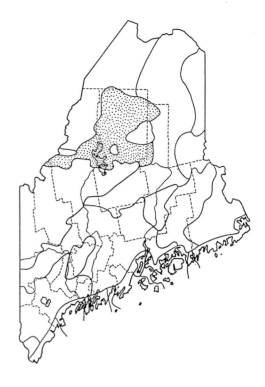

Northern lakes subregion

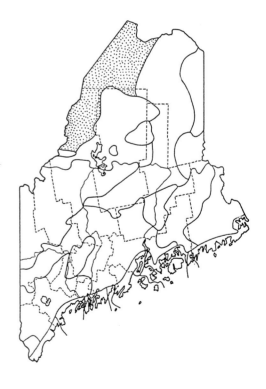

Allagash / St. John River subregion

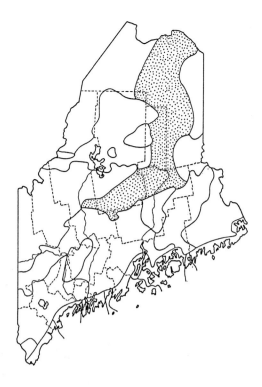

Forest lowlands subregion

Although no outstandingly large lakes occur in the forest lowlands subregion, there are many lakes and ponds. Some of the larger ones are Sebec, Schoodic, Squa Pan, and the Eagle-Square-Cross-Long lake chain. The major river is the East Branch of the Penobscot. Marshes, peatlands, and swamps are common. Some of the best examples of ribbed fens are found in this subregion. The wetlands and waters, in combination with the spruce-fir forest and the more prevalent hardwoods to the south, provide habitat for many species of wildlife.

Of special interest are two public lots owned by the state. One, the Deboullie-Red River area, contains a 22,000-acre township (T 15, R 9) sixty miles north of Baxter State Park and fifteen miles from the Canadian border in central Aroostook County. It is remote and isolated, containing over twenty deep, spring-fed ponds and rugged mountains with sheer cliffs and ice caves. These features are primarily the result of a granitic pluton that forced its way through a large overlying belt of Seboomook slate 360 to 400 million years ago. Such an intrusion is rare in northern Maine.

In more recent times, glaciers carved at least a dozen sheer cliffs from the mountains and left a layer of till, or unsorted rock, in lowland areas. The most unusual plant communities lie in cracks and crevices of these cliffs and among the rocks of the talus slopes below them. The arctic sandwort and smooth woodsia fern are two nationally rare plants found in this region. Other rare plants include fragrant cliff fern and showy lady's-slipper. The public lot also contains old-growth stands of northern white cedar. Interesting wildlife includes loons, bald eagles, and the uncommon blueback charr.

The other public lot, Squa Pan, is a tract of land over eleven thousand acres in extent, located seven miles east of Ashland and encompassing portions of Squa Pan Lake and Squa Pan Mountain. The mountainous and hilly portions are underlain by volcanic rocks, while siltstones and sandstones lie beneath the lowland areas.

Squa Pan is fully forested with the red spruce, balsam fir, and northern white cedar of the coniferous boreal forest, and the sugar maple, beech, white ash, and eastern hemlock of the northern hardwood forest. Wildlife includes the white-tailed deer, moose, black bear, fisher, bobcat, otter, common goldeneye, red-breasted merganser, loon, pine grosbeak, boreal chickadee, gray jay, and black-backed three-toed woodpecker.

Aroostook Limestone Region

Along the Canadian border, in the upper northeastern corner of Maine, lies the Aroostook limestone region, an area unusual because of its soils. Here, on a bedrock of metamorphosed limestone, lie well-drained deep loams that are less acid than Maine's typical soils. As one would expect in a locale so eminently suited for agriculture, much of the forest has vanished, having been converted years ago to farmland. What remains is spruce and fir, found on some poorly drained sites, and sugar maple, beech, birch, and white ash on higher ground.

Along the Aroostook River, outcrops of limy bedrock contribute to the presence of several rare species of plants. These include variegated scouring-rush, northern woodsia, Dudley's rush, false asphodel, shining ladies'-tresses, sandbar willow, Brunet's milk-vetch, Seneca snakeroot, sweet-broom, and Mistassini primrose.

The rolling landscape, with its occasional eskers, kame terraces, till, and

Mars Hill, rising above the gently rolling landscape in the limestone belt of northeastern Aroostook County, is one small mountain of resistant rock. Fox Hollow photo.

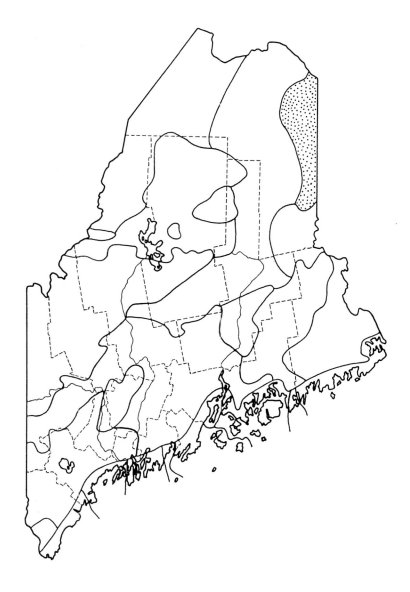

Aroostook limestone region

outwash indicating the influence of past glaciation, more recently has been carved by the Aroostook and other rivers and streams. Lakes, ponds, and peatlands are not as plentiful in this region as in certain others.

Below the surface, preserved in the strata of relatively unaltered sedimentary rock, are plant and animal fossils—more numerous here than in any other part of Maine. Some are over 400 million years old, dating into the Ordovician period. Today, the open land and hardwood forests are home for wildlife species quite different from those encountered in the predominant coniferous forest of northern Maine. Here one finds the eastern meadowlark and indigo bunting—and, more rarely, the upland sandpiper—nesting in the open land.

Eastern Peatlands Region

In eastern Maine is an area of lowlands with an unusual abundance of peatlands. The Norumbega Hills, which rise out of the relatively flat terrain, divide the region into western, northern, and southeastern sections. The southeastern section, including a major portion of Washington County, is actually more hilly than the Norumbega Hills, but elevations are not as high.

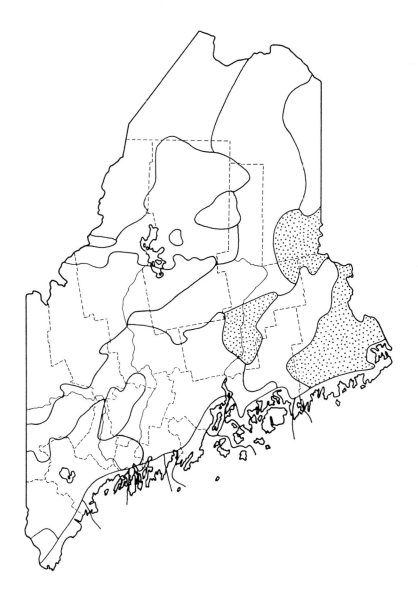

Eastern peatlands region

The thousands of wetlands in this region are associated with numerous lakes and ponds, most of which are rather shallow. The largest of these include West Grand Lake, Big Lake, Nicatous Lake, Baskahegan Lake, and Chiputneticook Lake—the last shared with Canada. Rivers that drain the region include the Penobscot, upper Narraguagus, Machias, Dennys, and lower St. Croix. Along the Penobscot River are important freshwater marshes.

Underlying the eastern peatlands region are diverse bedrock types, most of which are metamorphosed sedimentary rock. These include siltstone, sandstone, shale, limestone, and conglomerate. In the northern portion, metamorphosed volcanic ash is also present, and in the eastern section, granite and other intrusive igneous rocks.

Of special note are the glacial eskers running north to south across the region. Nowhere else in the United States are these features so numerous and well defined. Washington County contains ancient shorelines complete with raised beaches, wave-cut cliffs, terraces, and deltas. Excellent examples of washboard moraines are also present. As one might expect with so much evidence of glacial activity, many of the peatlands lie in kettleholes.

The lowland topography and shallow ponds of the glaciated landscape

Maine possesses a wide variety of significant peatlands throughout the state. Macwahoc Stream is in the Eastern Peatlands Region. Ronald B. Davis photo.

provided the necessary physical setting for the abundant peatlands, but climatic factors were primarily responsible for their development. These factors include low evapotranspiration in conjunction with cool temperatures during the growing season, high frequency of fog and precipitation, intermittent snow cover, and higher mineral content of precipitation near the sea.

The largest peatland in Maine, the Great Heath, is located north of Columbia by the Pleasant River. This is a raised peatland, formed by the coalescing of numerous dome-shaped peat bogs. Its distinctive features include ponds, ridges, hollows, and small islands of trees.

The forest cover surrounding the peatlands is primarily spruce-fir, with northern hardwoods on the drier sites. Closer to the bogs—and even in them—are tamaracks and black spruces. Other distinctive vegetation includes the blueberry barrens east of Deblois, maintained for hundreds of years through periodic burning by the pre-Colonial Indians.

Some nesting birds, including Lincoln's sparrow, palm warbler, and ring-necked duck, appear to be particularly associated with peatland ecosystems. Many eagles nest in the region around the lakes, as do ospreys. Bass are plentiful in the lakes, and Atlantic salmon runs occur in some of the rivers.

Thinking about Maine in terms of natural regions cultivates a view of nature that is intrinsically ecological. Such a view is essential to understanding the peculiarities of the land and its life. It is in this context that the foregoing discussion of Maine's seven natural regions provides the ecological platform from which to consider the conservation of the state's geological and biological rarities.

Conservation

Perspective

Who would not rise to meet
the expectations of the land?

—Henry David Thoreau

Just what, we might ask, could be the expectations of the land, and why should we rise to meet them? In our human egoism we would probably address the second question first. Because, we might answer, we are the land; we are made from it and it of us. Therefore, are we not, like all life, merely extensions of the land, despite our vaunted higher form of organization? And are not the expectations and needs of the land our own: an environment that is life nurturing as well as life giving? If so, to rise to meet them is to serve (and preserve) ourselves as well.

In terms of intelligence, we are, among our fellow organisms, gifted. For us, the preservation of nature can be a matter of consciousness and conscience. But we must accept that our health and survival require clean water and air, green plants, and any number of other essentials, many of which we are aware of but also many more about which we know little or nothing. Such an acceptance implies a responsibility. Aldo Leopold, one of our country's great conservationists, called it a land ethic. In his classic work, *A Sand County Almanac,* he wrote, "We abuse land because we regard it as a commodity belonging to us. When we see land as a community to which we belong, we may begin to treat it with love and respect."[1] Perhaps this is at the heart of what we call conservation.

Conservation is an elusive term to which we attach several meanings and, often, strong emotional overtones. It can mean using a resource in ways that avoid waste, or it can be defined as "preservation by protecting from loss or harm." Both interpretations implicitly contain a strong commitment to future generations.

Conservation of a natural area, such as a salt marsh or heron rookery, can be guided by several intents, depending on what we know about it and what value we attach to it. On these points there is often much disagreement; thus,

Rachel Carson, a Maine summer resident, wrote several major books on marine biology and the environment. The 3,160-acre Rachel Carson National Wildlife Refuge in York County is named in her honor. Erich Hartmann photo.

conservation decisions are sometimes accompanied by heated public debates, like those engendered in the 1980s by proposals to dam the West Branch of the Penobscot and to legalize moose hunting.

The real debate, however, must first be resolved in the minds of individuals, for conservation is fundamentally an individual responsibility before it is a collective one. What one identifies as worthy of discretionary use, preservation, or protection depends upon what one values. The philosophical decision to become actively involved in conservation is one of conscience, involving one's code of ethics. At the very heart is how one views his or her relationship with the rest of nature. A person who feels as one with the natural world, physically and emotionally interdependent, exhibits quite a different set of values and actions than does someone for whom this connection is weak or

The late George "Pete" Sawyer, of Ashland, and old-growth cedar. As manager of the Dunn Heirs land, he received the 1985 Critical Areas Award for his vision and pioneering efforts to identify and protect old-growth forests. Hank Tyler photo.

missing. In the former case one promises to conserve nature first, knowing that thereby the human condition will be served, whereas in the latter, prosaic human wants are considered paramount to the needs of nature. A commitment to the preservation of people should also be a commitment to conservation of the land, for the two are inseparable.

15

Protectors of Maine's Natural Areas

For those who love the land, some heartwarming moments lie waiting to be discovered in the popular accounts of Maine's history: moments of vision, of unselfish concern, patience, and generosity; times when unselfish human behavior meant the difference between losing a bit of nature and allowing it a future. Although Maine has experienced its share of losses, its record of accomplishment is extraordinary, reflecting dedicated effort in both public and private sectors.

In the public sector, the concept of protecting unique natural areas for preservation of their special characteristics and for the enjoyment of future

Screw Auger Falls in Gulf Hagas was acquired in 1985 by the National Park Service as part of its effort to protect significant natural features along the Appalachian Trail. Thomas Brewer photo.

A kettlehole pond and sphagnum bog in Kennebec County. This exemplary kettlehole was purchased by The Nature Conservancy and donated to Colby College, which uses it for education and research. This area has been designated a Maine Critical Area as well as a National Natural Landmark. Hank Tyler photo.

generations was pioneered at the national level in 1872 with the designation of Yellowstone as a park and forest preserve. A quarter of a century later, in 1897, the national park system, which today extends into all corners of the nation, became a reality. Maine's Acadia National Park, located on Mt. Desert Island and twelve smaller islands, is one of the most visited national parks in the country. The National Park Service has designated fifteen National Natural Landmarks in the state: Crystal Bog, New Gloucester Black Gum Stand, Bigelow Mountain, Colby-Marston Preserve, Penny Pond-Joe Pond Complex, Monhegan Island, Orono Bog, Passadumkeag Marsh and Boglands, Gulf Hagas, Mount Katahdin, the Hermitage, Carrying Place Cove Bog, Meddy-bemps Heath, Number 5 Bog, and Appleton Bog.

In 1903, President Theodore Roosevelt established the first wildlife refuge on Pelican Island in Florida to protect a magnificent colony of brown pelicans and other colonial nesting birds threatened by plumage hunting. Today, nearly 90 million acres of lands in the United States and its territories are set aside for wild animals. A total of 424 refuges in the National Wildlife Refuge System are managed by the United States Fish and Wildlife Service.

A cobble beach at Petit Manan Point National Wildlife Refuge. The refuge protects a diversity of rare habitats on the Washington County coast, including wetlands, peatlands, and cobble beaches. Hank Tyler photo.

Public lands on Upper Richardson Lake, managed by the Maine Bureau of Public Lands. The bureau manages over 450,000 acres of public lands in all, including many Critical Areas. Hank Tyler photo.

In Maine, eight refuges, totaling 31,301 acres, protect such important areas as Bois Bubert Island, Petit Manan Point, Cross Island, Moosehorn Wildlife Refuge in Baring, and Rachel Carson Wildlife Refuge in Wells.

Other efforts at the federal level also have affected the conservation of natural areas in Maine. Forty-five thousand acres in the western mountains are in the White Mountain National Forest—the only national forest land in the state. The roots of the national forest concept go back to 1891, when Congress passed an act to establish forest reserves. In 1964, the Wilderness Act was enacted to protect wild lands in the National Wilderness Preservation System. In Maine, part of the Moosehorn National Wildlife Refuge is being considered for inclusion in this system. The Wild and Scenic Rivers Act of 1968 designated the already state-protected Allagash as a wild river. Other rivers being considered for this designation include the Penobscot and the St. Croix. In spite of these efforts, however, the amount of federally protected and managed acreage in Maine remains relatively small. Fortunately, state and private interests have been more active in acquiring and protecting lands containing important natural areas.

The State of Maine itself is the largest single owner of critical and significant natural areas. These are managed by several state agencies, principally the Department of Conservation and the Department of Inland Fisheries and Wildlife.

Within the Department of Conservation, the Bureau of Parks and Recreation is one of the major land managers. The bureau had its beginning in 1935, when the legislature created the State Park Commission. Three years later, the state accepted a gift of one hundred acres of land in Presque Isle and hired its first superintendent of parks. Today, the bureau manages upward of seventy thousand acres, contained in 110 state parks and memorials and forty-four boat-launching areas. The Allagash Wilderness Waterway alone consists of more than twenty-two thousand acres, and the Bigelow Preserve covers another 30,498 acres. Many of the parks encompass unique natural features identified by the Critical Areas Program. These include: a least tern and piping plover nesting area at Popham Beach, an exposure of the Cape Elizabeth geological formation at Two Lights, and a significant stand of tupelo and the only site for American lotus north of Massachusetts at Ferry Beach in Saco. Baxter State Park, administered by a separate authority, contains over two hundred thousand acres and many Critical Areas.

Several other state agencies are also involved in the protection of natural areas. The Bureau of Public Lands, also in the Department of Conservation, was instrumental in consolidating state-owned lands and today manages about four hundred thousand acres. Through the Department of Inland Fisheries and Wildlife, the state also manages forty-one wildlife management areas covering more than forty-five thousand acres and including undeveloped shorefront properties, wetlands, upland areas, and islands. The agency's Nongame Project is responsible for helping to identify and protect endangered and threatened animal species.

Another agency with specific responsibilities for the protection of rare and unusual natural features is the Maine State Planning Office. Its Critical Areas Program, established in 1974, has inventoried and reported on over one hundred geological features and plant and animal species. The State Planning Office maintains the official listing of special natural sites, the Register of Critical Areas.

Although accomplishments of the public sector are impressive, the majority of Maine's critical areas are owned today by private organizations,

Great Spoon Island, in Penobscot Bay, is one of over two hundred coastal islands owned and managed by the Maine Department of Inland Fisheries and Wildlife to protect the state's significant seabird resource. Hank Tyler photo.

corporations, and individuals. Since most of these areas are expected to remain in private hands, the continued cooperation of the private sector is essential to their long-term protection. Based on past accomplishments, the prospects look hopeful for future help from Maine's private landowners.

A number of private nonprofit organizations have a history of involvement in protecting natural areas. The Nature Conservancy is one of these. A national organization, the conservancy identifies and protects significant natural areas throughout the country. Some it acquires by gifts; many of them it purchases outright. In addition, it provides advice and assistance to individuals, organizations, and government agencies regarding preservation of natural areas. Through chapters in more than thirty states, The Nature Conservancy protected some 1.5 million acres nationwide between 1950 and 1985.

The Maine Chapter of The Nature Conservancy, one of the first, was formed in 1956. By the mid-1980s, over twenty-three thousand acres of land had been protected by this chapter's efforts: nearly fourteen thousand acres in seventy preserves owned directly by the chapter, almost seventy-six hundred

Seawall Beach, one of Maine's most significant natural sand beach systems, is protected by a conservation easement granted to The Nature Conservancy. Hank Tyler photo.

Wight Brook Waterfalls (also called Step Falls), Newry, was the first nature preserve acquired and protected by The Nature Conservancy in Maine. E.T. Richardson, Jr., photo.

Harbor Island, Muscongus Bay, is protected by a series of conservation easements granted by the landowner to the National Audubon Society. Hank Tyler photo.

An extensive salt marsh borders the Maine Audubon Society headquarters at Gilsland Farm in Falmouth. Rand Raabe photo.

Great rhododendron, a rare plant in Maine, is protected in a New England Wildflower Society sanctuary in southern Maine. Hank Tyler photo.

acres in twenty-three areas transferred to other agencies for management and protection, and thirteen hundred acres in twenty-five privately owned tracts protected by conservation easements generally requiring that the areas remain forever wild. In 1984 the Maine chapter published a guide to more than fifty of its preserves, giving directions to features that would not be harmed or disturbed by careful visitation.

The National Audubon Society is another national organization that acquires and protects natural areas with special value as wildlife habitat or that offer outstanding resources for education or research. In Maine, the society maintains 608 acres in eleven sanctuaries, primarily in Muscongus Bay, where it operates a popular summer nature study program on Hog Island. In addition, the society holds fourteen easements on islands and coastal lands, totaling 1,618 acres. Maine's six chapters (Merrymeeting, Mid-Coast, Prouts Neck, Western Maine, Northeast, and York County) assist in the organization's conservation efforts.

Not to be confused with the National Audubon Society is the Maine Audubon Society, which is entirely separate from the national group. The Maine society, a vigorous statewide organization, is involved in a wide range of conservation activities, including land acquisition and protection, studies of wildlife species and natural habitats, political and legal action, energy conservation, and environmental education. It also owns and manages fourteen sites, totaling 756 acres, of which six have trail systems open to the public. The society also has four chapters: Schoodic, Penobscot, Down East, and Dover-Foxcroft. The Down East chapter has two sanctuaries, totaling 690 acres, on Mt. Desert Island.

The New England Wildflower Society, Inc., owns and protects New England habitats harboring flora of special significance. It was established as a nonprofit organization in 1922. Among the Maine areas it owns or has been instrumental in preserving are an unusually large northern stand of rhododendron in Springvale; an extensive tract of woodland, shore, and tidal marsh on Merrymeeting Bay in Woolwich; and a central Maine bog and woodland containing numerous rare orchids.

The Maine Coast Heritage Trust was founded in 1970 to promote the conservation of the state's islands and coastline by negotiating conservation easements and gifts of land from property owners to conservation organizations. As of 1986, the trust had assisted with 281 land transactions that protected 21,820 acres, and had itself begun to hold interests in property. The organization also provides technical advice, generally at no cost, to landowners, land trusts, communities, and other agencies.

The Maine Association of Conservation Commissions serves as a source of information for communities considering land protection. It also assists landowners with land protection plans, such as easements, for community benefit.

Almost 50 percent of the Maine's forest land is owned by a small number of large businesses, so it should come as no surprise to learn that over forty of the state's Critical Areas are in corporate ownership. These private landowners have often demonstrated awareness of the public's interest in the conservation of natural areas. Several companies have donated land for such uses as state and local parks, recreational areas, and preserves. Scott Paper, for example, donated most of the land for Lily Bay State Park on Moosehead Lake; International Paper donated Dunn's Notch Falls along the Appalachian Trail; the Huber Corporation gave Crystal Bog to The Nature Conservancy; and

Central Maine Power Company purchased Cathedral Pines and gave it to the town of Eustis. In addition, corporate landowners have also swapped lands with the state to facilitate efforts to consolidate public lots.

In other cases, companies have themselves developed properties for nature study and outdoor recreation. Central Maine Power Company, for example, created the Hiram Nature Study Area to promote and encourage an interest in conservation. This wooded sixty-acre site near Hiram Falls on the Saco River is open to nature students, bird watchers, photographers, picnickers, and anglers.

Especially inspiring are cases in which individuals embody the spirit of conservation through their personal actions. For example, hundreds of people have participated in the identification, documentation, and monitoring of Maine's critical natural areas, many of which are on the property of private landowners who voluntarily watch over them. Numerous areas are now protected thanks to the actions of future-thinking individuals who gave them to the state or to conservation organizations. The Freeman-Waterhouse Conservation Camp at Bryant Pond is one example.

In 1955, Lillian R. Waterhouse gave land and buildings in Woodstock (Bryant Pond is a village in that township) to the Maine Fish and Game Association for the operation of a conservation camp. Two years later, ownership was transferred to the Conservation Education Foundation of Maine, which was established to conduct conservation programs at the camp. Today, Maine's Conservation School continues to offer conservation and environmental education programs to young people and educators—all due to the generosity and environmental concern of one woman.

Perhaps no human act of conservation is more inspiring than the story of how Percival P. Baxter spent thirty years of his life patching together one of the most beautiful wilderness parks in the nation—Baxter State Park—and then presented it as a gift to the people of Maine. It took much more than financial resources to accomplish this task; it was a demonstration of vision, of determination, and of patience—qualities that form the foundation of any successful effort to conserve natural areas.

The process of acquiring and protecting natural areas also takes an understanding of the available legal methods or tools. Three techniques are

Mt. Katahdin, in Baxter State Park, is the crown jewel of Maine's protected natural areas. Governor Percival Baxter spent three decades acquiring and donating this 200,000-acre park to the people of Maine. Hank Tyler photo.

Great Duck Island, one of Maine's most significant seabird nesting islands, was purchased by The Nature Conservancy and Maine Department of Inland Fisheries and Wildlife in the early 1980s. Leach's storm-petrels, eider ducks, and black guillemots are important nesters on this island. Hank Tyler photo, courtesy of Maine Fish and Wildlife *Magazine.*

particularly popular and effective: purchase, donation, and easement. These are described in *The Landowner's Options,* a booklet for the layperson obtainable from the Maine State Planning Office.[1]

Outright purchase is a major way of acquiring land for conservation purposes and has been used effectively by individuals, organizations, and government agencies at all levels. For example, Falmouth residents who wanted a natural area for the school and community raised money to buy the Falmouth Foreside Preserve. State and federal agencies, such as the Maine Bureau of Parks and Recreation and the United States Department of the Interior, and a number of private organizations, such as The Nature Conservancy, also acquire land through purchase as well as by accepting gifts.

Donation is probably the simplest way to transfer land title to one of these organizations or agencies, and Maine has an impressive history of land giving. In some cases, landowners donate their property but retain the right to use the land or part of it during their lifetimes. In other instances, land is given with conditions of use attached to it. For example, Governor Baxter set forth a number of restrictions to ensure that Baxter State Park would remain "forever wild," and Katherine P. Tinker, a public-minded citizen and strong advocate of education, gave twenty acres to the town of Yarmouth to be used for environmental education—with the stipulation that if the land is not used under the terms of the agreement it will revert to The Nature Conservancy.

Under a conservation easement, the owner continues to own and use the land but chooses to write into the deed legal restrictions on its development. These covenants can specify the type of land use and the proportion of the property under easement. The owner can still sell the land, but its use remains subject to the terms of the agreement. Easements granted in perpetuity legally bind all present and future owners, thus affording permanent protection.

This type of land protection has been used effectively throughout Maine. Organizations such as the Maine Coast Heritage Trust provide free assistance to landowners who are considering this option. For example, one family with whom the trust worked owned part of an island and found the conservation easement a solution to a problem both they and the state faced: the threatened loss of the attractive natural, undeveloped character of the coast. Generations of the family have summered on the island, and although they had erected several cottages, about sixty acres, including a mile of waterfront, remained natural. However, as the owners grew older, they faced the possibility that each of their several heirs might wish to build a separate cottage, slowly eroding the beauty and naturalness that originally attracted the family to the island. In addition, the skyrocketing assessed value of island real estate raised the possibility that some of the land would have to be sold in order to pay inheritance taxes.

With help from the Maine Coast Heritage Trust, they decided that a conservation easement would solve their problem. The easement prohibited all building except on three small shore lots deleted from the protected area and provided for a right-of-way to gain access to the lots. Only recreational and conservation activities were permitted; all commercial activity was forbidden, including the cutting of standing timber. The easement was granted to and accepted by the National Park Service. By removing the possibility of development, the land's market value dropped, thus stabilizing property taxes and lowering the probable inheritance tax. The difference in value before and after the easement was also an allowable income tax deduction. Most important of all, the natural qualities of the area would be conserved for future generations to enjoy.

Between 1970, when the law allowing conservation easements was enacted, and 1984, over two hundred easements in perpetuity were granted to various public and private agencies in Maine. These established guidelines for the use of nearly fifty thousand acres of land. Currently, conservation easements protect a number of Maine's Critical Areas, including those located in Number 5 Bog in Jackman, along the West Branch of the Penobscot, on the shores of Attean Pond and Seboomook and Lobster lakes, and on the islands of Acadia National Park. As a tool for balancing personal and public interests in protecting the land, conservation easements have proven to be extremely effective.

A Final Word

Today we live in a world where the resources of the planet must be shared by more and more people, where technology has opened earth and space to our needs and opened our minds to new possibilities. It's a time in which each we find ourselves in a web of increasingly complex relationships, where a single action can ripple throughout the world.

Strangely enough, the very technology that is opening the world to us can also insulate us from it. We are in danger of closing our minds to the natural world and forgetting how strongly we are physically, intellectually, and emotionally attached to it. More and more, our lives are shaped and cocooned by technological fences that have allowed us to throw off some of the constraints imposed on us as members of natural communities. In our urban settings nature too often becomes simply another recreational outlet, to enjoy or not as we choose—not something of which we are but a small part, not something to be cared for as we care for ourselves.

But still, down deep, we really do know that our survival depends on such things as green plants, pure water, and clean air. We know how refreshing and renewing experiences close to nature can be. And intuitively we know that there is something satisfying and secure about an environment in which diversity is the order of things.

It's all too easy to put that knowledge aside or to avoid acting on it, and sometimes we need to be reminded. That is the purpose of this book: to remind us of our natural heritage and of our responsibility to meet the "expectations of the land."

Natural Areas Open to the Public

Many of the unique natural features described in this book may be found in the natural areas listed below (grouped by natural region). Some of these areas charge entrance fees. The sites are keyed to the following guides, which provide additional information concerning their location, access, and character:

(AC) *The Audubon Society Field Guide to the Natural Places of the Northeast: Coastal,* by Stephen Kulik, Pete Salmansohn, and Heidi Welch (New York: Pantheon Books, 1984).

(AI) *The Audubon Society Field Guide to the Natural Places of the Northeast: Inland,* by Stephen Kulik, Pete Salmansohn, and Heidi Welch (New York: Pantheon Books, 1984).

(AT) *Appalachian Trail Guide 1: Maine, and Maps* (Augusta: Maine Appalachian Trail Club, 1983).

(MA) *The Maine Atlas and Gazetteer* (Freeport, Me.: DeLorme Publishing Company, 1986).

(MC) *The Maine Coast: A Nature Lover's Guide,* by Dorcas S. Miller (Charlotte, N.C.: East Woods Press, 1979).

(MF) *Maine Forever: A Guide to Nature Conservancy Preserves in Maine,* by Mary Minor C.S. Lannon (Topsham, Maine: The Maine Chapter of The Nature Conservancy, 1984).

(NS) *Natural Sites: A Guide to Maine's Natural Phenomena,* by Bernie Monegain, Maine Geographic Series (Freeport, Me.: DeLorme Publishing Company, 1985).

Coastal Region

Sandy Beach Coastal Subregion

Biddeford Pool (MA, NS). Mile-wide tidal pool, habitat for many shorebirds, good winter seabird area.

Blowing Cave, Kennebunkport (MA, NS). Spouts of water and mist up to 30-feet high from wave pressure in sea cave.

Butler/Marshall Preserve, The Nature Conservancy, Kennebunk and Arundel (MF). Varied habitats on tidal waters of the Kennebunk River. Picnic Rock—large glacial boulder.

Cape Neddick Park, York (MA). Woodland park.

East Point Sanctuary, Maine Audubon Society, Biddeford (AC, MA). Thirty-acre sanctuary on Biddeford Pool peninsula, birdlife, rocky shore, pebble beaches.

Ferry Beach State Park, Saco (MA). Wooded area with sand beach, tupelo stand.

Goose Rocks Beach, Kennebunkport (MA, MC). One of Maine's largest sand beaches.

Ogunquit Beach, Wells (MA, MC). Longest barrier spit sand beach in Maine (when combined with Moody Beach).

Perkins Cove / Marginal Way, Ogunquit (MA, MC). Paved path along rocky shore.

Rachel Carson National Wildlife Refuge, Wells (MA, MC). White pine forest, salt marsh, birdlife.

Scarborough Beach (MA). Closed barrier sand beach protecting marsh.

Scarborough Marsh State Wildlife Management Area and Nature Center, Managed by Maine Audubon Society (AC, MA, MC, NS). Largest salt marsh in Maine, trails, canoe tours.

Seapoint, Kittery (MC). Small peninsula, marsh, birdlife.

Sohier Park, York (MA, MC). Exposure of gabbro of the Acadian Orogeny, winter birds.

Vaughns Island Preserve, Kennebunkport (MA, NS). Uninhabited island, rocky shoreline, pebble beach, marshes, separated from mainland by tidal creeks.

Wells National Estuarine Reserve (MA, MC, NS). Nearly 2000 acres protecting wetlands, beaches, and upland fields and forest along Wells Bay.

Transition Coastal Subregion

Back Cove Sanctuary, Portland (MA, MC). Tidal flats, birdlife.

Basket Island Preserve, The Nature Conservancy, Cumberland (MA, MF). Shell and gravel beaches, extensive intertidal zone.

Bates Morse Mountain Coastal Research Area, Inc., managed by Bates College and The Nature Conservancy, Phippsburg (MA, MF). Seawall Beach—undeveloped barrier beach system—nesting least terns and piping plovers.

Baxter Woods, Portland (MA). Wooded park and bird sanctuary.

Bowdoin Pines, Brunswick (MA, MC, NS). Impressive grove of white pine over 140 years old.

Bradbury Mountain State Park, Pownal (MA, MC). Granitic mountain with views of Casco Bay and the White Mountains.

Crescent Beach State Park, Cape Elizabeth (MA, MC). Fringing pocket sand beach.

Damariscotta Reversing Falls, Damariscotta / Newcastle (MA, NS). Tidal reversal of river flow, alewife population.

Damariscove Island Preserve, The Nature Conservancy, Boothbay (MF). Seabird nesting island, one of earliest settlement sites in Maine. (Visitors requested to stay south of isthmus from April 15 to August 15.)

Desert of Maine, Freeport (MA, MC, NS). Large sandy glacial outwash plain revealed by erosion of topsoil.

Gilsland Farm, Maine Audubon Society headquarters, Falmouth (MA, MC). Woods, fields, pond, estuary.

Harkness Preserve, The Nature Conservancy, Rockport (MF). Stand of American chestnuts.

Hockomock Nature Trail, National Audubon Society, Bremen (MA, MC). Self-guiding trail along shore, fields, and woods.

Hog Island, National Audubon Society Camp, Bremen (MA). Todd Wildlife Sanctuary, spruce-fir forest on island just off the mainland.

Josephine Newman Wildlife Sanctuary, Maine Audubon Society, Georgetown (MA, MC). Coastal habitats, wooded ledges overlooking Robin Hood Cove, cattail pond, meadow.

La Verna Preserve, The Nature Conservancy, Bristol. (MA, MF) Rugged shoreline, tidal pools.

Maquoit Bay, Brunswick (MC). Shallow, warm-water bay with abundance of shellfish—clams, mussels, quahogs—and shorebirds.

Mast Landing Sanctuary, Maine Audubon Society, Freeport (MA, MC). Tidal river, woods, fields.

Merrymeeting Bay, Bath, Woolwich, Bowdoinham, Topsham (MC, NS). Largest fresh-water tidal bay north of the Chesapeake. Migratory birds, eagles.

Montsweag Preserve, The Nature Conservancy, Woolwich (MA, MF). Salt-water estuary.

Musquash Pond Preserve, The Nature Conservancy, Jefferson (MA, MF). Freshwater wetlands and forests.

Pemaquid Beach State Park, Bristol (MA, MC). Pocket barrier sand beach.

Pemaquid Point, Bristol (AC, MA, MC, NS). Coastal peninsula with fascinating bedrock formations and patterns.

Popham Beach State Park, Phippsburg (AC, MA, MC). One of Maine's largest and most complex beach systems, marshes, Fox Island Tombolo.

Rachel Carson Salt Pond Preserve, The Nature Conservancy, New Harbor (MA, MC, MF). One-quarter acre tidal pool.

Reid State Park, Georgetown (MA, MC). Maine's northernmost large sand beach system, two beaches—Mile Beach (closed barrier) and Half Mile Beach (open barrier spit), marshes.

Robert P.T. Coffin Wildflower Reservation, New England Wildflower Society, Inc., Woolwich (MA, MC). Secluded forest sanctuary overlooking Merrymeeting Bay.

Royal River Park, Yarmouth (MA). Riverside path between two falls.

Steve Powell Refuge and State Wildlife Management Area, Perkins Township (MA, MC). Islands at head of Merrymeeting Bay in Kennebec River, fields, woodlands, deer, bald eagle nest.

Two Lights State Park, Cape Elizabeth (MA, MC). Rocky shoreline of weathered, metamorphosed bedrock of the Casco Bay Group's Cape Elizabeth Formation.

Upper Goose Island Preserve, The Nature Conservancy, Harpswell (MA, MF). Blue heron colony, nesting osprey, 200-year-old maple and yellow birch. (Visitors are requested not to explore the island's interior between April and mid-August.)

Winslow Park, Freeport (MA). Wooded peninsula and beach on Casco Bay.

Wolf Neck Woods State Park, Freeport (AC, MA, MC). Small wooded park on coastal peninsula.

Penobscot Bay Coastal Subregion

Acadia National Park, Mt. Desert Island and surrounding area. (AC, MA, MC, NS) Highly scenic and uniquely diverse coastal area.

> **Acadia Mountain:** Overlooks Somes Sound.
>
> **Baker Island:** Glacially scarred island, large blocks of pink granite form feature known as the "dance floor," meadows, spruce-fir forest.
>
> **Cadillac Mountain:** Maine's highest coastal mountain, scenic views of Frenchman Bay.
>
> **Dorr Mountain:** Views of Frenchman Bay and Cadillac Mountain.
>
> **Flying Mountain:** Views of Somes Sound and Cadillac Mountain.
>
> **Gorham Mountain:** Interesting geology and scenic views.
>
> **Jordan Pond and Penobscot Mountain:** Scenic area rich in glacial history.
>
> **Great Head:** High coastal headland.
>
> **Isle au Haut:** Steep cliffs, forested shores, cobble beaches, beautiful coves.
>
> **Otter Cliffs and Otter Point:** Shoreline of pink granite.
>
> **Sand Beach:** Pocket beach with high percentage of shell fragments.
>
> **Schoodic Point:** Rocky point with basaltic dikes, granite cliffs, tide pools, jack pine.
>
> **Somes Sound:** Only fjord on the East Coast.
>
> **South Bubble Erratic:** Precariously perched glacial boulder.
>
> **The Beehive:** Mountain with stepped granite cliffs, scenic views.
>
> **Thunder Hole:** Thunderous sounds and water spouts from waves trapped in rocky cavern.
>
> **Wild Gardens of Acadia:** Over two hundred species of plants indigenous to Acadia National Park.
>
> **Witch Hole Pond Carriage Path:** Access to pond in glacially formed basin, beaver habitat.

Bar Harbor Bar, Maine Bureau of Parks and Recreation (AC). Rocky tidal bar between Mt. Desert Island and Bar Island.

Big Garden and Big White Island preserves, The Nature Conservancy, Vinalhaven (MF). Rugged islands forested with spruce and fir, variety of songbirds and seabirds.

Birdsacre Sanctuary, Ellsworth (MA, MC). Woodlands and pond.

Bradbury Island and Sheep Island preserves, The Nature Conservancy, East Penobscot Bay (MF). Bradbury Island: one-hundred-foot cliffs, deer, osprey; Sheep Island: thunder hole, osprey nests; gray seals in area.

Camden Hills State Park, Camden (AC, MA, MC). Wooded hills overlooking Penobscot Bay. Mount Megunticook is Maine's second highest coastal mountain, Maiden Cliff—high cliff overlooking Megunticook Lake.

Crockett Cove Woods and Barred Island preserves, The Nature Conservancy, Stonington and Deer Isle (MF). Classic example of coastal spruce-fir forest with abundant lichens and mosses.

Fernald's Neck Preserve, The Nature Conservancy, Camden and Lincolnville (MF). Large forested peninsula jutting into Megunticook Lake, wetland, more than 1800 feet of shoreline.

Fort Point State Park, Stockton Springs (MA). Peninsula location.

Indian Point-Blagden Preserve, The Nature Conservancy, Bar Harbor (AC, MF). Forested preserve on Western Bay, harbor seal haulout ledges.

Lamoine State Park, Lamoine (MA). Park on Frenchman Bay, views of Mt. Desert Island mountains, beach.

Lane's Island Preserve, The Nature Conservancy, Vinalhaven (MF). Open, relatively low island with evidence of early Indian habitation.

Moose Point State Park, Searsport (MA). Field, coniferous forest.

Mullen Head Park, North Haven (MA). Shoreland park.

Schoodic Mountain, Township 9 SD (AC, MA). Prominent mountain at the head of Frenchman Bay.

Sheep Island Preserve, The Nature Conservancy, Vinalhaven (MF). Small, wooded, low-lying island.

Ship Harbor Nature Trail, Southwest Harbor (MA). Granite ledges, shore, spruce woods.

Ship Island Group preserves (Ship, Bar, and Trumpet islands), The Nature Conservancy, Tremont (MF). Seabird nesting islands. (Visitors requested not to visit between May 15 and July 15.)

Smith Island Preserve, The Nature Conservancy, Vinalhaven (MF). Small island with rocky shore, two small cobble beaches, low vegetation.

The Brothers and Hay Ledge Preserve, The Nature Conservancy, St. George (MF). Seabird nesting colonies. (Visitors requested not to visit from May 1 to August 15, during nesting season.)

Turtle Island Preserve, The Nature Conservancy, Winter Harbor (MF). Old dense spruce forest, great blue heron colony, tidepools, seal haulouts. (Visitors requested not to explore the island interior between April and mid-August.)

Warren Island State Park, Islesboro (MA). Spruce-covered island.

Wreck Island and Round Island preserves, The Nature Conservancy, Stonington (MF). Old fields, woods, gravel beaches, rocky shores.

Eastern Coastal Subregion

Cobscook Bay State Park, Edmunds Township (MA, MC). Beautiful wooded park, rocky shore, high tides, shorebirds, offshore seal haulouts, occasional sightings of harbor porpoise.

Great Wass Island Preserve, The Nature Conservancy, Beals (MF). Coastal raised peatlands, rare marine invertebrates and algae, jack pine woodlands, subarctic maritime plants.

Larrabee Heath Preserve, The Nature Conservancy, Machiasport (MF). Coastal raised peatland.

McLellan Park, Millbridge (MA). Scenic views, trails.

Mistake Island Preserve, The Nature Conservancy, Jonesport (MF). Subarctic maritime plants and coastal heath community.

Petit Manan National Wildlife Refuge, Steuben (AC). Narrow, islandlike peninsula with old blueberry fields, jack pine, wetland.

Quoddy Head State Park, Lubec (MA, MC). Windswept peninsula with cliffs, large intertidal zone, and coastal raised peatland.

Roque Bluffs State Park (MA, MC). Pocket barrier sand beach with shallow freshwater lagoon.

Southern Oak-Forest Region

Mount Agamenticus, York (MA, MC, NS). Monadnock of significant botanical interest, at the northern boundary of many species of southern plants.
Spring Hill Recreation Area, South Berwick (MA). Park on pond.
Vaughan Woods Memorial, Maine Bureau of Parks and Recreation, South Berwick (AC, MA, MC). Small, historic woodland park on Salmon Falls River.

Upland-Hilly Region

Pine Forest Subregion

Douglas Mountain Preserve, The Nature Conservancy, Sebago (AI, MA, MF). Wooded mountain, panoramic view of mountains and lakes.
Dry Mills State Fish Hatchery and Game Farm, Gray (MA). Natural area with trails, captive wild animals, visitor's center.
Gray Delta, Gray–New Gloucester area. Maine Turnpike crosses this prime example of ancient river delta of glacial origin.
Harvey Butler Rhododendron Sanctuary, New England Wildflower Society, Inc., Springvale. Mixed hardwoods forest with great rhododendron.
Hiram Falls, Hiram (MA, NS). Geologically interesting falls.
Hiram Nature Study Area, Central Maine Power Company, Baldwin (MA). Wooded site adjacent to Saco River.
Kezar Falls Gorge, Kezar River, Lovell (MA). Deep, winding gorge containing falls.
Range Ponds State Park, Poland (MA). Wooded park by lake.
Sebago Lake State Park, Naples and Casco (MA). Forested park on lake, sand beaches, large white oak forest.
Thorncraig Bird Sanctuary, Lewiston (MA). Over two hundred acres of natural habitat within city limits.

Upland-Foothills Subregion

Annie Sturgis Sanctuary, New England Wildflower Society, Inc., Vassalboro. Forty acres of mixed hardwoods and softwoods on Kennebec River. Protects a stand of wild ginger.
Augusta Nature Area. Diversity of habitats in hilly terrain within city limits.
Brownfield Bog State Wildlife Management Area. Wetlands and upland forests in scenic area.
Chesterville Esker (MA). Narrow esker between two ponds.
Chesterville State Wildlife Management Area (MA). Ponds, wetlands, and wooded uplands.
Craig Brook National Fish Hatchery, Orland. Natural area with trail.
Damariscotta Lake State Park, Jefferson (MA). Wooded lakeside park, sandy beach.
Frye Mountain State Wildlife Management Area, Montville (MA). Forest and field habitat for diversity of wildlife.
Indian and Fowl Meadow Islands Preserve, The Nature Conservancy, Embden (MF). Two small floodplain islands in Upper Kennebec River.
Lake St. George State Park, Liberty (MA). Park on spring-fed lake.

Maine's Conservation School, Conservation Education Foundation of Maine, Bryant Pond Village, Woodstock. Hilly, deciduous wooded area on lake.

Mendall Marsh State Wildlife Management Area, Frankfort (MA). Tidal wetlands, migrating waterfowl.

Mercer Bog State Wildlife Management Area. Canoe access to wetlands, diversity of wildlife.

Mullen Woods Preserve, The Nature Conservancy, Newport (MF). Old-growth white pine.

North Anson Gorge (MA). Large exposure of bedrock, twelve-foot-high walls, on Carrabassett River.

Ruffingham Meadow Wildlife Management Area, Searsmont (MA). Wetlands, waterfowl nesting.

Sheepscot Reversing Falls, Alna (MA, NS). Tidal change of water flow.

Snow Falls Gorge, West Paris (MA, NS). Scenic roadside waterfalls and gorge on Little Androscoggin River.

Sucker Brook Preserve, The Nature Conservancy, Lovell (MF). Brook, beaver pond, freshwater marsh.

Swan Lake State Park, Swanville (MA). Small park with beach.

Norumbega Hills Subregion

The Whalesback, Aurora (MA, MC, MS). Outstanding esker aligned with direction of glacial retreat, forms roadbed of Route 9 for 2.5 miles.

Mountain Region

Appalachian Trail. Trail system across Maine's highest mountains and most rugged wilderness country, spectacular scenic views, 276 miles from New Hampshire border to Mt. Katahdin.

Baxter State Park (AI, MA, AT).

>**Baxter Peak, Mt. Katahdin:** Maine's highest point, at 5,267 feet. National Natural Landmark.

>**The Chimney:** Deep mountainside gully.

>**Grand Falls:** Cascading falls in gorge.

>**Great Basin:** Glacially carved cirque.

>**Green Falls:** Secluded mountain waterfall over moss-covered bedrock.

>**Howe Brook:** Wooded stream with potholes and secluded waterfall.

>**Katahdin Esker:** Ancient glacial streambed in relief traversed by Baxter Park Perimeter Road.

>**Katahdin Stream Falls:** High falls in granite ravine.

>**The Knife Edge:** Spectacular arete—thin high ridge.

>**Little and Big Niagra Falls:** Scenic falls on Nesowadnehunk Stream over pink granite.

>**Northwest Basin:** Remote cirque and tarn.

>**Sandy Stream Pond:** Excellent moose habitat.

>**South Turner Mountain.** Spectacular views.

>**The Tableland.** Rock-strewn alpine plateau, rare alpine plants.

>**Traveler Mountain.** Volcanic mountain, old-growth forests, alpine vegetation.

Bigelow Mountain, Maine Bureau of Parks and Recreation, Wyman, Dead

River (AI, MA, AT). Massive mountain range with four conical peaks, National Natural Landmark.

Big Squaw Mountain, Scott Paper Company, Big Squaw Township (AI, MA). Panoramic view of Maine's north woods and Moosehead Lake.

Boarstone Mountain, National Audubon Society, Elliotsville (AI, MA). Mountainous and wooded wildlife sanctuary with fine views.

Cathedral Pines, Stratton. Old-growth stand of red pine.

Coos Canyon, Byron. (MA, NS) Scenic roadside gorge with falls and potholes along the East Branch of the Swift River.

Crocker Cirque, Carrabassett Valley (MA, AT). Glacial cirque and pool near Appalachian Trail.

Dunn Falls, Andover North Surplus (MA, AT). Spectacular series of waterfalls and cascades on West Branch Ellis River along Appalachian Trail. Two large vertical drops, steep bedrock walls.

Grafton Notch State Park, Grafton (AI, MA, NS, AT).

    Moose Cave Gorge. Deep 300-foot gorge in granite bedrock.

    Mother Walker Falls Gorge. Large V-shaped gorge with cascades and natural bridge.

    Old Speck (AT). Third highest mountain in Maine.

    Screw Auger Falls Gorge. Twisting gorge in granite on Bear River.

    Table Rock. Lookout ledge with scenic views of nearby mountains.

Gulf Hagas, Bowdoin College Grant East (AI, MA, NS, AT). Impressive, deep, narrow and twisting slate gorge, sometimes called the Grand Canyon of the East. National Natural Landmark. Near Appalachian Trail.

Height of Land, Township D (MA). Scenic views of White Mountains and Rangeley Lakes from roadside overlook.

The Hermitage Preserve, The Nature Conservancy, T7 R10 (MF). Old-growth white pine, National Natural Landmark, at entrance to Gulf Hagas.

Kennebec River Gorge, The Forks (MA, NS). Ten-mile turbulent gorge, up to 240 feet deep.

Little Wilson Falls Gorge, Prentiss and Carlisle Company, Elliotsville Plantation (AI, MA, AT). One of the highest falls in Maine at head of narrow slate gorge.

Mahoosuc Notch and Arm, Brown Company, Gilead, Maine, and Berlin, New Hampshire (AI, AT). Rugged, spectacular mountain habitat along the Appalachian Trail.

Mount Blue State Park, Weld (MA, NS). Forested park by lake. Mountain is fine example of a monadnock.

Moxie Falls, Moxie Gore (MA). One of Maine's highest falls, over 110 feet in several drops, on Moxie Stream.

Rangeley Lake State Park, Rangeley (MA). Wooded park in mountains by lake.

Screw Auger Falls, Bowdoin College Grant East. (MA, AT). Series of falls on Gulf Hagas Stream as it enters Gulf Hagas. Near Appalachian Trail.

Smalls Falls, Sandy River, Township E (MA). Two scenic falls at junction of two streams.

Step Falls Preserve, The Nature Conservancy, Newry (AI, MA, MF). Scenic waterfalls.

Swift River Falls, Roxbury (MA). Two small drops, outstanding example of hydraulic sculpting of granite bedrock.

Tumbledown Mountain, Weld (AI, MA, NS). High, rugged, glaciated mountain with fascinating rock patterns and alpine lake.

White Mountain National Forest, Stoneham, Albany, Mason.

Bachelders Grant (AI, MA, NS).
Bickford Slides. Two scenic waterfalls along Bickford Brook.
Caribou Mountain. Overlooking Evans Notch, panoramic view of White Mountains, old-growth forests.

Northern Forest Region

Northern Lakes Subregion

Holeb Falls, Attean (MA). Falls over blocky granite on Moose River, largest drop over twenty-five feet.
Ice Caves, T8 R14 WELS (MA). Deep, cold caves near Allagash Lake.
Lily Bay State Park, Beaver Cove (MA). Park on shore of Moosehead Lake in beautiful wilderness region.
Little Allagash Falls, Maine Bureau of Parks and Recreation, T3 R13 WELS (MA). Scenic falls on Little Allagash Stream, drop of about twelve feet over ledge into pool.
No. 5 Bog, Attean, Bradstreet, T5 R7. Large peatland, jack pine, red pine, National Natural Landmark.
Ripogenus Gorge, T3 R11 (MA, NS). Spectacular 200-foot-deep gorge on West Branch Penobscot River.

Allagash/St. John River Subregion

Allagash Wilderness Waterway, Maine Bureau of Parks and Recreation (AI, MA). Scenic wilderness canoe area, old-growth white pine.
Allagash Falls. Scenic falls on Allagash River—turbulent rapids above and below twenty-foot-high falls.

Forest Lowlands Subregion

Mattawamkeag Wilderness Park (MA). Forested park along the Matta-wamkeag River.
Peaks-Kenny State Park, Dover-Foxcroft (MA). Forested park on lake, views of mountains.
Seboeis River Gorge Preserve, The Nature Conservancy, T5 R7 and T6 R7 (MF). Major river gorge in an eight-mile unspoiled river corridor.

Aroostook Limestone Region

Aroostook State Park, Presque Isle (MA). Park by lake, good views from mountain.
Lt. Gordon Manuel State Wildlife Management Area, Hodgdon (MA). Marsh habitat.

Eastern Peatlands Region

Columbia Falls Delta, Columbia Falls, Jonesboro, Centerville (AC). Outstanding example of an ancient river delta formed at contact of glacial ice and the sea.
Enfield Horseback, Passadumkeag (MA, NS). Sixty-foot-high esker rising out of swamp and traversed by a road.
The Great Heath, Columbia (AI, MA, MC). Largest raised bog in Maine, bisected by the Pleasant River.

Great Works State Wildlife Management Area, Edmunds (MA). Diversity of habitats—marsh, pond, wooded upland.

Moosehorn National Wildlife Refuge, Baring (AC, MA, MC). Diversity of habitats, migrating waterfowl, other wildlife. Two designated Wilderness Areas: Baring (4680 acres) and Edmunds (2782 acres).

Orono Bog, University of Maine and private. Orono (AI). Large 600-acre peatland, National Natural Landmark.

Sunset Park, Orient (MA). Small park by lake.

Agencies and Organizations

Following are some of the agencies and organizations interested in the conservation of Maine's natural areas, geological features, plants, and animals.

Federal Agencies

Acadia National Park
P.O. Box 177
Bar Harbor, Maine 04609

U.S. Fish and Wildlife Service
One Gateway Center, Suite 700
Newton Corner, Mass. 02158

U.S. Fish and Wildlife Service
Ralph Hill Market Place, Room 400
22 Bridge Street
Concord, New Hampshire 03301

White Mountain National Forest
Evans Notch Ranger District
Bethel, Maine 04217

State Agencies

Critical Areas Program
Maine State Planning Office
State House Station 38
Augusta, Maine 04333

Maine Department of Conservation
State House Station 22
Augusta, Maine 04333
Includes:
    Maine Forest Service; Maine
    Geological Survey; Bureau
    of Parks and Recreation;
    Bureau of Public Lands

Maine Department of Inland
Fisheries and Wildlife
284 State Street
Augusta, Maine 04333

Maine Endangered and Nongame
Wildlife Project
Maine Department of Inland
Fisheries and Wildlife
P.O. Box 1298
Bangor, Maine 04401

Maine Department of Marine
Resources
State House Station 21
Augusta, Maine 04333

Educational Institutions

College of the Atlantic
Bar Harbor, Maine 04609

UNIVERSITY OF MAINE

Center for Marine Studies
14 Coburn Hall
University of Maine
Orono, Maine 04469
Includes:
    Ira C. Darling Center;
    The Joint Institutional
    Sea Grant Program

College of Forest Resources
240 Nutting Hall
University of Maine
Orono, Maine 04469

Cooperative Fish and Wildlife
Research Unit
Fisheries-Zoology Department
313 Murray Hall
University of Maine
Orono, Maine 04469

Institute for Quaternary Studies
University of Maine
Orono, Maine 04469

Land and Water Resources Center
11 Coburn Hall
University of Maine
Orono, Maine 04469

Private Organizations

Maine Audubon Society
Gilsland Farm
118 U.S. Route One
Falmouth, Maine 04105

Maine Coast Heritage Trust
P.O. Box 426
Northeast Harbor, Maine 04662
and
P.O. Box 416
Topsham, Maine 04086

The Nature Conservancy,
Maine Chapter
P.O. Box 338
122 Main Street
Topsham, Maine 04086-1220

National Audubon Society
950 Third Avenue
New York, New York 10022

Natural Resources Council of Maine
271 State Street
Augusta, Maine 04330

New England Wildflower Society, Inc.
Garden-in-the-Woods
Hemenway Road
Framingham, Massachusetts 01701

Publications of the Maine Critical Areas Program

The following educational brochures are available from the Maine Critical Areas Program, Maine State Planning Office, State House Station #38, Augusta, Maine 04333. A complete listing of publications of the Critical Areas Program is also available upon request.

Plants

Nodding Pogonia
Orchids
Sassafras
Mountain Laurel
Rhododendron
Tupelo
Atlantic White Cedar
Shagbark Hickory

Baxter State Park:
 Flowering Ground Plants
 of the Northern Forest
Sassafras
Alpine Vegetation
Old-Growth White Pine
White Oak
Furbish's Lousewort

Birds

Alcids
Common Eider
Terns
Black Tern

Least Tern
Piping Plover
Leach's Storm-Petrel
Wading Birds

Invertebrates

American Oyster
Horseshoe Crab

Marine Invertebrates

Geology

Waterfalls
Gorges
Whitewater Rapids

Eskers
Sand Beaches
Fossils

Wells National Estuarine Reserve

Wells Sanctuary
Estuaries

Birds
Sand Beaches

Bibliography

The following references are particularly related to Maine and New England. Many other books and guides of a general nature are also available that describe plants, animals, and other natural features found in Maine.

General Natural History

Bouthillette, Guy. *Tidal Zones: A Guide to Plants and Animals Where the Sea Meets the Shore*. Edited by Barbara Feller-Roth. Freeport, Me.: Delorme Publishing Company, 1983. A pocket reference describing marine invertebrates, seaweeds, sponges, and fish of the intertidal zone.

Conkling, Philip. *Islands in Time: A Natural and Human History of the Islands of Maine*. Camden, Me.: Down East Books, 1981. A lively account of Maine's islands.

Cronin, William. *Changes in the Land: Indians, Colonists, and the Ecology of New England*. New York: Hill and Wang, 1983. An excellent ecological history of colonial New England and how the land and people changed each other.

Cupo, Joe. *Weather: Records, Patterns and Phenomena*. Freeport, Me.: DeLorme Publishing Company, 1983. A pocket reference clearly explaining the reasons for Maine's weather.

Gosner, Kenneth L. *A Field Guide to the Atlantic Seashore*. Boston: Houghton Mifflin Company, 1979. A comprehensive field guide to invertebrates and seaweeds of the Atlantic coast from the Bay of Fundy to Cape Hatteras.

Jorgensen, Neil. *A Guide to New England's Landscape*. Chester, Ct.: Globe Pequot Press, 1977. A very readable description of New England's geology and vegetation.

Miller, Dorcas S. *The Maine Coast*. Charlotte, N.C.: Fast & McMillan Publishers, Inc., 1979. Includes a brief, clear presentation of Maine's coastal human history, natural resources, geology, wildlife, and ecosystems.

Geology

Blakemore, Jean. *We Walk on Jewels: Treasure Hunting in Maine for Gems and Minerals*. Rockland, Me.: Courier of Maine Books, 1976. A guide to rock and mineral collecting in Maine.

Chapman, Carleton A. *The Geology of Acadia National Park*. Old Greenwich, Ct.: Chatham Press, Inc., 1970. Provides an excellent description of the geological history and features of Acadia National Park.

Hussey II, Arthur M. *The Geology of Two Lights and Crescent Beach State Parks Area, Cape Elizabeth, Maine*. Bulletin 26. Augusta: Maine Geological Survey, Dept. of Conservation, 1982. Provides a clear explanation of the geological history and features of the Cape Elizabeth coastal area.

Kendall, David L. *Glaciers and Granite: A Guide to Maine's Landscape and Geology*. Camden, Me.: Down East Books, 1987.

Osberg, Philip H., et al. *Bedrock Geological Map of Maine*. Augusta: Maine Geological Survey, 1985.

Perham, Jane C. *Gems and Minerals: A Guide to Rockhounding in Maine*. Edited by Laura Sawyer. Freeport, Me.: DeLorme Publishing Company, 1983. A pocket reference illustrating and describing over forty Maine minerals and gems.

Thompson, Woodrow B., ed. *Surficial Geological Map of Maine*. Augusta: Maine Geological Survey, 1985.

Fresh Water and Wetlands

Caduto, Michael J. *Pond and Brook: A Guide to Nature Study in Freshwater Environments*. Englewood Cliffs, N.J.: Prentice-Hall, Inc., 1985. An excellent introduction to all common freshwater environments—ponds, lakes, streams, rivers, and wetlands.

Johnson, Charles W. *Bogs of the Northeast*. Hanover, N.H.: University Press of New England, 1985. A very thorough and readable treatment of the ecology of peatlands.

Snow, John O. *Secrets of a Saltmarsh*. Portland, Me.: Guy Gannett Publishing Co., 1980. A revealing account of life in a salt marsh.

Plant Life

Campbell, Christopher S., and Hyland, Fay. *Winter Keys to Woody Plants of Maine*. Orono: University of Maine at Orono Press, 1978. A well-illustrated guide to the winter identification of both woody plants indigenous to Maine and those established following escape from cultivation.

Dwelley, Marilyn. *Spring Wildflowers of New England*; *Summer Wildflowers of New England*; *Trees and Shrubs of New England*. Camden, Me.: Down East Books, 1973, 1977, 1980. Nontechnical identification guides to New England wildflowers, trees, and shrubs categorized by families within color groups.

Hyland, Fay, and Hoisington, Barbara. *The Woody Plants of Sphagnous Bogs of Northern New England and Adjacent Canada*. Orono: University of Maine at Orono Press, 1981. A key to the identification of the woody plants of peatlands.

Irland, Lloyd C. *Wildlands and Woodlots: The Story of New England's Forests*. Hanover, N.H.: University Press of New England, 1982. A nontechnical description of New England's forest geography and discussion of the social and economic issues related to forests.

Keenan, Philip E. *Orchids: A Complete Guide to Maine's Orchids*. Edited by

L.M. Eastman. Freeport, Me.: DeLorme Publishing Company, 1983. A pocket reference for the identification of all forty-six species of orchids found in Maine.

Fishes

Maine Fish. Thorndike, Me.: Thorndike Press, n.d. A booklet containing reprints of articles from *Maine Fish and Wildlife* Magazine on the life histories of a wide variety of Maine fish.

Thompson, Peter. *The Game Fishes of New England and Southeastern Canada.* Camden, Me.: Down East Books, 1980. An excellent guide to saltwater, anadromous, catadromous, and freshwater fishes. Illustrated in color. (Out of print.)

Amphibians and Reptiles

DeGraaf, Richard M., and Rudis, Deborah D. *Amphibians and Reptiles of New England: Habitats and Natural History.* Amherst, Mass.: Univ. of Massachusetts Press, 1983. A detailed guide to the life histories and habitat associations of the nearly sixty species of salamanders, frogs, toads, turtles, and snakes of the New England region.

Epple, Anne Orth. *The Amphibians of New England.* Camden, Me.: Down East Books, 1983. A handbook describing the appearances, habitats, and life cyles of the twenty-two amphibians inhabiting the woods, ponds, streams, and wetlands of the Northeast.

Birds

Adamus, Paul R., principal author and compiler. *Atlas of Breeding Birds in Maine, 1978-1983.* Augusta: Maine Department of Inland Fisheries and Wildlife, 1987. Provides maps and other information on distribution of the 201 species breeding in the state.

Kidwell, Al. *Coastal Birds: A Guide to Birds of Maine's Beautiful Coastline.* Freeport, Me.: DeLorme Publishing Company, 1983. A pocket reference to birds seen throughout the year along the coast of Maine.

Maine Birds. Thorndike, Me.: Thorndike Press, 1978. A booklet of reprints of articles from *Maine Fish and Wildlife* Magazine on the life histories of many of Maine's upland game, migratory, and nongame birds.

Pettingill, Jr., Olin Sewall, ed. *Enjoying Maine Birds.* Falmouth, Me.: Maine Audubon Society, 1960. An introductory guide booklet to many of Maine's birds.

Pierson, Elizabeth, and Pierson, Jan. *A Birder's Guide to the Coast of Maine.* Camden, Me.: Down East Books, 1981. A guide to twenty-one bird-watching sites along the Maine coast.

Mammals

Godin, Alfred J. *Wild Mammals of New England.* Freeport, Me.: DeLorme Publishing Company, 1983. A very complete and interestingly written field guide to New England's mammals. Includes descriptions, information on distribution and behavior, drawings, and maps.

Katona, Steven K.; Rough, Valerie; and Richardson, David T. *A Field Guide to the Whales, Porpoises and Seals of the Gulf of Maine and Eastern Canada: Cape Cod to Newfoundland.* New York: Charles Scribner's Sons, 1983. A thorough, well-illustrated account of the whales, porpoises, and seals in the Gulf of Maine. Provides detailed information on the characteristics, feeding habits, behavior, and reproductive cycles of thirty-one species in the region.

Kidwell, Al. *Whales and Seals: A Guide to Coastal and Offshore Mammals.* Freeport, Me.: DeLorme Publishing Company, 1983. A pocket reference to whales and seals along the coast of Maine and in its offshore waters.

Maine Mammals. Thorndike, Me.: Thorndike Press, n.d. A booklet of reprints of articles from *Maine Fish and Wildlife* Magazine on over twenty-five species of Maine's mammals.

Notes

Preface

1. Kenneth Roberts, *Trending into Maine* (Camden, Maine: Down East, 1938), p. 3.

2. James Rosier, *A True Relation,* quoted in Kenneth Roberts's *Trending into Maine*, p.4.

1 • Patterns in the Rock

1. Arthur M. Hussey II, Professor of Geology at Bowdoin College, helped with the identification and sequencing of many of the geologic events outlined in this chapter. In addition, this text draws upon his description of events in *The Geology of the Two Lights and Crescent Beach State Parks Area, Cape Elizabeth, Maine,* Bulletin 26 (Augusta, Maine Geological Survey, Department of Conservation, 1982). Professor Hussey and many other scientists continue to collect data and develop new hypotheses as they reconstruct the scenario of geologic events that shaped Maine.

2. References to the Casco Bay Group were provided by Arthur M. Hussey II, *Significant Geologic Localities in the Casco Bay Group and Southern Maine,* Planning Report 37 (Augusta: Maine Critical Areas Program, State Planning Office, 1977).

3. Information on the serpentine formations in central western Maine came from Eugene L. Boudette, "Ophiolite Assemblage of Early Paleozoic Age in Central Western Maine," *Structural Zones and Faults of the Northern Appalachians,* ed. P. St-Julian and J. Beland, Special Paper 24 (Geological Association of Canada, 1982), pp. 209–230.

4. The description of the Shin Brook Formation was based on Robert B. Neuman, *Fossils in Ordovician Tuffs Northeastern Maine,* Geological Survey Bulletin 1181-E (Washington, D.C.: U.S. Government Printing Office, 1964) and his description in *Decade of North American Geology* (Boulder, Colo.: Geological Society of America, 1988).

5. Information on the fossil groups in Maine was found in William H. Forbes, *Significant Bedrock Fossil Localities in Maine and Their Relevance to*

the *Critical Areas Program,* Planning Report 46 (Augusta: Maine Critical Areas Program, State Planning Office, 1977).

6. References to significant outcrops in the Kingsbury, Skowhegan, and Waterville area were based on Allan Ludman and Philip H. Osberg, "Site No. 169: Stratigraphy and Structure of the Central Maine Turbidite Belt in the Skowhegan-Waterville Region," in *Decade of North American Geology.*

7. The description of formations in the Rangeley area came from Robert H. Moench and Eugene L. Boudette, "Stratigraphy of the Rangely Area, Western Maine," in *Decade of North American Geology.*

8. The description of the volcanic complex preserved in the Katahdin and Traveler Mountain area was based on a personal communication from Rudolph Hon, Professor of Geology at Boston College, and from his article, "Petrology of Igneous Bodies Within the Katahdin Pluton," *New England Intercollegiate Geological Conference Guidebook* (Chestnut Hill, Mass.: Department of Geology and Geophysics, Boston College, 1980), pp. 65–79.

9. Information on the Mapleton Formation came from David C. Roy, Professor of Geology at Boston College, in a personal communication and from Kenneth J. White, "The Mapleton Formation; and Immediately Post-Acadian Basin Fill," (MS thesis, Boston College, 1975)

2 • *The Works of Glaciers*

1. Descriptions of the origin of the Knife Edge and other glacial features of Baxter State Park, along with a general explanation of the glacial geology of Maine, were given in Dabney W. Caldwell, *The Geology of Baxter State Park and Mt. Katahdin,* Bulletin 12 (Augusta: Maine Geological Survey, 1972).

2. Details on the formation and character of the state's major glaciomarine deltas were provided by Harold W. Borns, Jr., *Emerged Glaciomarine Deltas in Maine,* Planning Report 53 (Augusta: Maine Critical Areas Program, State Planning Office, 1981).

3. The identification of significant eskers in Maine and a brief description of Maine's glacial history were obtained from Harold W. Borns, Jr., *Eskers in Maine,* Planning Report 67 (Augusta: Maine Critical Areas Program, State Planning Office, 1979).

4. References to kettleholes are based on Kathlyn I. Marsh, *Development of a Methodology for Inventorying Kettleholes in Maine,* Miscellaneous Report 7 (Augusta: Maine Critical Areas Program, State Planning Office, 1978).

3 • *Inland Waters*

1. A detailed analysis of the significant natural and recreational values of the state's river systems was found in the *Maine Rivers Study* (Augusta: Maine Department of Conservation, and National Park Service, U.S. Department of Interior, 1982).

2. Descriptions of Maine's outstanding waterfalls were based on Thomas Brewer, *Waterfalls in Maine and Their Relevance to the Critical Areas Program,* Planning Report 60 (Augusta: Maine Critical Areas Program, State Planning Office, 1978).

3. Information on Maine's significant whitewater rapids was drawn from Janet McMahon, *Maine's Whitewater Rapids and Their Relevance to the Critical Areas Program,* Planning Report 74 (Augusta: Maine Critical Areas Program, State Planning Office, 1981).

4. Detailed descriptions of Maine's gorges were found in Thomas Brewer,

Gorges in Maine and Their Relevance to the Critical Areas Program, Planning Report 64 (Augusta: Maine Critical Areas Program, State Planning Office, 1978).

5. The account of dam development in the Penobscot region of northern Maine during the 1800s was based upon Alfred Greer Hempstead, *The Penobscot Boom* (privately published, 1931; reprinted by Down East Books, 1975). Out-of-print.

6. Information on the Maine Tourmaline Necklace was provided by Ronald J. Kley, Registrar/Curator at the Maine State Museum.

7. Henry D. Thoreau, *The Maine Woods* (New York: Thomas Y. Crowell & Co., 1906), p. 97.

8. Descriptive information on the lakes in Deboullie Township was provided by Mark J. Kern, *Natural Resources Inventory of T15, R9,* Miscellaneous Report 17 (Augusta: Maine Department of Conservation and Maine State Planning Office, 1984).

4 • The Coast

1. Much of the information on sand beaches came from Bruce W. Nelson and L. Kenneth Fink, Jr., *Geological and Botanical Features of Sand Beach Systems in Maine,* Maine Sea Grant Publications Bulletin 14 and Planning Report 54 (Augusta: Maine Critical Areas Program, State Planning Office, 1980).

2. Background on gravel beaches in Maine, and especially Jasper Beach, was provided by Barry S. Timson, *Jasper Beach, Machiasport, Maine,* Planning Report 75 (Augusta: Maine Critical Areas Program, State Planning Office, 1981).

3. Information on marine features in Maine, including sea caves, spouting holes, thunderholes, and marine arches, was obtained from Paul R. Adamus and Garrett C. Clough, Principal Investigators for the Center for Natural Areas, *A Preliminary Listing of Noteworthy Natural Features in Maine,* Miscellaneous Report 2 (Augusta: Maine Critical Areas Program, State Planning Office, 1976).

4. Descriptive information pertaining to some of southern Maine's unusual marine features was provided by Arthur M. Hussey II, *Significant Geologic Localities in the York County Coastal Zone,* Planning Report 56 (Augusta: Maine Critical Areas Program, State Planning Office, 1978).

Section II • Perspective

1. F. Morris and E.A. Eames, *Our Wild Orchids: Trails and Portraits* (New York: Charles Scribner's Sons, 1929).

2. Information on arethusa came from Susan C. Gawler, *Arethusa* (Arethusa bulbosa), *A Rare Orchid in Maine and Its Relevance to the Critical Areas Program,* Planning Report 76 (Augusta: Maine Critical Areas Program, State Planning Office, 1982).

3. Much of the general information on Maine's rare plants, including types, listing criteria, significance levels, and threats to their survival, came from Susan C. Gawler, *An Annotated List of Maine's Rare Vascular Plants,* with assistance from L. M. Eastman, Charles D. Richards, and the Endangered Species Committee of the New England Botannical Club and with additions by Barbara St. John Vickery, Miscellaneous Report 25 (Augusta: Maine Critical Areas Program, State Planning Office, 1984).

4. The description of slender cliff-brake drew upon L. M. Eastman, Maine Audubon Society, *Slender Cliff-brake* (Cryptogramma stelleri) *in Maine and*

Its Relevance to the Critical Areas Program, Planning Report 22 (Augusta: Maine Critical Areas Program, State Planning Office, 1976).

5. References to great rhododendron were provided by Harry R. Tyler, Jr., *Great Rhododendron* (Rhododendron maximum) *in Maine and Its Relevance to the Critical Areas Program,* Planning Report 3 (Augusta: Maine Critical Areas Program, State Planning Office, 1975).

6. Information on mountain laurel came from Harry R. Tyler, Jr., *Mountain Laurel* (Kalmia latifolia) *in Maine and Its Relevance to the Critical Areas Program,* Planning Report 7 (Augusta: Maine Critical Areas Program, State Planning Office, 1976)

5 • *Alpine Plant Communities*

1. Much of this chapter is based upon the study by Diane Ebert May and Ronald B. Davis, *Alpine Tundra Vegetation of Maine Mountains and Its Relevance to the Critical Areas Program,* Planning Report 36 (Augusta: Maine Critical Areas Program, State Planning Office, 1978).

2. Information on the fir waves in Baxter State Park came from Dabney W. Caldwell, *The Geology of Baxter State Park and Mt. Katahdin,* Bulletin 12 (Augusta: Maine Geological Survey, 1972) and from W. Donald Hudson, Jr., *Old-Growth Forests, Subalpine Forests, and Alpine Areas in Baxter State Park,* Miscellaneous Report 31 (Augusta: Maine Critical Areas Program, State Planning Office, 1985).

6 • *Woodland Plant Communities*

1. The division of Maine into three major forest zones is based upon a modification of the Natural Forest Vegetation Zones map in *Forest Cover Types of North America* (Washington, D.C.: Society of American Foresters, 1955).

2. Many of the references to old-growth forests drew upon *Natural Old-Growth Forest Stands in Maine and Their Relevance to the Critical Areas Program,* Planning Report 79 (Augusta: Maine Critical Areas Program, State Planning Office, 1982).

3. Henry D. Thoreau, *The Maine Woods* (New York: Thomas Y. Crowell & Co., 1906), p.301.

4. Information on many of the rare plant species described in this chapter came from *A Compilation of the Critical Areas Program Botanical Fact Sheets,* Miscellaneous Report 33 (Augusta: Maine Critical Areas Program, State Planning Office, 1985).

5. Background information on jack pine was provided by *Jack Pine* (Pinus banksiana) *in Maine and Its Relevance to the Critical Areas Program,* Planning Report 77 (Augusta: Maine Critical Areas Program, State Planning Office, 1983).

6. The description of white pine drew upon Philip W. Conkling, *Old-Growth White Pine* (Pinus strobus) *Stands in Maine and Their Relevance to the Critical Areas Program,* Planning Report 61 (Augusta: Maine Critical Areas Program, State Planning Office, 1978).

7. Details about ram's-head lady's-slipper came from A. E. Brower, *Ram's-head Lady's-slipper* (Cypripedium arietinum) *in Maine and Its Relevance to the Critical Areas Program,* Planning Report 25 (Augusta: Maine Critical Areas Program, State Planning Office, 1977).

8. Details on small whorled pogonia came from L. M. Eastman, *Small Whorled Pogonia* (Isotria medeoloides) *in Maine and Its Relevance to the*

Critical Areas Program, Planning Report 24 (Augusta: Maine Critical Areas Program, State Planning Office, 1977).

9. Facts about nodding pogonia came from L. M. Eastman, *Nodding Pogonia* (Triphora trianthophora) *in Maine and Its Relevance to the Critical Areas Program,* Planning Report 19 (Augusta: Maine Critical Areas Program, State Planning Office, 1976)

10. Data on tupelo were provided by L. M. Eastman, *Tupelo* (Nyssa sylvatica) *in Maine and Its Relevance to the Critical Areas Program,* Planning Report 39 (Augusta: Maine Critical Areas Program, State Planning Office,1977).

11. Information on old-growth shagbark hickory was obtained from Roger J. Stern, *Old Growth Shagbark Hickory* (Carya ovata) *Stands in Maine and Their Relevance to the Critical Areas Program,* Planning Report 66 (Augusta: Maine Critical Areas Program, State Planning Office, 1979).

12. The description of old-growth white oak was based on Roger J. Stern, *Old Growth White Oak* (Quercus alba) *Stands in Maine and Their Relevance to the Critical Areas Program,* Planning Report 65 (Augusta: Maine Critical Areas Program, State Planning Office, 1979).

13. Background on chestnut oak was provided by L. M. Eastman, *Chestnut Oak* (Quercus prinus) *in Maine and Its Relevance to the Critical Areas Program,* Planning Report 14 (Augusta: Maine Critical Areas Program, State Planning Office, 1976).

14. Information on scarlet oak came from L. M. Eastman, *Scarlet Oak* (Quercus coccinea) *in Maine and Its Relevance to the Critical Areas Program,* Planning Report 59 (Augusta: Maine Critical Areas Program, State Planning Office, 1976).

15. The description of flowering dogwood is based on L. M. Eastman, *Flowering Dogwood* (Cornus florida) *in Maine and Its Relevance to the Critical Areas Program,* Planning Report 9 (Augusta: Maine Critical Areas Program, State Planning Office, 1976).

16. The reference to sassafras drew upon L. M. Eastman, *Sassafras Trees in Maine and Their Relevance to the Critical Areas Program,* Planning Report 8 (Augusta: Maine Critical Areas Program, State Planning Office, 1976).

17. Data on spicebush came from L. M. Eastman, *Spicebush* (Lindera benzoin) *in Maine and Its Relevance to the Critical Areas Program,* Planning Report 23 (Augusta: Maine Critical Areas Program, State Planning Office, 1976).

18. The brief reference to spotted wintergreen drew upon L. M. Eastman, *Spotted Wintergreen* (Chimaphila maculata) *in Maine and Its Relevance to the Critical Areas Program,* Planning Report 21 (Augusta: Maine Critical Areas Program, State Planning Office,1976).

7 • *Freshwater Wetland Plant Communities*

1. General background information on wetlands was provided by Timothy Zorach, *Freshwater Wetlands in Maine*, Planning Report 70 (Augusta: Maine Critical Areas Program, State Planning Office, 1979).

2. Information describing many of the rare plants in this chapter came from *A Compilation of the Critical Areas Program Botanical Fact Sheets,* Miscellaneous Report 33 (Augusta: Maine Critical Areas Program, State Planning Office, 1985).

3. The primary source of information on peatlands was Ian A. Worley, *Maine Peatlands—Their Abundance, Ecology, and Relevance to the Critical*

Areas Program, Planning Report 73 (Augusta: Maine Critical Areas Program, State Planning Office, 1981).

4. The description and explanation of patterned fens were taken from Eric R. Sorensen, *Ecology and Distribution of Patterned Fens in Maine and Their Relevance to the Critical Areas Program,* Planning Report 81 (Augusta: Maine Critical Areas Program, State Planning Office, 1986).

5. Information on prairie white fringed orchid came from A. E. Brower, *The Prairie White Fringed Orchid* (Platanthera leucophaea) *in Maine and Its Relevance to the Critical Areas Program,* Planning Report 34 (Augusta: Maine Critical Areas Program, State Planning Office, 1977).

6. Details on the Great Heath were taken from Caren Caljouw, *A Preliminary Natural Areas Description of the Great Heath and Environs,* Miscellaneous Report 13 (Augusta: Bureau of Public Lands, Maine Department of Conservation, State Planning Office, 1982).

7. The characterization of No. 5 Bog was provided by Harry R. Tyler, Jr., and Christopher V. Davis, *Evaluation of No. 5 Bog and Jack Pine Stand, Somerset County, Maine, as a Potential National Natural Landmark,* Miscellaneous Report 14, prepared for the National Park Service, U.S. Department of the Interior (Augusta: Maine Critical Areas Program, State Planning Office, 1982).

8. Information on coastal raised bogs came from Ian A. Worley, *Botanical and Ecological Aspects of Coastal Raised Peatlands in Maine and Their Relevance to the Critical Areas Progam,* Planning Report 69 (Augusta: Maine Critical Areas Program, State Planning Office, 1980).

9. Facts about small round-leaved orchis came from L. M. Eastman, *Small Round-leaved Orchis* (Orchis rotundifolia) *in Maine and Its Relevance to the Critical Areas Program,* Planning Report 52 (Augusta: Maine Critical Areas Program, State Planning Office, 1977).

10. Notes on clammy azalea were taken from L. M. Eastman, *Clammy Azalea* (Rhododendron viscosum) *in Maine and Its Relevance to the Critical Areas Program,* Planning Report 33 (Augusta: Maine Critical Areas Program, State Planning Office, 1977).

11. Descriptive information on Atlantic white cedar came from L. M. Eastman, *Atlantic White Cedar* (Chamaecyparis thyoides) *in Maine and Its Relevance to the Critical Areas Program,* Planning Report 38 (Augusta: Maine Critical Areas Program, State Planning Office, 1977).

12. General information on rare vascular plants related to Maine's rivers was obtained from Maine Rivers Study (Augusta: Maine Department of Conservation and U.S. Department of Interior, National Park Service, Mid-Atlantic Regional Office, 1982).

13. Notes on Furbish's lousewort came from Charles D. Richards, *Furbish's Lousewort* (Pedicularis furbishiae) *in Maine and Its Relevance to the Critical Areas Program,* revised by Susan C. Gawler, Planning Report 13 (Augusta: Maine Critical Areas Program, State Planning Office, 1986).

14. Information on cut-leaved anemone came from Charles D. Richards, *Cut-leaved Anemone* (Anemone multifida) *and Its Relevance to the Critical Areas Program,* Planning Report 48 (Augusta: Maine Critical Areas Program, State Planning Office, 1977).

15. Data on northern painted-cup were obtained from Charles D. Richards, *Northern Painted-Cup* (Castilleja septentrionalis) *in Maine and Its Relevance to the Critical Areas Program,* Planning Report 49 (Augusta: Maine Critical Areas Program, State Planning Office, 1977).

8 • Coastal Plant Communities

1. Information on rare plants in the coastal zone from Casco Bay to Passamaquoddy Bay was contributed by the following sources: Norman Famous and Craig Ferris, "Endangered, Threatened and Rare Plants," in An Ecological Characterization of Coastal Maine, Vol. 3, Stewart I. Fefer and Patricia A. Schettig, Principal Investigators (Newton Corner, Mass.: Department of the Interior, U.S. Fish and Wildlife Service, Northeast Region, 1980) and A Compilation of the Critical Areas Program Botanical Fact Sheets (Augusta: Maine Critical Areas Program, State Planning Office, 1985).

2. Much of the botanical information related to sand beaches came from Bruce W. Nelson and L. Kenneth Fink, Jr., Geological and Botanical Features of Sand Beach Systems in Maine, Maine Sea Grant Publications Bulletin 14 and Planning Report 54 (Augusta: Maine Critical Areas Program, State Planning Office, 1980).

3. References to plants associated with gravel beaches came from Barry S. Timson, Jasper Beach, Machiasport, Maine, Planning Report 75 (Augusta: Maine Critical Areas Program, State Planning Office, 1981).

4. Information on Long's bitter cress was provided by L. M. Eastman, Long's Bitter Cress (Cardamine longii) in Maine and Its Relevance to the Critical Areas Program, Planning Report 17 (Augusta: Maine Critical Areas Program, State Planning Office, 1976).

5. Background information on Merrymeeting Bay was provided by Reed & D'Andrea, Merrymeeting Bay (Augusta,: Maine Department of Conservation, 1975).

6. John O. Snow, Secrets of a Salt Marsh (Portland, Maine: Guy Gannett Publishing Co., 1980).

7. The description of slender blue flag was based on L. M. Eastman, Slender Blue Flag (Iris prismatica) in Maine and Its Relevance to the Critical Areas Program, Planning Report 12 (Augusta: Maine Critical Areas Program, State Planning Office, 1976).

8. Information on several of the subarctic plants came from Frederick C. Olday, Susan C. Gawler, and Barbara St. John Vickery, Seven Unusual Sub-Arctic Plants of the Maine Coast, Planning Report 78 (Augusta: Maine Critical Areas Program, State Planning Office, 1983).

9. Data on luminous moss came from Harry R. Tyler, Jr., Luminous Moss (Schistostega pennata) in Maine and Its Relevance to the Critical Areas Program, Planning Report 2 (Augusta: Maine Critical Areas Program, State Planning Office, 1975).

10. The description of inkberry was based on L. M. Eastman, Inkberry (Ilex glabra) in Maine and Its Relevance to the Critical Areas Program, Planning Report 10 (Augusta: Maine Critical Areas Program, State Planning Office, 1976).

Section III

1. Aldo Leopold, A Sand County Almanac (New York: Oxford Univ. Press, 1966), p. xvii.

2. Paul R. Adamus, comp., Atlas of Breeding Birds in Maine, 1978–1983 (Augusta: Maine Department of Inland Fisheries and Wildlife, n.d.).

3. Richard Lorey Day, "The Wildlife of Maine—A Geographic Study" (MA diss., Clark University, 1950), p. 455.

4. A brief overview of animal species that have disappeared from Maine

was provided by Donald F. Mairs and Richard B. Parks, "Once Common . . . Now Gone," *Maine Fish and Game* (Spring, 1964).

5. Leopold, *A Sand County Almanac*, pp. xviii-xix.

6. A listing of Maine's vertebrate animal species categorized according to level of endangerment was provided by "Fish and Wildlife Species of Special Interest to Maine (Draft)" (Bangor: The Endangered and Nongame Wildlife Project, Maine Department of Inland Fisheries and Wildlife, April 1, 1986).

9 • *Invertebrates*

1. Information on the bog elfin came from A. E. Brower, *Bog Elfin* (Incisalia lanoiaieensis) *in Maine and Its Relevance to the Critical Areas Program,* Planning Report 63 (Augusta: Maine Critical Areas Program, State Planning Office, 1978).

2. The description of the Katahdin Arctic butterfly is based on A. E. Brower, *Katahdin Arctic Butterfly* (Oeneis polixenes katahdin) *in Maine and Its Relevance to the Critical Areas Program,* Planning Report 35 (Augusta: Maine Critical Areas Program, State Planning Office, 1977).

3. Information on Maine's intertidal zone and its invertebrate species and unique characteristics came from Lee F. Doggett, Peter F. Larsen, and Susan C. Sykes, *Intertidal Bedrock Areas of High Species Diversity in Maine, and Their Relevance to the Critical Areas Program,* Planning Report 55 (Augusta: Maine Critical Areas Program, State Planning Office, 1978).

4. Facts about the horseshoe crab were drawn from John W. Born, *Significant Breeding Sites of the Horseshoe Crab* (Limulus polyphemus) *in Maine and Their Relevance to the Critical Areas Program,* Planning Report 28 (Augusta: Maine Critical Areas Program, State Planning Office, 1977).

5. Background on the American oyster was provided by Joel Cowger, *Natural Occurrence of the American Oyster* (Crassostrea virginica) *in Maine and Its Relevance to the Critical Areas Program,* Planning Report 4 (Augusta: Maine Critical Areas Program, State Planning Office, 1975).

6. Details on quahogs came from A. H. Gustafson, *Quahogs* (Mercenaria mercenaria) *in Maine and Their Relevance to the Critical Areas Program,* Planning Report 43 (Augusta: Maine Critical Areas Program, State Planning Office, 1977).

7. Particulars about the dwarf tellin were taken from Mary Ann Gilbert, *The Dwarf Tellin* (Tellina agilis) *in Maine and Its Relevance to the Critical Areas Program,* Planning Report 30 (Augusta: Maine Critical Areas Program, State Planning Office, 1977).

8. The description of the gaper clam is from Mary Ann Gilbert, *The Gaper Clam* (Mya truncata) *in Maine and Its Relevance to the Critical Areas Program,* Planning Report 29 (Augusta: Maine Critical Areas Program, State Planning Office, 1977).

9. Data on the discordant and little black mussels came from Mary Ann Gilbert, *The Discordant Mussel* (Musculus discors) *and the Little Black Mussel* (Musculus niger) *in Maine and Their Relevance to the Critical Areas Program,* Planning Report 45 (Augusta: Maine Critical Areas Program, State Planning Office,1977).

10. Information on species of Astarte came from Mary Ann Gilbert, *The* Astarte *spp. Complex in Maine and Its Relevance to the Critical Areas Program,* Planning Report 44 (Augusta: Maine Critical Areas Program, State Planning Office, 1977).

11. Background on smooth top shell was provided by Mary Ann Gilbert, *The Smooth Top Shell* (Margarites helcinicus) *in Maine and Its Relevance to*

the *Critical Areas Program,* Planning Report 51 (Augusta: Maine Critical Areas Program, State Planning Office, 1977).

10 • *Fishes*

1. Descriptive information on several of the species of fish discussed in this chapter was provided by W. Harry Everhart, *Fishes of Maine* (Augusta: Maine Dept. of Inland Fisheries and Game, 1958).

2. Many details concerning the striped bass, Atlantic and short-nosed sturgeons, and the American shad were provided by *The Fisheries Resources of the Kennebec River: Discover the Kennebec* (n.p., Kennebec River Council, 1986).

3. Information on the arctic charr came from *Landlocked Arctic Charr in Maine* (Augusta: Maine Dept. of Inland Fisheries and Wildlife and State Planning Office, 1985).

11 • *Amphibians and Reptiles*

1. Much of the data concerning the rarity and distribution of Maine's reptiles and amphibians came from the records of the Maine Amphibian and Reptile Atlas Project, a collaborative undertaking by the Maine Chapter of The Nature Conservancy's Natural Heritage Program, the University of Maine's Wildlife Department, the Maine Audubon Society, and the Maine Department of Inland Fisheries and Wildlife.

12 • *Birds*

1. Background information on many of the species discussed in this chapter came from Paul R. Adamus and Garrett C. Clough, *A Preliminary Listing of Noteworthy Natural Features in Maine,* Miscellaneous Report 2 (Augusta: Maine Critical Areas Program, State Planning Office, 1976), pp. 266–317.

2. Information on Maine's bald eagle population and related management efforts came from the Maine Endangered and Nongame Wildlife Project and from the Maine Bald Eagle Project, a cooperative venture of the University of Maine's Wildlife Division, the Maine Dept. of Inland Fisheries and Wildlife, and the U. S. Fish and Wildlife Service.

3. The account of the peregrine falcon in Maine and efforts to restore it to the state drew heavily on materials describing the Peregrine Falcon Reestablishment Program of the Maine Endangered and Nongame Wildlife Project, Dept. of Inland Fisheries and Wildlife.

4. Data on Maine's coastal terns came from the following sources: Harry R. Tyler, Jr., *Common Terns* (Sterna hirundo), *Arctic Tern* (Sterna paradisaea), *and Roseate Terns* (Sterna dougalli) *in Maine,* Planning Report 1 (Augusta: Maine Critical Areas Program, State Planning Office, 1975); and Dale K. Dorr, *Least Tern* (Sterna albifrons) *Nesting Habitat in Maine and Its Relevance to the Critical Areas Program,* Planning Report 11 (Augusta: Maine Critical Areas Program, State Planning Office, 1976).

5. Information on Maine's alcids, including the razorbill and common puffin came from Joel Cowger, *Alcid Nesting Habitat on the Maine Coast and Its Relevance to the Critical Areas Program*, Planning Report 5 (Augusta: Maine Critical Areas Program, State Planning Office, 1976).

6. Information on the Eastern Egg Rock puffin project came from reports in Egg Rock Update, Newsletter of the Fratercula Fund of the National Audubon Society.

7. Details about the Leach's storm-petrel came from Joel Cowger, *The*

Nesting Habitat of the Leach's Storm-petrel in Maine and Its Relevance to the Critical Areas Program, Planning Report 6 (Augusta: Maine Critical Areas Program, State Planning Office, 1976).

8. Particulars about the common eider were drawn from Stewart Fefer, *The American Eider* (Somateria mollissima) *in Maine and Its Relevance to the Critical Areas Program,* Planning Report 27 (Augusta: Maine Critical Areas Program, State Planning Office, 1977).

9. Information on Maine's wading birds came from reports published by the Critical Areas Program, including Harry R. Tyler, Jr., *Wading Birds in Maine and Their Relevance to the Critical Areas Program,* Planning Report 26 (Augusta: Maine Critical Areas Program, State Planning Office, 1977).

10. Data on mainland great blue heron colonies were provided by Naomi Edelson, *Maine Inland Great Blue Heron Nesting Colonies,* (Augusta: Maine Critical Areas Program, State Planning Office, 1987).

11. The description of the piping plover was based on Dale K. Dorr, *Piping Plover* (Charadrius melodus) *Nesting Habitat in Maine and Its Relevance to the Critical Areas Program,* Planning Report 15 (Augusta: Maine Critical Areas Program, State Planning Office, 1976).

12. Facts about the black tern were provided by Dale K. Dorr, *Black Tern* (Chlidonias niger) *Nesting Habitat in Maine and Its Relevance to the Critical Areas Program,* Planning Report 18 (Augusta: Maine Critical Areas Program, State Planning Office, 1976).

13. Information on the status of the grasshopper sparrow in Maine came from Peter Vickery, "The Making of an Endangered Species," *Habitat: Journal of the Maine Audubon Society,* vol. 4, no. 1 (November–December, 1986): 41–43.

13 • Mammals

1. Brief notes on several of the species described in this chapter came from Paul R. Adamus and Garrett C. Clough, *A Preliminary Listing of Noteworthy Natural Features in Maine.* Miscellaneous Report 2 (Augusta: Maine Critical Areas Program, State Planning Office, 1976), pp. 318–336.

2. Background information for preparation of the section on marine mammals was provided by the following reports: Patricia Schettig and Cheryl Klink, "Marine Mammals," in *An Ecological Characterization of Coastal Maine,* vol. 3, Stewart I. Fefer and Patricia A. Schettig, Principal Investigators (Newton Corner, Mass.: Dept. of the Interior, U. S. Fish and Wildlife Service, Northeast Region, 1980); John H. Prescott, Scott D. Kraus, and James R. Gilbert, *Report: East Coast/ Gulf Coast Cetacean and Pinniped Research Workshop* (Washington, D.C.: Marine Mammal Workshop, 1979).

3. Estimates of the right whale population were found in Howard W. Braham and Dale W. Rice, "The Right Whale, *Balaena glacialis,*" *Marine Fisheries Review* 46, no. 4 (1984): 43.

4. Population estimates of the humpback whale were found in James H. Johnson and Allen A. Wolman, "The Humpback Whale, *Megaptera novaeangliae,*" *Maine Fisheries Review* 46, no. 4 (1984): 35.

5. The 1985 discoveries of the northern bog lemming in Baxter State Park by John Albright and Garrett Clough were reported by C. Hasty Thompson, "On Nature," *Maine Sunday Telegram,* 25, (August 1985).

6. Some details about the cottontail rabbit in Maine were provided by Douglas L. Marston, "Maine's 'Cooneys,'" *Maine Fish and Game* (Fall 1967).

7. The description of the Canada lynx in Maine drew upon the article by John H. Hunt, "The Little Known Lynx," *Maine Fish and Game* (Spring 1974).

8. Much of the information on the yellow-nosed vole came from Ruth C. Chodrow and Robert L. Martin, *The Yellow-nosed Vole in Maine and Its Relevance to the Critical Areas Program,* Planning Report 57 (Augusta: Maine Critical Areas Program, State Planning Office, and Maine Dept. of Inland Fisheries and Wildlife, 1978).

9. Some background information on Maine's bats was obtained from Robert L. Martin, "Bats," *Maine Audubon News* (June 1975).

Section IV • Perspective

1. Ian L. McHarg, *Design with Nature* (Garden City, N. Y.: The Natural History Press, 1969), p. 56.

14 • A Richly Varied Landscape

1. Much of the material in this chapter is based on Paul R. Adamus, *The Natural Regions of Maine,* Miscellaneous Report 2 (Augusta: Maine Critical Areas Program, State Planning Office, 1978).

Section V • Perspective

1. Aldo Leopold, *A Sand County Almanac* (New York: Oxford Univ. Press, 1966), pp. x–xix.

15 • Protectors of Maine's Natural Areas

1. Janet E. Milne, *The Landowner's Options,* 3rd ed. rev. (Augusta: Maine Critical Areas Program, State Planning Office; Topsham: Maine Chapter of The Nature Conservancy and Maine Coast Heritage Trust, 1985).

Index

Rhododendron, 221
Rhyolite, 54
Right whale, 196, 197–98, **197**
Ring-necked duck, 233
Ripogenus Dam, 29; Gorge, 29, 257
Robert P.T. Coffin Wildflower Reservation, 251
Rock bridge, 56
Rock vole, 205
Roosevelt, Theodore, 241
Roque Bluffs, 50
Roque Bluffs State Park, 254
Roseate tern, 174, 176
Roseroot stonecrop, 128, **128**, 220
Royal River Park, 251
Ruddy turnstone, 187, **187**
Ruffed grouse, 168
Ruffingham Meadow Wildlife Management Area, 255
Rush dwarf shrub heath, 73
Rusty woodsia, 81

S

Saco Heath, 110
St. Croix River, 41, 242
St. John oxytrope, 116, **117**, 119
St. John River, 40, **41**, 115–18, **116**, 156, 229
St. John rose, 118
St. John tansy, 116, **117**
Salamanders. *See* Four-toed salamander, Northern spring salamander, Tremblay's salamander
Salt marshes, 126
Saltwort, 121, **121**
Sand Beach, 252
Sanderling, **187**
Sandpiper, 187
Sandy beach coastal subregion, 217–18, **218**, 250
Sandy Stream Pond, 255
Sassafras, 66, **66**, 95
Sawyer, George "Pete," 238
Scantily flowered sedge, 104, 105
Scarborough Beach, 250
Scarborough Marsh, 126, 169, 218; State Wildlife Management Area, 250
Schoodic Point, 83, 129, 143, 169, 222, 252
Schoodic Mountain, 253
Scott Paper Company, 244
Screw Auger Falls Gorge, **4**, 35, **35**, 38, **240**, 256
Screw Auger Falls (Gulf Hagas), 256
Seabeach sandwort, 121
Sea caves, 54–55
Sea-floor spreading, 9–11, 15–17
Sea lungwort, 123, **123**. *See* Oysterleaf

Seapoint, 250
Sea rocket, 121
Seaside spurge, 122, **122**
Seawall Beach, **48**, 51, 52, **243**
Sebago Lake, 42; State Park, 254
Seboeis River Gorge Preserve, 257
Seboomook Lake, 247
Sedge, 71, 104
Sedge wren, 191, **191**
Sei whale, 197, 198, 200, **200**
Semipalmated plover, 187
Seneca snakeroot, 230
Shagbark hickory. *See* Hickory, shagbark
Sharp-tailed sparrow, 193
Sheep Island Preserve, 253
Sheep laurel, 106
Sheepscot Reversing Falls, 255
Shin Brook Formation, 11
Shining ladies'-tresses, 230
Ship Harbor Nature Trail, 253
Ship Island Group preserves, 253
Shipstern Island, 58, **58**
Shoals Marine Laboratory, 144
Short-nosed sturgeon, 154, **154**, 219
Showy arnica, 118
Showy lady's slipper, 65, **65**, 66, 104, 105, 230
Showy orchis, 64, 66
Silver-haired bat, 206, 207, **207**
Slender blue flag, 126–27, **126**
Slender cliff brake, 64, **64**
Small-footed myotis, 206, 209, **209**
Smallmouth bass, 224
Small round-leaved orchis, 113–14, **113**
Smalls Falls, 256
Small whorled pogonia, 67, **67**, 87
Smith Island Preserve, 253
Smooth top shell, 149–50, **150**
Smooth winterberry, 89
Smooth woodsia fern, 81, **81**, 119, 230
Snakes. *See* Black racer, Eastern ribbon snake, Northern brown snake, Timber rattler
Snow, John, 126
Snow Falls Gorge, 255
Snowy egret, 183–84, **183**, 218
Sohier Park, 250
Somes Sound, 219, 252
Sour gum. *See* Tupelo
South Branch Ponds, 156
South Bubble Erratic, 252
Southern bog lemming, 209
Southern flying squirrel, 205, **205**
Southern oak-forest region, 220–21, **221**, 254
South Turner Mountain, 255
Spartina, 126
Speck Pond, 42, **42**
Sperm whale, 200, **200**

Sphagnum moss, 74, 102, **106**
Spicebush, 95–96, **95**
Spotted turtle, 166, 167, **167**
Spotted wintergreen, 96, **96**
Spouting hole. *See* Blow hole
Spring Hill Recreation Area, 254
Spring peeper, 159
Spruce, red, 84–85, 84
Squa Pan area, 230
Stair Falls Whitewater Rapids, **36**, 37
Step Falls Preserve, 256
Steve Powell Refuge and State Wildlife Management Area, 251
Striped bass, **152**, 153
Sucker Brook Preserve, 255
Summer grape, 97
Sunapee charr, 155, 156, **156**
Sundew, 74
Sunset Park, 258
Swamp darter, 156, **156**
Swamp valerian, 119
Swan Lake State Park, 255
Sweet-broom, 230
Swift River, 38–39; Falls, 256

T

Tableland, The, 71, 72, 73, 255
Table Rock, 256
Taconic Orogeny, 12, **12**
Tall wormwood, 122, **122**
Talus, 43
Tarr, Ralph S., 20
Terns, 174–75. *See also* Arctic tern, Black tern, Common tern, Least tern, Roseate tern
Thoreau, Henry David, 79, 136
Thorncraig Bird Sanctuary, 254
Thunder Hole, 252
Timber rattlesnake, 161
Timber wolf. *See* Gray wolf
Tinker, Katherine P., 246
Tourmaline, 38, 223
Transition coastal subregion, 218–19, **218**, 250–52
Traveler Mountain, 73, 255
Tremblay's salamander, 159–60, **159**
Tree-ring analysis, 78
Tricolored heron, 184–85
Trilobite, **9**
Tumbledown Mountain, 256
Tupelo, 89–90, **90**
Turtle Island Preserve, 253
Turtles. *See* Eastern box turtle, Atlantic leatherback turtle, Atlantic logerhead turtle, Atlantic Ridley turtle
Two Lights State Park, 144, 242, 251

U

U.S. Department of the Interior, 115, 154, 246
U.S. Fish and Wildlife Service, 241, 259
U.S. Food and Drug Administration, 95
University of Maine, Center for Marine Studies, 260; College of Forest Resources, 260; Cooperative Fish and Wildlife Research Unit, 260; Institute for Quaternary Studies, 260; Land and Water Resources Center, 260; Wildlife Department, 159
Upland foothills subregion, 224, **225**, 254–55
Upland-hilly region, 222–25, **223**, 254–55
Upland sandpiper, 186–87, **186**, 231
Upper Goose Island Preserve, 251–52
Upper Pockwockamus Falls Whitewater Rapids, **35**
Upper Richardson Lake, **241**

V

Variegated horsetail, 118, **118**

Variegated scouring-rush, 230
Vaughns Island Preserve, 250
Vaughan Woods Memorial, 254
Verrill, Addison Emery, 147
Vesper sparrow, 193
Virginia Lake, 213

W

Wabanaki, 37, 134, 146, 157
Warren Island State Park, 253
Water pimpernel, 125
Water pipit, 191–92, **192**, 227
Water snake, 162
Waterhouse, Lillian R., 245
Wells National Estuarine Reserve, **50**, **124**, 127, 250
West Quoddy Head, 143
Wetlands, types of, **98**
Whales. *See* Finback whale, Humpback whale, Minke whale, Right whale, Sperm whale, Sei whale.
Whalesback, The (esker), **25**, 255
Whalesback, The (shell midden), **145**
White Mountain National Forest, 256, 259

White Mountains, 225
Wide-leaved ladies' tresses, 64
Wight Brook Waterfalls, **243**
Wild and Scenic Rivers Act, 242
Wild Gardens of Acadia, 252
Wild ginger, 89
Wild indigo, 97
Wilderness Act, 243
Willow, bearberry, 69, 71; dwarf, 69, 71; sandbar, 119, 230
Winslow Park, 252
Witch Pond Carriage Path, 252
Wolf Neck Woods State Park, 252
Wood duck, 101
Wood turtle, 167, **167**
Woodland caribou, 136, 137–38, **138**
Wreck Island and Round Island preserves, 253

Y

Yellow jewelweed, 64
Yellow-nosed vole, 205–6, **206**
Yellow-throated vireos, 224
Young, Aaron, 94